THE
NEW AMERICAN
JUDAISM

THE
NEW AMERICAN
JUDAISM

---

*The Way Forward on
Challenging Issues from
Intermarriage to Jewish Identity*

Rabbi Arthur Blecher

THE NEW AMERICAN JUDAISM
Copyright © Rabbi Arthur Blecher, 2007.

First published in 2007 by
PALGRAVE MACMILLAN™
175 Fifth Avenue, New York, N.Y. 10010 and
Houndmills, Basingstoke, Hampshire, England RG21 6XS.
Companies and representatives throughout the world.

PALGRAVE MACMILLAN is the global academic imprint of the
Palgrave Macmillan division of St. Martin's Press, LLC and of Palgrave
Macmillan Ltd. Macmillan® is a registered trademark in the United States,
United Kingdom and other countries. Palgrave is a registered trademark in
the European Union and other countries.

ISBN–13: 978–1–4039–7746–5
ISBN–10: 1–4039–7746–1

Library of Congress Cataloging-in-Publication Data is available from the
Library of Congress.

A catalogue record of the book is available from the British Library.

Design by Letra Libre, Inc.

First edition: October 2007
10 9 8 7 6 5 4 3 2 1

Printed in the United States of America.

For Jim

מים עמקים עצה בלב־איש ואיש תבונה ידלנה.

The man of insight draws meaning from the deep waters of the human mind.

—*Proverbs 20:5*

CONTENTS

ACKNOWLEDGMENTS

Many friends and associates kindly provided support, read drafts and offered useful suggestions during the various stages of this project. Among them are: Bill Adler, Florence Clay, James Clay, Pauline Clay, Joel Elvery, Anthony Flacco, Samuel Fleishman, Anne Glusker, Lee Goldman, Diane Goldstein, Wendy Gradison, Sharon McDaniel, Mary Ellen Petrisko, Peter Pizzalongo, Carlos Prugue, Joanna Rom, Richard Rubenstein, Hugh Schwartz, Reginald Wilson, and Rain Zohav.

My research assistant, Byron Hulcher, managed my bibliography and tracked down Internet sources.

The members of my congregation, Beth Chai, and everyone who attended my lectures at the Jewish Cultural School of Washington stimulated me with fascinating ideas, challenged me with very interesting questions and inspired me by their openness to new concepts.

MacRae Ross, of blessed memory, provided professional expertise and personal encouragement.

Marjory Ross advised me and graciously opened some valuable doors for me.

My literary agent, Sharlene Martin, skillfully opened other important doors for me.

My editor, Amanda Moon, and her colleagues at Palgrave Macmillan astutely helped refine my concepts and carefully guided the project through the publication process.

Debby Manette applied a sharp eye and a discerning mind to the manuscript.

My friend and mentor, Kenneth Jacobson, generously gave me the benefit of his considerable intelligence, keen insight and editorial experience.

INTRODUCTION

On New Year's Eve of 2000, I realized that I was approaching the twenty-fifth anniversary of my ordination as a Conservative rabbi. I had long ago left the Conservative movement, earned a doctorate in psychology and began leading a satisfying life as a therapist and an independent rabbi. As a traditionally trained rabbi, I was accustomed to quoting the ancient sages to match everyday situations, easily exhaling smoky plumes of Hebrew wisdom. But if I were to carefully unpack the comfortable container of my American Judaism, what would I find? Because I grew up in Judaism's Conservative movement, taught in its Hebrew schools, held degrees from its seminary and led its synagogues, I was familiar with the workings of the Jewish establishment. On the other hand, because I had been part of no denomination for twenty years, I was something of a maverick. I made a resolution: From my vantage point as both insider and outsider, I would verify everything I thought I knew about the Jewish religion. I would use the scholarly tools I had acquired in rabbinical school, along with my training in psychotherapy. I would set aside all my previous assumptions in order to see Judaism—its meta-structures and its subtexts—in a clear light.

I found that a distinct pattern emerges from the printed pages of almost all Judaica published in America since the beginning of the twentieth century. Whether a book is about God, or Scripture, or Jewish history or ritual observance, writers tend to reiterate a few specific concerns. One is continuity: The author takes pains to show that some particular manifestation of current Jewish practice is directly linked to ancient Judaism. Another topic is authenticity: The book makes assumptions about whether something is either intrinsically Jewish or the result of outside influence. Finally, writers are preoccupied with worries about the survival of the Jewish way of life. In fact, the specific words *continuity, authenticity* and *survival,* with a few variations, appear repeatedly. These concepts are recorded everywhere in works produced in America after the beginning of the twentieth century—journal articles, rabbis' sermons, Hebrew school textbooks. Isolated examples might crop up in writing from other times or other places, but not the overall pattern.

Clearly, there is an undercurrent of anxiety in American Judaism. It is a common theme in books, articles, sermons and lectures today, but is especially true of works from the early part of the twentieth century. The founders of American Judaism were reacting to fears—the kind of fears that would be endemic to an immigrant generation. The theme of continuity was really a response to the fear that ties to the past had been severed. The theme of authenticity was an expression of fear that the present had been compromised. And the theme of survival arose from the fear that there would be no future. Obviously, a profound transformation took hold of Jews in America at the beginning of the previous century.

———

Right after the Jewish New Year, Rosh Hashanah, the Lerners made an appointment to see me for counseling. Debra Lerner* runs her own consulting business; she is successful, sophisticated and socially astute. Alan Lerner, a partner in one of Washington's top law firms, has a reputation as a well-informed intellectual and a

---

* I have fictionalized the identities of the people in this account, but the events are real.

skillful litigator. The Lerners were longtime members of one of Washington's oldest and largest Conservative synagogues. Their only child, Jeff, had gone to Hebrew school there, become a member of United Synagogue Youth and spent summers at the Conservative movement's Camp Ramah. During college, Jeff was president of his campus Hillel group and had even studied for a year in Israel. Everyone, including Jeff, assumed he would marry a girl with a strong Jewish background and raise a model family, but in his second year of medical school, Jeff fell in love with Catherine. Catherine was not Jewish. In spite of their misgivings, Jeff's parents decided to take the high road and welcome Catherine as their prospective daughter-in-law.

Rosh Hashanah started out as a beautiful day for the Lerners. The synagogue service was inspiring; the singing was spirited; the sound of the ram's horn was thrilling. However, the rabbi's sermon was devastating. Speaking with both charisma and conviction, Rabbi Bookman announced to his assembled congregation of two thousand people that intermarriage was threatening the survival of American Jewry. He cited impressive statistics that most children of mixed couples grow up to be gentiles and predicted that at the present rate of intermarriage, the American Jewish community would disappear within two generations. He forcefully stated that rabbis who perform mixed marriages were charlatans and mercenaries because such wedding ceremonies were shams. The only solution to the intermarriage epidemic was synagogue affiliation and ongoing Jewish education from the earliest age. Rabbi Bookman pointed out that his synagogue ran both a nursery school and an adult education series and insisted that every member had a moral obligation to perpetuate four thousand years of Judaism by enrolling in classes. The rabbi concluded his sermon by stating that any Jew who married a non-Jew would be responsible for continuing the Holocaust.

Now the Lerners were sitting in my office. Debra was in tears. Alan was obviously depressed. They revered Rabbi Bookman, and they were appalled by what he told them. They thought they had done everything parents could do to pass on Jewish tradition to the future generations. Maybe they should have insisted Jeff attend a graduate school with a higher percentage of Jews. Maybe they should have opposed his relationship with Catherine. Maybe they should have had more children. Even though I tried to suggest other ways to look at the situation, the Lerners could not believe their rabbi was entirely wrong. He was, after all, a very learned and sincere man. Finally Alan said to me, "I know it doesn't make any sense, but I can't get over the feeling that I have somehow failed my ancestors and that my own son has betrayed his people."

There is nothing unusual about a rabbi using guilt and fear to promote attendance at services and classes. Clerics do this sort of thing all the time, and so have I. But when a rabbi invokes the Holocaust—that is pulling out the heavy artillery. Here in my office was the same pattern I have seen in almost everything I have read in English about the Jewish religion. We were talking about Judaism in terms of continuity, authenticity and survival. As I looked at the faces and postures of this couple, as I listened to the intonations of their voices, I instinctively knew that something is amiss with how my colleagues and I go about our jobs as religious leaders. How can a community thrive based on a discourse of anxiety and guilt and on members who feel defeated and helpless?

My meeting with the Lerners made me wonder about my own preaching. I would never accuse my members of bringing a scourge upon the Jewish people, but how different was I really from their rabbi? If I were to go through my old notes and manuscripts, I know I would find the same patterns and themes that populate most American Jewish thinking. Which is not surprising, since I studied with the same professors as Rabbi Bookman; I read the same textbooks. Like the other two or three thousand American rabbis, my ideas about Judaism were shaped by institutions that were founded in the United States at the beginning of the twentieth century.

How did American Judaism come to be so infused with anxiety during its formative period? What effect did this pervasive apprehension have on the teachings of American Judaism's founders, and what is its influence today? What hopeful and empowering messages can by found within the experiences of the twentieth century to point the way forward to a new American Judaism? Finding the answers to these questions took as much work as I had spent in rabbinical school. The project turned out to be far more difficult than I imagined because it forced me to disassemble the very structures that were most familiar to me. It led me to reexamine the literature that had shaped me as a Jew, from ancient Hebrew sources to contemporary American writing. My research uncovered information that challenged my basic assumptions about the Jewish religion and called into question everything I had learned from the teachers I revered and the books I respected.

I discovered that somehow a number of significant historical inaccuracies invaded the information American Jewish teachers have been presenting for over a century. This phenomenon is very troubling to me because I have always considered intellectual enlightenment and meticulous scholarship to be the hallmarks of American Judaism. It is hard to believe that American Judaism was founded on several false concepts, yet there can be no question that fiction has been mingled with fact. Unwarranted claims of institutional power and unjustified claims of rabbinic power, misrepresentations about historical origins, illusions about the Old World and false alarms about the New World, misinterpretations of Hebrew sources and misunderstandings about intermarriage—these all were woven into the fabric of American Judaism in the twentieth century. They are myths in the sense of collective ideas that are untrue. As myths, they continue to influence American Judaism in the twenty-first century, preserving the very guilt and anxiety that engendered them. And as myths, they also contain valuable truths about the collective spirit of an enduring civilization.

Disassembling myths removes their power to generate apprehension and despair. At the same time, myths endow life with meaning. I believe that recognizing myths for what they are does not diminish their power to capture the imagination or to enliven the soul; rather, it provides a way forward. The American Jewish people can be trusted to know what is fact and what is fiction about their own civilization. They are fully able to discern the redemptive values of the Jewish religion and appreciate the lessons of its history without the mediation of rabbis and denominational authorities. They can accept the human frailty of Judaism's most respected institutions while continuing to benefit from the valuable resources those institutions are able to provide.

Writing this book was a transforming experience for me. As I looked at American Judaism in a clear light, I become more intrigued—and more inspired—by Jewish civilization than ever before. My research gave me a fresh outlook on Judaism that I could bring to my congregation and my classes and that I could incorporate into my personal life. I have written this book with the firm conviction that clearing away myths will reveal a new American Jewish religion whose vitality and diversity far exceed the ability of any institution to contain or any rabbi to define. I offer these pages in the hope they will serve as the beginning of a conversation.

1

INVENTING JUDAISM IN AMERICA

Three of the most consequential events in all of Jewish history occurred during the first half of the twentieth century: the mass migration of half of European Jewry to America, the destruction of most of Europe's remaining Jews and the establishment of the modern State of Israel. The impact of any one these episodes by itself would be powerful enough to permanently alter the self-concept of the people caught up in it. Yet all three took place within the span of a single lifetime. A fourth event, the creation of a new form of Judaism in the early years of the century, is rarely mentioned even though it was one of the most radical transformations in the existence of the Jewish people. Instead, Jewish historians emphasize the establishment of post-exilic Judean society 2,500 years ago and the development of rabbinic Judaism two thousand years ago. Each of these metamorphoses took centuries to unfold. The formation of a new Jewish religion in America is as monumental a change as anything the Jewish people have experienced, yet not only did it take place just a hundred years ago, it happened within a single generation.

Like other religions, Judaism is a structure of concepts and practices organized around a worldview. In response to sweeping historical forces at the beginning of the twentieth century, American rabbis developed a new institutional structure for the Jewish religion. Reacting to the powerful psychological factors of mass migration, the rabbis also introduced new concepts. The new institutions in turn generated new practices, while the new concepts generated a new worldview for the Jewish people. By devising new structures, new concepts, new practices and a new worldview, American rabbis—whether they intended to do so or not—succeeded in inventing a new Jewish religion.

It is no surprise that major historical events, social upheaval and mass psychological trauma would shape the religious beliefs and practices of a people. Yet even though the twentieth century is the most important century in the history of the Jewish people, rabbis, teachers and textbooks tend to give the opposite impression: that Judaism was formed long ago in faraway places, that Judaism in the New World was carried here from the Old World and that Judaism has tended to remain consistent in its beliefs and practices despite cataclysmic experiences.

Ironically, the same sociological factors that gave birth to a new Jewish religion a hundred years ago produced a mind-set so enduring that Jewish thinkers today often insist Judaism in America is not new at all. At the end of the nineteenth century, Europe was the center of Judaism. Of the estimated 7.5 million Jews in the world at that time, approximately 7 million lived in Europe. Only a relative handful lived in North America.[1] By the beginning of the twentieth century, the number of Jews living in Eastern Europe had risen to around 9 million, but another million had immigrated to North America. Only about 50,000 Jews lived in Palestine. In response to both oppressive conditions in Eastern Europe and expanding opportunities in America in the early 1900s, a total of 3 to 4 million Jews moved to the United States and Canada, thereby creating a second major Jewish community. By numbers alone, the migration to America was much more extensive than the biblical accounts of

the Exodus from Egypt or the exile to Babylonia. After the Holocaust destroyed two-thirds of the Jews of Europe, America became
the main homeland for Judaism. Although the birth of a second
homeland followed when the modern State of Israel was founded in
1948, America remained the largest Jewish population center for
the rest of the century. In 2000, 6 million Jews lived in America,
compared with about 5 million in Israel and 1.5 million in Europe.[2]

This was the most monumental transformation in the course
of Jewish history, not only because of how many people were affected but also because of its rapidity. Judea had been the political
and religious capital of the Jewish people from the time of the establishment of the Second Commonwealth in the sixth century
BCE until the Roman destruction of the Jewish state in the year 70.
Gradually, incrementally, over the next thousand years, the Jews
became a Diaspora spreading across the countries of Europe. They
remained a European people for another thousand years. But at
the beginning of the twentieth century, the world of Judaism very
quickly began to shift from the old to the new. By the middle of the
century, the Holocaust made the shift complete: America, not Europe, was the Jewish homeland. Even though there would be two
centers of Jewish population by the end of the century—Israel and
America—the fact remained that the Jews were no longer a European people.

The particular history of the European Jewish community
made the experience of mass migration especially traumatic. Like
other immigrants, the Jews had settled in some of the most densely
populated neighborhoods in one of the largest cities in the world.
Endemic disease and the violence of crowded conditions added to
the stress. Not only had they moved to a new society with a new
language, they had entered a new era. In the brief time it took to
sail across the Atlantic, they went from feudalism to the Industrial
Age. Like other immigrants, they brought with them no internal
reference points to guide them as they adapted to their new lives.
But in some ways they were very different from all other immigrant populations of the period.

The Jews of Eastern Europe had lived for centuries as an oppressed and alien ethnic population. Their history as strangers began with the Jews who settled in central Europe in the Middle Ages and spoke their own Hebraic version of German. After they migrated eastward and established themselves in Poland, their numbers grew. They lived as a nation within a nation, with their own language and their own religion; the Jews of Poland were not Poles. When Catherine the Great of Russia took over the eastern half of Poland in the late 1700s, the Jews became stranger still: They lived in Polish towns within czarist Russia but were neither Russians nor Poles. Then a century of czarist edicts crippled them economically. Inevitably their fate affected their self-concept as a community. Generations of Eastern European Jews lived as aliens and as victims. The passage to America would lift their oppression and relieve their isolation. But by promising them prosperity and offering them citizenship, America also threatened to erase their identity. By becoming Americans, would they cease to be Jews?

The mass migration of European Jews to America presented a daunting challenge for both the rabbis who were already comfortably established in America and the immigrant rabbis. The American Jewish community, which at that time was predominantly Reform, would have to find a way to absorb an Orthodox population four times its size. The Old World rabbis who came to America joined their New World colleagues in helping the transplanted Jews practice Judaism in a new environment. Many rabbis, fearing that traditional Judaism would be lost in the passage across the Atlantic, were convinced that they would have to invent a new Judaism. When the renowned rabbinic scholar Solomon Schechter moved to America from Europe in 1902, he warned his colleagues that "unless we succeed in effecting an organization which, while loyal to the Torah, to the teachings of our sages, to the traditions of our fathers, to the usages and customs of Israel, shall at the same time introduce the English sermon and adopt scientific methods in our seminaries, in our training of rabbis and schoolmasters . . . traditional Judaism will not survive another generation in this country."[3] His words encapsulated the overall mentality of that time: The Jewish way of life was at risk in the New World, and it was up to the rabbis to resolve the critical tension between tradition and modernity. As they set about their task, Jewish leaders became so preoccupied with thoughts of the continuity of Jewish tradition in the new era, the ideological authenticity of Jewish practice in America and the survival of the Jews as a distinct people, that *continuity*, *survival* and *authenticity* became the central themes of Judaism in America.

Even though they shared a common vision of their role as the preservers of Judaism in America, the rabbis did not agree on the specific form that religion should assume. Nor could they agree on who would lead it. They founded rival movements and built competing institutions and national organizations, forging a new form of Judaism: denominational Judaism. Reform Judaism in Germany had paved the way by borrowing the structures of the Lutheran church. Now American rabbis recast Judaism following the model that had already proved successful for the Protestant denominations in America. They created new Jewish denominations using a three-part blueprint: Each denomination would have a national federation of congregations, a central school to train rabbis for the movement and a national association of rabbis. (See chapter 6 for a fuller discussion of the denominations.)

This three-part institutional structure represented a significant departure from Old World Judaism. First of all, it meant that the denomination would provide the rabbis to lead its member congregations, the teachers and cantors to staff them and the prayer books for use at services. This was a new concept for Jews. Traditionally in Europe, rabbis were ordained privately in local schools by other individual rabbis; no national institutions granted ordination the way a university grants a degree. In the Old World, prayer books were produced by individual congregations, individual rabbis or private publishers. Second, although the denominations maintained the tradition of the local synagogue as the center of

Jewish life, there was a key difference. The new national bodies would decide the standards of both congregational membership and congregational religious life. Each denomination would set the rules for who could or could not belong to its congregations; the denomination would prescribe the professional practices its rabbis would follow; denominational law would affect the rituals performed in its synagogues. The autonomy that synagogues had enjoyed for a thousand years in Europe would have no place in denominational Judaism.

Denominational Judaism created a new kind of rabbi as well. Continuing the path begun in the mid 1800s by German Reform Judaism, the progressive movements in America copied Christian practice by developing elaborate synagogue services and life-cycle ceremonies presided over by the rabbis. In Old World Judaism, rabbis ruled on the standards for Jewish practice, but any adult male who knew what to do could carry out the rites and rituals. The rabbis preached in the synagogues, but they were not the official leaders of the synagogues. (See chapter 7 for a discussion of rabbis.) Under denominational Judaism, the rabbis retained their historical role as the teachers of Judaism, but they performed new functions as well. Rabbis led prayer services, conducted bar mitzvah ceremonies, blessed babies and houses and officiated at funerals. They became indispensable to the ritual life of American Judaism.

DENOMINATIONAL DIFFERENCES

Despite their shared themes and their identical structures, there are certain doctrinal differences among the denominations. These philosophical distinctions are not hard to figure out. A lot of people assume that Orthodoxy occupies the traditional camp, Reform the liberal one and Conservative Judaism the middle. Reconstructionism would fall somewhere between Conservative and Reform. The denominations formally define themselves by their interpretations of certain central subjects of discourse within Judaism. These core elements are God, Torah, Jewish law (*Halachah*) and Israel. Although different thinkers bundle the elements of Judaism differently, anyone defining Judaism must interpret these terms. *God* includes not only theological teachings, but also the range of philosophical speculation about reality, both perceived and intuited. *Torah* primarily refers to the first five books of the Old Testament, which record the oldest of the preserved laws and stories of Judaism; the word also is used to mean all of Jewish sacred writing. *Halachah* is Jewish law, primarily derived from the Talmudic discussions of the commandments of the Torah; the Shulchan Aruch is the major authoritative codification of the *Halachah*. (The appendix discusses the sacred texts of Judaism.) By extension, *Halachah* refers to all the rituals and other religious practices of Judaism. *Israel* is the classic literary term for the Jewish people, both in the ancestral homeland and throughout the Diaspora. So *God* refers to beliefs of Judaism, *Torah* to the sacred literature of Judaism, *Halachah* to the practices of Judaism and *Israel* to the people of Judaism. Within each of these four areas, there is a traditionalist approach and a modernist approach.

There has been a wide range of beliefs about God throughout Jewish history, and Jews in general are tolerant of a wide variety of personal understandings about the nature of God. Nevertheless, it is possible to sketch some general principles. Essentially, the traditionalist view is theistic and supernatural. God is a distinct living entity who created the world by an act of will, is aware of everything that happens in the world, is concerned about human actions, distinguishes between good and evil and expresses thoughts and feelings. God is present everywhere in the universe but also has an existence that transcends ordinary reality; God is all-powerful and all-knowing.

The modernist view is naturalist. God is a process within human existence, a redemptive force within society. Mystical understandings about God—which transcend distinctions between the natural and the supernatural—are found in both traditionalist and modernist thinking. None of the denominations is especially doctrinaire about God, but all are dogmatic about the other three core elements of Judaism.

The traditionalist belief is that the Torah was dictated by God—letter by letter—to Moses at Sinai and that the Hebrew text of the Torah in use today comprises the same words that Moses received from God. The Torah can be interpreted by applying the formal principles of rabbinic logic, as discussed in chapter 7. This view is called *Torah Misinai*—Torah from Sinai. It is important to understand that Jewish traditionalists are not literalists. That is, they believe that every word of the Torah has multiple meanings, that God uses metaphors and that personal interpretations are valid. In fact, as I explain in chapter 7, classical rabbinic Judaism adopted a system of logical inference specifically designed to generate multiple meanings from the Torah.

Modernists believe that the Torah was compiled over a period of time from different sources, both written and oral; its teachings may have been inspired by God, but its words were composed by Israel's ancestors. Later generations of Jews redacted and organized the material into five books. Modernists study Torah by applying archeological, linguistic and anthropological tools as well as traditional approaches. They believe that every passage of the Torah is open to interpretation by the reader, whereas traditionalists rely on authoritative commentaries. However, traditionalists insist that all Jews must conform to Jewish law when it comes to the observance of the Torah's commandments, as opposed to discussion of its ideas.

Although the *Halachah* is the formal codified body of Jewish law, in reality it cannot have the force of law for any Jew in America because everyone residing in America is governed by the laws of the state; it can only be binding upon Jews who voluntarily accept it as such. Traditionalists consider Jewish law to be fully binding on all Jews today; modernists do not. Accordingly, traditionalists expect every Jew to follow the *Halachah* not only with regard to religious observances but in all aspects of daily life as well. The *Halachah* regulates what Jews may eat and what they may wear, what activities are prohibited on the Sabbath, how they make love.

Israel is the Jewish people, the nation that descended from the tribe of Judah. All Jews agree that anyone born to Jewish parents is a member of the House of Israel. The difference of opinions arises when only one parent is Jewish. During the biblical period, status as an Israelite was transmitted through the father; this is known as patrilineal descent. During the rabbinic period, the law was changed; status was to be conferred through the mother, or matrilineal descent. The traditionalist view maintains the rabbinic ruling: Jewish identity depends on the individual's mother. The liberal view is actually a hybrid of the biblical and rabbinic positions: Jewish identity may be transmitted through the mother *or* the father.

The denominations can be distinguished from one another by whether they endorse the traditionalist or the modernist view of the classic issues of Judaism. Orthodox Judaism takes the traditional position on all four. The Conservative movement accepts a range of understandings about God, but officially maintains the traditional belief in a theistic, supernatural God. The Reform view is no different from the Conservative when it comes to belief in God. Reconstructionism, however, was founded on the philosophy of Mordecai Kaplan, who in the 1950s proposed a non-supernatural understanding of God as "the power that makes for salvation."

The Conservative, Reform and Reconstructionist movements all take the modernist position regarding the Torah. They teach scientific methods of biblical criticism along with the classical rabbinic commentaries. However, the modernist movements part company over Jewish law and Israel. Like the Orthodox, the Conservative movement holds that the *Halachah* is binding. However, Conservative Judaism believes that rabbinic edicts of the past must be understood within the social context of their times and that its Committee on Law and Standards has the authority to change the *Halachah* in response to new circumstances. The Orthodox denomination believes that modern rabbis may enact only those modifications that make the law *more* stringent. The Reconstructionist and Reform movements teach that the Jewish law is not binding; ritual practice is accepted as part of Jewish civilization, and each movement establishes its own standards.

Regarding the issue of membership in the House of Israel, the Conservative movement agrees with the Orthodox that Jewish identity is transmitted through the individual's mother. The Reconstructionist and Reform movements take the liberal position that an individual may be accepted as a Jew if either mother or father is Jewish and the person is raised as Jew. All four movements accept the idea of conversion to Judaism, and all four agree that a Jew who chooses to convert to another religion is no longer a member of the House of Israel.

Discussions about the meaning of God, Torah, Jewish law and Israel have been essential aspects of Judaism for many centuries. In comparison, both the structure of American Judaism and its themes are quite recent. Yet the invention of a new Judaism is still hard to see against the dramatic backdrop of the other events, not because it was any less significant or transformative, but because its very intent was to remain invisible. The rabbis who created denominational Judaism found it difficult to acknowledge the extent of their innovations because of their own internal conflict between tradition and modernization. They needed to reassure the immigrants—and themselves—that American Judaism had not discarded anything. So rather than say that New World Judaism had replaced Old World Judaism, the founders of American Judaism preferred to say that Old World Judaism had been modified in light of new circumstances. The cautiousness of the rabbinate mirrored the emotions of the laity.

The rabbis who migrated to America did not escape the culture shock of their compatriots, nor were the rabbis already here immune to its effects. They absorbed the anxiety of their fellow Jews and echoed the fear about the future and the mourning for the past in their own teachings. But because these men were intellectuals and students of the Enlightenment, they reflexively expressed their emotions as intellectual constructs. Hidden within the themes of continuity, survival and authenticity, their worries infused what they wrote and spoke about the Jewish religion in America and are very much a part of American Judaism today. These concepts constitute the embedded ideology of denominational Judaism, although they have never been formally acknowledged. These elements of denominational thinking were never central to Judaism prior to the twentieth century, even though they are quite characteristic of Judaism in America today. Today worries about continuity, authenticity and survival have become so prevalent in discourse about the meaning of Jewishness and the fate of the Jewish people that it is nearly impossible to think about Judaism in other terms. Nor is it easy to move forward from the attitudes of despair, apprehension and self-doubt these notions have instilled in the American Jewish community.

Unrecognized emotions lead to faulty thinking, and this is exactly what has happened in American Judaism. Anxiety and grief clothed as ideology have produced a constellation of false assumptions about the Jewish civilization. With its theologians, its seminaries, its rabbis, its publishing houses and its youth camps, denominational Judaism has ground the lenses through which most contemporary thinkers view Judaism past, present and future. It has produced a worldview that is dominated by the belief that the existence and authenticity of American Jews is tenuous. As a result of this perspective, subjective interpretations of both Jewish history and Jewish literary sources by denominational Judaism are so convincing that most people believe they are objective facts. Thus denominational Judaism continues to preserve concepts that were generated by the psychological trauma of cultural dislocation a century ago. None of them is true, yet they are rarely questioned. In this sense, they are myths. They are the myths of American Judaism, and they strongly affect its self-concept as a community. Consider these myths:

- Judaism is a four-thousand-year-old religion whose beliefs and practices originated in the Bible.

- Judaism in America is disappearing through assimilation and the Jewish population is at risk of dying out.
- An ideal Jewish life existed years ago in the small towns of Eastern Europe, and the popular image of the shtetl reflects a real world.
- The Jewish religion was founded on reason, and Jews have been a people of law and logic throughout their history.
- The denominations are Judaism's historical governing bodies, and they represent normative Judaism in America.
- Rabbis are Judaism's official practitioners.
- The Jewish population will be sustained if Jews marry other Jews exclusively, and intermarriage is a threat to the survival of Judaism.

Even though none of these claims is true, they dictate the day-by-day policies and practices of American Judaism. Nonetheless, for the well-being and growth of Judaism in America, it is essential that we recognize these lingering anxieties and correct these misconceptions.

What psychological and historical forces affecting Jews in the beginning of the twentieth century caused these particular myths to arise? How did they become so entrenched that they dominate Jewish discourse today? Why are they being preserved without question, and what price is being paid for perpetuating them? And what would Judaism—and Jewishness—look like if these notions could be set aside? These are the questions I hope to address throughout the pages that follow as we explore the myths of the old American Judaism and how Jews today are finding their way to a new American Judaism.

2

HISTORY, CONTINUITY AND PERSPECTIVE

Most American Jews today imagine their religion to be far older than it actually is. The genealogies in the Hebrew Bible lead back four thousand years to Abraham, and while some rabbis and textbooks treat the story of Abraham as historical fact and some do not, they all teach that Judaism as practiced in America today began with the first Hebrew ancestors. Although the Bible's accounting of the ages of the patriarchs is not realistic, and Jewish tradition has never depended on a literal interpretation of Scripture, when it comes to the age of Judaism even modern Jewish authorities say it is four thousand years old.

Whether the stories in Genesis are true or not, Judaism was not created out of whole cloth in the distant past. Although some threads of oral literature may go back four thousand years, and such essential principles as monotheism and social justice have remained constant throughout Jewish history, many of the beliefs and almost all of the customs of that era would be totally unfamiliar to Jews today. Two thousand years ago, the Jewish religion involved a centralized system of priests and animal sacrifices. The fundamental institutions of American Judaism—the denomination and the modern rabbi—developed within the past 150 years, and many of their concepts and practices are entirely twentieth-century American products.

Along with misconceptions about Judaism's age, unfounded theories about historical continuity color how most Jews in America understand their religion today. Despite the fact that denominationalism itself is a modern invention, American Judaism imagines a link between the present and the ancient past for every concept, whether God or Israel or Torah or Jewish law. The same bias compels denominational thinkers to portray all instances of change and innovation within the Jewish religion—no matter how momentous—as some sort of gradual evolution that has been occurring without interruption for four thousand years. No voices from the past talk about Judaism in terms of organic development over time; the concept itself is a twentieth-century American phenomenon.

There is a price to be paid for perpetuating the myth of Judaism's four-thousand-year age. Aside from the fact that it misrepresents the history of the Jewish religion, it hinders relations with the Christian community. Even though Christianity's history parallels that of modern, post–Second Temple Judaism, Jews and gentiles alike have come to believe that Judaism is the parent of Christianity rather than its sibling. By granting Judaism unfair seniority, religious leaders obstruct meaningful interreligious dialogue. A similar barrier may affect future dialogue with the Islamic community. Furthermore, the imbedded theme of continuity hampers denominational Judaism's relationship with its own members. By describing the institutions and concepts it introduced as an organic process of gradual evolution rather than a bold response to a new society, American Judaism presents a timid picture of itself, devoid of spirit and originality.

From Jewish denominations to Ivy League universities, the age of Judaism is accepted without question, even though there is no evidence for it outside the Book of Genesis. According to Reconstructionist leader Milton Steinberg, "Judaism has four thousand years of history behind it and in it,"[1] and the Conservative movement proclaims that Judaism has, "for four thousand years, emphasized a strong sense of family and the value of a close community."[2] The Orthodox movement Aish Hatorah teaches that Jewish women "have been lighting candles every Friday night for 4,000 years."[3] Reform rabbi Morris Kertzer describes Judaism as "one of the oldest religions known to man, with a tradition that reaches back to the dawn of recorded history."[4] The independent website About Judaism calls it "a four-thousand-year-old treasure."[5] Brown University informs its faculty and students that "Jews understand Judaism in terms of its 4,000-year history,"[6] while the BBC reports that "Judaism originated in Israel around four thousand years ago."[7]

In addition to teaching that Judaism began in ancient times, denominational authorities insist that Judaism gradually grew from its biblical origins into the civilization that it is today. For example, although a recent textbook produced by the Reconstructionist movement acknowledges that Judaism has changed constantly throughout its history, it goes to great lengths to interpret all change within the context of evolution. The authors explain that Jewish "holidays, practices, and even beliefs have evolved, and they must continue to evolve." In other words, contemporary Judaism is not the result of any sudden transformation imposed by outside forces; the change has always been incremental, and all change comes from within the community. The authors claim that in order to "keep up" with a changing world, Judaism has "undergone adaptation," but at the same time "we must continue to be deeply immersed in the worlds of our ancestors."[8] They conclude their discussion by invoking the usual denominational themes of both survival and continuity with a reference to the "process of continuing Jewish survival."

American Judaism has always been uneasy about acknowledging its own originality. Even the founders of the Reform movement in the 1800s, who had introduced radical departures from tradition, wanted American Jews to see all changes as "organic, growing out of the historic fabric of Judaism."[9] Their concept of cultural evolution and continuity with ancient times is so much a part of American Judaism's worldview that Jewish thinkers today automatically try to establish a four-thousand-year history for every idea. For instance, Rabbi Arthur Green in his theological exposition *Seek My Face, Speak My Name* talks about how people can experience God's presence in their lives: "[Abraham's] faith in following this [divine] voice marks the first step in the path we still seek to walk. His and his beloved Sarah's longing for children shapes for all time the Jewish concern for offspring, and our devotion to passing down our tradition from one generation to another. To break that link between generations is to break faith with this wonderful old couple who put so much trust in us, the descendants for whom they prayed."[10] Ostensibly Green is talking about the personal redemption that comes from finding God, but his plea for unbroken continuity with ancient times could have come from any of hundreds of textbooks, rabbis' sermons or synagogue newsletters on any topic. His image of the "wonderful old couple" praying for their children is like a scene from *Fiddler on the Roof*. When Green was a newly ordained rabbi, he demonstrated unusual vision and courage by abandoning denominationalism to explore new paths. As one of the founders of the postdenominational Havurah movement, he helped create a robust and thriving new form of Judaism in America. Yet his need to give the impression of a seamless continuity from past to present is characteristic of twentieth-century American Judaism. This is not surprising, since Green is a product of denominational Judaism; he was trained as a rabbi in the Conservative movement. The fact that the denominational worldview is so engrained in the writing of even nonconforming thinkers like Green shows how difficult it is for today's Jews to break free of the myths of American Judaism.

DISASSEMBLING THE MYTH

Although it is possible that ancestors of the Hebrews lived four thousand years ago, the only record of any of the patriarchs is the biblical narrative, which itself was not committed to parchment until centuries later. While many details in the story of Abraham reflect ancient Babylonian society, the Bible also says that he lived to be 175 years old and that his wife, Sarah, was 100 years old when she gave birth to Isaac. Since the Book of Genesis lists even older ages for other individuals, it is possible that the numbers were meant to be symbolic rather than literal. In any case, the stories in Genesis are not a reliable source for establishing an historical timeline. There is no way to know for certain how much of Abraham is history and how much is folklore. Fragments of Sumerian legends preserved in the Hebrew Bible, along with isolated Uggaritic and Akkadian words and allusions to the Code of Hammurabi, point to the Fertile Crescent four millennia ago. However, no archeological evidence confirms the existence of the Hebrews at that time. In fact, no Jewish document or other artifact has been discovered so far that is more than three thousand years old. Possible references to Hebrews are found in the Amarna tablets (1300s BCE) and the Merneptah tablet (1200s BCE), but these are far from clear. There is scant if any archeological evidence to confirm the existence of Solomon or David as powerful kings who ruled around 1000 BCE. Yet in spite of the lack of unambiguous evidence outside the stories in the Bible for Hebrew ancestry dating back to the time of Abraham, scholars both Jewish and gentile repeat the number four thousand as if it were an established historical fact rather than a tradition or a theory.

So if Judaism is not four thousand years old, how old is it? Actually, it is not easy to assign any one specific age to Judaism because there are many separate entities that can be called "Judaism." The Jews are a civilization with a country of origin, languages, laws, literature, folkways, history, art, social institutions and dynasties. Religion is part of that nationhood, and history has seen several different manifestations of Jewish civilization. Even if there was a confederation of Israelites in Canaan around 1500 BCE, as described in the Hebrew Bible, that society all came to an end with the Babylonian conquests of Judea in 586 BCE. The Judean nation that began with the return from Exile ended with the destruction of the Second Temple and the Second Commonwealth in the year 70 CE. The world of the rabbinic academies ceased to exist by the Middle Ages. The culture of Eastern European Jewry that began in the fourteenth century was destroyed forever in the twentieth.

As the civilization of the Jewish people has changed dramatically over the centuries, its religious practices have taken on different forms. In fact, the religion of the Jewish people has had several distinct incarnations: the practices of the patriarchal period of the Bible, priestly Judaism, rabbinic Judaism and Diaspora Judaism. The Judaism of twentieth-century America, denominational Judaism, is the fifth version of the Jewish religion. These different forms of Judaism are readily identified by certain defining characteristics: the mode of worship, the time and place of worship, and the individuals who perform the worship. The differences between biblical practices and modern Judaism are so great that they cannot be considered the same religion.

The stories of the patriarchs in Genesis may be mythic, but the Bible does provide a realistic picture of one major aspect of ancient Near Eastern religion: the practice of sacrifice. The Torah describes the sacrifices performed by Cain and Abel and the Hebrew patriarchs Abraham and Jacob. These accounts match what is known about the religious rituals of other ancient Near Eastern peoples. First the person who wanted to offer a sacrifice built an altar or structure for the fire, typically on top of a hill. Then the object to be sacrificed—human, animal or farm produce—was placed on the altar and burned. Unlike their neighbors, the Hebrews did not sacrifice humans. According to the details in the Torah, the smoke would rise up and God would smell the aroma of the cooked food. As recounted in Genesis 8:20–12: "Then Noah built an altar to the Lord and brought of every clean animal and every clean bird for sacrifice as burnt offerings on the altar. The Lord smelled the pleasing odor." In this case God responded by vowing not to bring another catastrophic deluge upon the world. Several passages in Genesis—such as 12:8—describe Abraham and Jacob building altars and invoking the name of God. This was the religion of the patriarchal period: decentralized, sacrificial, private, with no set times or places. Interestingly, the Book of Genesis provides us with the history of a very different form of communion with God for women during the patriarchal period. Women did not build altars; rather, they would cry out, and God would hear and respond. The stories about Hagar and Rachael are fascinating illustrations.

The religion described in the Book of Genesis no longer exists, if it ever did exist. It was replaced by other modes of worship thousands of years ago. To the extent that the accounts in the Bible reflect historical reality, priestly Judaism became the religion of Israel when the Jewish people became a nation. Extensive passages in the later four books of the Torah—Exodus, Leviticus, Numbers and Deuteronomy—prescribe the centralized system of highly formalized sacrifices that replaced the patriarchal mode. Although there is evidence that during the early stages of priestly Judaism there was more than one altar, the worship of God was no longer a private act. Instead, there was a public altar for the entire community. The priestly tribe of the Levites was designated to perform the rituals exclusively. The line of Kohen within the tribe of Levi conducted the actual sacrifices; the ordinary Levites were responsible for other functions, such as singing and instrumental music. The sacrifices were performed at set times of the day, of the week, of the month and of the year. After the Exodus from Egypt, the commandments in Deuteronomy forbade individual sacrifices. Once a permanent sanctuary was built in Jerusalem, Jews would have to travel to the capital for worship. The sacrifices were accompanied by musical instruments and a choir of Levites. There were a few specified prayers led by the priests with the people responding. The element of the aroma of the sacrifices, which is emphasized in

Genesis, remained a feature of the priestly system: "Let [Aaron and his sons] turn the ram completely into smoke upon the altar. It is a burnt offering to the Lord, a pleasing odor, a sacrifice by fire to the Lord" (Exodus 29:18). The priestly mode of Jewish religious practice was still based on sacrifices of animals and produce, but centralized worship was conducted on behalf of the nation by a bloodline of priests and Levites. Priestly Judaism was the religion of the Jewish people when David established Jerusalem as the political and religious capital of his kingdom and when Solomon built the First Temple. The Temple period as described in the Hebrew Bible resembles the nationalized and highly formalized ritual systems of the great Babylonian, Greek and Roman empires that dominated the region in ancient times.

The religious system of the First Temple period is gone as well. The Hebrew Bible describes the conquest of Judea and the destruction of its Temple in the year 586 BCE. The Jews who were transplanted to Babylonia after the fall of Jerusalem found ways to maintain their religion without the Temple. Although by biblical law the sacrifices could be performed only in Jerusalem and only by the priests, these Jews created other rituals they could practice in their homes at the same sacred times designated by the Torah. The communities they built in exile thrived and eventually became major centers of Jewish life that survived long after the end of the exile and the building of the Second Temple.

According to the Bible, when the exiles returned and established a second Jewish commonwealth in Judea, they introduced a major change to the Temple service: the reading of the Torah. This new practice paved the way for the forms of the Jewish religion that would follow, and today the formal reading of the Torah is a central ritual of Judaism. During the five-hundred-year period of the Second Temple, the profession of Torah scribe evolved into the class of the rabbis, who would meet in local study centers to interpret both the written and oral Torah and to expound on Jewish law. Major rabbinic centers existed in Babylonia, far from the reach of the priests of Jerusalem or the kings of Judea. This new institution of the local house of study and worship—the synagogue—existed in tandem with the Temple in Jerusalem.

When the Second Temple was destroyed in 70 CE, and both the Jewish state and priestly Judaism ended, the synagogues in Judea and Babylonia were already fully functional. From that point on, the Jewish religion consisted of Torah study, prayer and non-sacrificial rituals conducted by private individuals in homes and local synagogues. Rabbinic Judaism replaced Second Temple priestly Judaism. Nothing remained of the Jewish modes of worship associated with the Bible except for the reading of the Torah. Rabbinic Judaism would be the religion of the Jewish people for the next five hundred years.

Over time, the Judean communities declined while surrounding communities thrived. As Jewish life in Judea disintegrated, Jews moved farther and farther into regions in the Arabian Peninsula, North Africa and the Mediterranean. By the Middle Ages, there were Jewish communities across Europe and in the Far East. The rabbinic academies were no more, but the other institutions of rabbinic Judaism worked very well for the new communities of the Diaspora. The text of the Torah was portable. The prayers and home rituals traveled with Jews as they spread around the world. As the Diaspora widened, the Jewish communities became more separated from one another. With increasing isolation, they became more autonomous. They built synagogues and gathered there at the prescribed times. They studied the classic rabbinic texts. The civilization of Judaism lived without a homeland, without a central government and without a center of worship. Instead, individual Jewish communities established themselves within the homelands of other peoples. These communities were generally self-governing, for until the 1800s Jews were not citizens of the lands where they resided. By the end of the nineteenth century, Diaspora Judaism represented the largest population, the broadest geographical extent, the widest cultural and ideological diversity and the longest span of years in all of Jewish history. The twentieth century changed all that when the center of Jewish life shifted from the Old World to the New and denominational Judaism became the religion of the Jews in America.

As I mentioned before, denominational Judaism has its roots in the German Reform movement of the 1800s. The key differences between denominational Judaism and earlier forms of worship are the centrality of the rabbis in Jewish ritual life (discussed in more depth in chapter 7) and the increased inclusion of women. Over the course of the twentieth century, all of the denominations made major accommodations in religious practice as women gradually became equal members of American society. Each denomination proceeded at its own pace along a continuum—some going farther than others—from equal education, to increased participation in ritual life, to congregational leadership, to the ordination of women as rabbis. By the end of the century, all three modernist movements were ordaining women. Although Orthodox Judaism does not ordain women and does not grant them the same legal status as men, many Orthodox congregations have instituted modernizations. For example, women no longer sit behind a *mechitzah* (partition) at the back of the synagogue or in a balcony; men and women sit on separate sides of the synagogue, the *mechitzah* between them. Some Orthodox women now wear distinctive women's *tallitot* (prayer shawls) at services,[11] a practice that was unheard of in the Old World. Most important, modern Orthodox girls receive an extensive Jewish education along with the boys.

There have been several major forms of the Jewish religion, each distinct from the other. Each one of them could be called "Judaism," but denominational Judaism is the predominant religion of American Jewry today.

JUDAISM'S TRUE AGE

Even though rabbis and textbooks are fond of making connections between contemporary Jewish customs and the Torah, almost all the customs and ceremonies of Judaism began well after the time of the Torah. In fact, the real formative period of what we know as

Judaism began in 586 BCE with the Babylonian conquest of Judea. Many of the most familiar elements of the religion, such as the Sabbath eve home rituals of candle lighting, sanctification of wine (kiddush) and sharing of loaves of challah, receive no mention in the Bible at all. They began in the Jewish communities living in Babylonia as substitutes for the priestly rites of the Temple in Jerusalem and developed over time. The practice of affixing the mezzuzah (a small box containing passages from the Pentateuch) to the door of a Jewish house and the ceremony of binding the tefillin (small leather cases containing Torah passages) to the arm and the forehead most likely began at that time and place as well.[12] The complex rabbinic debates about the details of these particular observances, meticulously recorded in the Mishnah and the Talmud, indicate that they were not firmly established until well after the Babylonian exile, many centuries after the time of the Five Books of Moses. While it is true that the Book of Numbers commands the Israelites to tie fringes on their garments, none of the other books of the Bible makes any reference to it as an Israelite practice. In any case, the configuration of knots tied into the corner tassels of the prayer shawl, as well as the tallit itself, are postbiblical developments.

Some historians believe that the entire Jewish liturgical calendar was established during the Babylonian exile and that it was the exile community that endowed the agricultural festivals of Passover, Sukkot (Tabernacles) and Shavuot (Pentecost) with their historical and theological meanings.[13]

Weddings and funerals are perhaps the most familiar rites of any religion today. Many people would be surprised to learn that the traditional Jewish wedding ceremony did not originate in biblical times. No wedding ceremonies of any kind are described in the Hebrew Bible. In fact, the Bible doesn't even use the term *wife*. A man simply "acquired" a woman—or women, for that matter—from her family. The sharing of wine, the giving of a ring, the statement of betrothal, the *huppah* (wedding canopy), the *ketubah* (marriage contract)—all of these were instituted by the rabbis around two thousand years ago, well after the time of the Bible. And monogamy—which is what most people think of when they think of Jewish marriage—did not become the standard practice until much later. Polygamy was not officially outlawed among the Ashkenazi Jews until 1000, in a famous *takkanah* (amendment) of Rabbi Gershom ben Judah. The Jews of Spain practiced polygamy until the 1400s, and some Sephardic groups practiced it into the twentieth century. Similarly, the Jewish funeral practices, from the preparation of the body to its internment, were developed during the rabbinic period. The laws of mourning originated during that period as well, but many of the customs came much later than that.

The practice of male infant circumcision, which is so characteristic of the Jewish people, is mentioned in the Bible. However, it did not become the elaborate ceremony it is today—with chair of Elijah and other rituals—until after the exile. Covering the head as a sign of piety is discussed for the first time in the rabbinic literature, but there is no evidence for the custom of wearing yarmulkes (skullcaps) prior to the medieval period. The Siddur, the Hebrew prayer book, developed after the 800s,[14] and the order of services was not standardized until the invention of printing. Tallit and yarmulke, life-cycle ceremonies, tefillin and siddur—these central religious observances of normative Judaism are no more than two thousand years old. And none of the ceremonies of Judaism today is four thousand years old.

Not only are the customs and ceremonies of Judaism far more recent than most people have been led to believe, the specific details of how these rituals were to be performed varied from community to community during the Diaspora. The Talmud, which records intricate legal discussions of all these matters, preserves multiple opinions of different rabbinic authorities, and generations of rabbinic scholars over the next several hundred years did not always agree about which opinions were binding. Several leading rabbis compiled organized codes of Jewish law. Maimonides' Mishneh Torah, compiled in the 1100s, is one of the most respected, but the Shulchan Aruch, published in the 1500s, became the standard.[15] The elaborate laws of kashruth—regulating how animal products may or may not be used for food—which are so much a part of Orthodox Jewish life, were not fixed until that time. In fact, what we recognize as Orthodox Judaism today is no more than several centuries old. The word *orthodox* means "uniform law," and it was the Shulchan Aruch that made Orthodox Judaism possible. Although many people believe Orthodoxy represents the oldest form of Judaism, in fact it is not very much older than the modernist movements.

The institutions and ideology that constitute denominational Judaism, of course, are no more than a hundred or so years old, and many important ritual practices were created during the modern era. The Hebrew liturgy was translated into English; Orthodox, Conservative, Reconstructionist and Reform prayer books are printed with Hebrew and English on facing pages. American rabbis composed contemporary readings in English for various religious, family, personal and civic occasions and published these in the denominational prayer books along with the traditional prayers. Along with modernized synagogue services led by rabbis, the denominations created important new ceremonies. They transformed the relatively simple custom of celebrating a young man's first *aliyah* (recitation of blessings at the reading of the Torah, typically during an ordinary weekday service) into the elaborate bar mitzvah ceremony held on the Sabbath. The Reform movement created the confirmation service for students who completed Sunday school at the end of high school years, and the Reconstructionist movement created the bat mitzvah ceremony to celebrate the coming-of-age of young women.

Even the word *Judaism* is a modern creation. There is no corresponding Hebrew term either in the Hebrew Bible or the classic rabbinic literature.[16] The Jews of the Old World used *yiddishkeit*, which means simply "Jewishness" and refers to the entire culture of the people, not just their religion. It was not until the emergence of the Reform movement in the nineteenth century in central Europe that Jews began to differentiate their religious concepts and observances from the rest of their civilization and therefore needed a name for their religion.

THE THEME OF CONTINUITY

American Jewish leaders do not deny that Judaism has changed over the centuries, but their claim that these changes have been the result of a continuous organic process within Judaism itself is just as inaccurate as the myth that Judaism is four thousand old. Not only is there as much discontinuity as continuity throughout the history of Judaism's communal structure and religious observance, for the most part these changes have been compelled by outside forces. Whatever the transforming power of ancestral beliefs, Judaism has also been affected by the actions of other nations, by the accidents of history and by the general arbitrariness of life on earth. Numerous historical experiences—and discontinuities—over many centuries were critical to the shaping of Jewish civilization. It is true for any nation that outside forces can have an effect on a people beyond its own ability to control them. Random and unforeseen events influence every society. When the actions of others impact the Jewish people, as they have throughout Jewish history, they are not part of any evolution of Judaism. If anything they interrupt Judaism, sidetrack it or lead it in a new direction.

If Nebuchadnezzar had not conquered Judea in the sixth century BCE and forced its middle class into exile in Babylonia, the Books of Jeremiah and of Ezekiel would never have been written and many Jewish institutions would not have been created. Suppose Cyrus the Great of Persia had not taken over Babylonia in 537 BCE. Ezra would not have established the Torah as the central law of a new Jewish commonwealth, and the Second Temple would never have been built. If the Greek empire had not overtaken Assyria and Assyria then overtaken Judea in the third century BCE, the Hellenistic values of scholarship and the veneration of classical texts might not have influenced the Jews as much as they did. The

Greek concept of interpreting classical texts by principles of logic would not have become the force behind the development of rabbinic law. If the Roman general Titus had not besieged Jerusalem and sacked the Second Temple in the year 70 CE, animal sacrifice might have continued to be the dominant Jewish mode of worship.

Since the earliest times, the fate of the Jewish people has been determined as much by the destinies of other peoples as by the vision of the Torah. There is no way to know exactly what present-day Judaism would look like if the Jews of Western Europe had never enjoyed the benefits of the Enlightenment that followed the French Revolution. Alternatively, if the French military had not falsely convicted their only Jewish officer of treason in 1895, inspiring Theodore Herzl to write *Der Judenstaat* and give birth to Zionism, Jewish intellectuals might not have established settlements in Palestine in the early 1900s. If Russia had not annexed parts of Poland in the late 1700s, there would not have been so many Jews under Russian rule; if Czar Alexander II had not been assassinated in 1881, the oppression of the Jews might not have been so severe, and millions of Eastern European Jews might not have migrated to America. If the Great Depression had not afflicted Germany in the 1930s, Adolf Hitler might not have become chancellor, millions of Jews would not have been murdered, the State of Israel might not have been established in 1948, and Judaism would be a very different religion than it is today.

It may be appealing to use evolution as a model for the history of Judaism, and human societies do indeed resemble living organisms in some ways. However, it makes just as much sense to adopt a geopolitical view of the basic facts of Jewish life over the centuries. The ancestral homeland of the Jewish people is situated on a narrow bridge of land that connects the Arabian Peninsula and the continent of Africa. A mere 130 miles of Judean territory marked the boundary between the empires of Assyria and Egypt, ensuring that the conquering armies of ambitious, aggressive nations would march back and forth across the land for ages. Judea's location on the Mediterranean Sea guaranteed that the rising civilizations of

Greece and Rome would compete for domination of the few thousand square miles that comprise the birthplace of Judaism. During the twentieth century, Israel's strategic front on both the Mediterranean Sea and the Gulf of Suez kept it on the front page of world news.

As the Roman empire declined, social conditions within Judea deteriorated to the point where Judaism no longer had a viable homeland. The Jews became a Diaspora. It was inevitable that Diaspora Judaism would be characterized by disruption and change as the result of the Jewish people's dispersion among the different races, cultures and religious civilizations of the world. The Judaism of the communities that settled in Babylonia was very different from the religion of Judea. The same is true of the Jewish communities that developed within Muslim, Catholic and Protestant lands. And the same is true of the Judaism that was born in America in the twentieth century.

THE BIRTH OF A MYTH

The myth of Judaism's great age came to America with the immigrants themselves. The vast majority of the Jews of Eastern Europe did not have broad secular educations, and they had no way to know that the laws and customs by which they lived their lives came from different times and different places. With no historical perspective about the development of Jewish civilization, they could not have realized that some practices were newer than others. Nor could they have appreciated the fact that very few of the elements of what they knew to be the Jewish way of life actually originated in the time of the Torah. It was easy for them to picture Abraham wearing a yarmulke and tallit and Sarah lighting candles on Friday night.

Although the faithful immigrants may have believed that all their customs and ceremonies originated in the Bible, the modern rabbinic scholars who assumed leadership of American Jewry at the beginning of the twentieth century did have historical perspective. It is likely that they knew that the custom of kindling Sabbath lights was not established before the sixth century BCE and that skullcaps and prayer shawls did not become the religious garb of Jews until the common era. They certainly appreciated that the institutions they were inventing—the denominational structure and the modern rabbinate—were new to the Jewish people. Why then did modern American rabbis reinforce, rather than dispel, the myth of Judaism's ancient heritage? The answer can be found in the psychological factors that affected the founders of denominational Judaism and in the cultural influences of America a century ago.

The Jewish immigrants who arrived in America at the beginning of the twentieth century wanted to bring at least some of their ancestral way of life into the new land. The rabbis who came with them sought ways to transfer to a new venue their centuries-old authority as determiners of Jewish law. Those rabbis who were already in America saw themselves as leaders of a displaced nation, responsible for adapting Old World Judaism to life in the New World. American rabbis believed that the survival of Judaism in America called for new approaches to religious life, but at the same time they were careful to downplay the extent of the changes they were introducing. They wanted the Eastern European immigrants to see the institutions of the new American Judaism as authentic, and they wanted the immigrant generation to accept the authority of denominational Judaism's leadership. In order to keep Jewish tradition alive, they felt it was important to claim an ancient pedigree for the institutions they were building and the concepts they were introducing. So American rabbis began to teach that the practices and organizations they created for a new generation of Jews were no less a fulfillment of God's covenant with Abraham than were the practices and institutions of Eastern Europe.

American rabbis also were affected by the general mood of their generation. The immigrants who emerged from Ellis Island entered an especially transformative culture. Early twentieth-century America was a brave new world singing an anthem of industrial innovation and social progress. American Judaism enthusiastically resonated with the optimistic music of modernism. American rabbis of the time accepted the modernist concept of progress as an innate force of nature propelling human society toward eventual perfection, adopting it as if it were a foundational belief of Judaism itself, even though no work of Jewish literature prior to the Industrial Age contains any such notion.

Swept up in the New World spirit of invention and modernity, American rabbis were inspired to undertake bold steps to construct a modern home for Old World Judaism. However, the very newness of the institutions they were creating aroused anxiety. Not only did the changes they were introducing represent a significant departure from the past, the very rapidity of the change was unnerving. The fact that new institutions could replace old practices in so short a time implied the new institutions themselves might be temporary. They could not help but wonder whether changing times would prove denominational Judaism to be a passing phenomenon. As part of the immigrant generation, American rabbis themselves struggled to balance the tension between modernity and tradition. But the very spirit of modernity and invention that had inspired them also intimidated them.

Ironically, modern Western culture came to their rescue. New theories about cultural evolution provided the founders of denominational Judaism with a reassuring way to look at the changes they were advocating. The movements combined modernism's optimistic faith that human society is constantly improving with their own need to link the present to the past, and they began to describe the Jewish religion as if it were a natural organism. Rabbis became fond of using the terms *evolve*, *grow* and *adapt*. This was a new way of thinking for Jews, but it quickly became a permanent part of twentieth-century American Judaism. Because denominational Judaism is constantly seeking to link everything within contemporary Judaism to the Jewish religion of previous times, while at the same time affirming its belief in human progress, denominational speakers and writers tend to express the theme of continuity in terms of evolution. This language is found in all kinds of material produced by the movements all through the twentieth century.

The rabbis who created denominational Judaism found the idea of evolution far more appealing than innovation because it helped them resolve their own internal conflict about tradition and modernity. They needed to reassure the immigrants—and themselves as well—that American Judaism had not discarded anything. So they taught that New World Judaism had not replaced Eastern European Judaism any more than Diaspora Judaism had replaced biblical Judaism. Rather, denominational Judaism had evolved from the religion of Abraham, and Eastern European traditions were simply one station along a four-thousand-year journey. But by claiming that denominational Judaism evolved from the religion of the Bible, American rabbis reinforced the traditional belief that Judaism began with Abraham. If American Judaism is the product of a continuing process of evolution from ancient times, then Judaism must indeed be ancient.

Of course, cultural evolution is a modern concept. However, the denominational theme of religious continuity is also a product of twentieth-century America. As I mentioned, prior to the early 1900s, Judaism in America was Reform Judaism, and the Reform movement in the nineteenth century had no need to reconcile with tradition. It took full credit for breaking from the past. In fact, when the movement published a formal statement of its principles in 1885, it made strong statements of *discontinuity*: "We . . . reject all such [ceremonies] as are not adapted to the views and habits of modern civilization. . . . Such Mosaic and rabbinical laws as regulate diet, priestly purity, and dress originated in ages and under the influence of ideas entirely foreign to our present mental and spiritual state. . . . Their observance in our days is apt rather to obstruct than to further modern spiritual elevation."[17] The statement simply asserted that newer forms of Judaism replace older forms. This was Reform ideology before the migration of the Eastern European

Jews and the advent of denominational Judaism. Prior to the twentieth century, Reform movement writings in America contained none of the themes of denominational Judaism—continuity, authenticity and survival. The arrival of millions of Eastern European Jews changed all that.

By the time the waves of immigration had ended at the outbreak of World War I, Reform Judaism had adopted the theme of continuity and the evolutionary rhetoric that is characteristic of denominational Judaism today. Its new formal statement of principles, published in 1937, stated: "Reform Judaism recognizes the principle of progressive development in religion and consciously applies this principle to spiritual as well as to cultural and social life. . . . Each age has the obligation to adapt the teachings of the Torah to its basic needs in consonance with the genius of Judaism."[18]

All of the branches of Judaism in America acknowledge in some way that Judaism must change as society changes. For example, the modernist movements granted women equal participation in congregational life. The Conservative movement permitted worshippers to drive to services on the Sabbath, while the Reform movement did away with the dietary laws entirely. Even Orthodoxy, which is founded on the claim that Jewish law was revealed by God to the rabbis of old, undertook with enthusiasm the task of applying traditional law to new technology and new situations: Is the use of birth control pills permissible? How should a Jewish astronaut maintain the cycle of morning and evening prayers in outer space? Is turning on an electric lamp the same as lighting a fire? The Orthodox rabbinate in America has issued hundreds and hundreds of such new rulings on matters of Jewish law.

Each of the movements is determined to provide the leadership that will steer Judaism through the changing ways of American life. The Reform, Conservative and Reconstructionist movements were founded with the stated mission of adapting Judaism to modern society. Nonetheless, all of the branches of twentieth-century American Judaism are reticent to talk about change within Judaism. Instead, denominational discourse employs a common list of euphemisms to describe the obvious fact that Judaism today is different from the Judaism of yesterday. It sounds better to denominational ears to say that modernist movements are adding to Jewish tradition or adjusting it rather than to say they are changing beliefs or trying out entirely new practices. It sits better with denominational sentiment to believe that older forms of Judaism evolved or grew than to think that they simply were replaced by newer forms.

Institutional needs also motivated the concept of evolutionary adaptation within Jewish civilization. There are predictable psychological reasons for denominational Judaism's insistence that twentieth- and twenty-first-century Jewish life is entirely the organic result of internal forces and for its proclivity to describe any change at all—especially its own innovations—in the most modest terms. It is an obvious fact that many changes within Jewish life—like changes within the life of any social group—come as unavoidable reactions to external forces and events of the world at large. Because three major historical events—the mass migration of European Jews to the United States, the Holocaust and the founding of the modern State of Israel—all took place within fifty years, the magnitude of change within the twentieth century was greater than in any other period of Jewish history. Just as it can be disturbing for people to think that some aspects of their lives are outside their control, it is disquieting to Jewish authorities to consider that the course of Jewish life might be beyond their control as leaders. So the movements find it reassuring to interpret *all* change within Judaism as the natural outgrowth of intrinsic Jewish processes.

When the Conservative movement published a formal statement of its ideology in 1988, it acknowledged the wide variety of religious literature and institutions that comprised Judaism over the ages. Yet its innate denominational bias toward organic continuity draws a portrait of Judaism free of internal disagreements: "[Israel] produced most of the Bible, the Mishnah, the [Jerusalem] Talmud, the major Midrashim, liturgy, and other great works while the Diaspora gave us the Babylonian Talmud, Hebrew poetry, philosophical writings, commentaries, law codes, and other lasting creations. The various communities interacted in a continual symbiotic process of mutual enrichment."[19] This formulation overlooks the political tensions and civil conflicts that traumatized both Israel and the Diaspora. For instance, during the Second Temple period, the Pharisees, a kind of political party representing the rabbis, fought a long, and sometimes violent, battle against the Sadducees, who represented the priesthood and the monarchy, over which group would assume the ultimate authority of law in ancient Israel. The historian Josephus claimed that in the first century BCE, the tyrannical Sadducee king of Judea, Alexander Jannaeus, crucified eight hundred Pharisees after cutting the throats of their wives and children.[20] As for religious development in the Diaspora, when some rabbis in the Middle Ages introduced mysticism to Jewish life, creating the Hasidic movement that continues to grow today, the mainstream rabbis of the classic Talmudic academies condemned the Hasidic masters in the most contemptuous terms. European Jewry became divided into the mystical Hasidim and rationalist Mitnagdim (the opponents); the two factions despised each other for centuries.

If change can be seen as coming from within Judaism itself, then there is a role for the authority of denominationalism. But if change is imposed by either outside forces or cataclysmic internal upheaval, it can be neither predicted nor controlled. In that case the denomination's influence would be far more limited than it would like to believe. Because it is a human institution, denominational Judaism does not want to accept limitations to its ability to administer Jewish religion in America; and because it is a human institution, it does not want to accept the inevitability of its own mortality. As much as denominational Judaism downplays its role in creating a new form of Judaism in America in the twentieth century to replace European Diaspora Judaism, recognizing that fact authorizes other groups of rabbis or lay leaders to create even newer forms of Judaism.

Beliefs about historical continuity and internal adaptation—the dual elements of cultural evolution—are essential to American Judaism's world view in the twenty-first century. According to Reform Judaism's *Statement of Principles*, published in 1999: "Throughout our history, we Jews have remained firmly rooted in Jewish tradition, even as we have learned much from our encounters with other cultures. The great contribution of Reform Judaism is that it has enabled the Jewish people to introduce innovation while preserving tradition."[21] By depending on such oblique references as "learned much from our encounters with other cultures" and "introduce innovation," these American Jewish leaders mask the fact that over the centuries, many civilizations have had major impacts on Judaism—both good and bad—and have forced wrenching transformations on Jewish life. When viewed through the denominational lens of continuity, Jewish history appears much less interesting than it actually is.

The denominational theme of continuity and evolution arose from the cultural forces of the immigrant experience. It was a valuable psychological mechanism that helped the founders of denominational Judaism to resolve their concerns about authenticity and authority. Reinterpreting change as continuity made it easier for American rabbis to balance tradition and modernity, and easier for the immigrant generation to accept American Judaism. The concept of the continuity of Judaism was useful in the early years of the twentieth century. Now that the immigrant generation is gone, the myth that all of Judaism is four thousand years old no longer serves its original purpose.

THE EFFECTS OF THE MYTH

It is natural for people to establish emotional links between present and past, to see current values grounded in ancient beliefs. Doing so can be both empowering and sustaining, but it must be balanced by respect for the truth. American Jewish leaders sometimes seem so preoccupied with keeping ancestral origins in sight that they unintentionally mislead their members about the very Judaism they are trying so hard to protect. In addition, the assumptions hidden within American Judaism can be barriers to Jewish leaders who seek to instill a sense of pride and excitement in new generations of Jews. Modern rabbis and textbooks present a sanitized Jewish history where internal crises and external cataclysms are reduced to processes of "adaptation." By insisting that the beliefs and practices of Judaism in America today are little more than evolved manifestations of a four-thousand-year-old religion, Jewish leaders create a picture of Judaism with little possibility of innovation, inspiration or surprise.

For example, the current website for the Reconstructionist movement restates its basic doctrine that Judaism is an "evolving religious civilization" and goes on to explain that "each generation subtly shapes the Jewish religion."[22] This shows the extent to which the dependence on denominational rhetoric produces inaccurate statements, because ironically such language as "subtly shapes" actually underplays Reconstructionist contributions to Jewish life. Reconstructionism, along with the other modernist movements, created significant innovations and brought major changes to Jewish religious practice in America. Translating the Hebrew prayers into English, ordaining women as rabbis, teaching the Bible from historical and sociological perspectives, building prestigious graduate schools of Judaic studies, organizing national youth groups and Hebrew summer camps—these were hardly subtle changes. Nor did they evolve gradually. They were created deliberately and boldly by American Judaism. The website reinforces the myth of historical continuity when its authors set out to describe the important role the quest for social justice has assumed within contemporary American Judaism. Instead of presenting a dynamic picture of courage and vision, the authors discount the process of change and innovation within Judaism. Even the historical significance of the social advances championed by the Reconstructionist movement itself, such as its policy of complete equality for women and sexual minorities, is blunted by the inevitable expression of reverence for the past: "generations of Jews have sharpened and distilled the ethical insights of Judaism as a result of their encounter with other cultures and traditions, and so it is in our time." Surely the contemporary Jewish view of social justice was more than just "sharpened" by the encounter with the Holocaust. "Distilled" hardly does justice to the American rabbis who marched with Martin Luther King, Jr.

Granted, these citations are taken from public relations literature intended to promote Judaism and inspire a strong sense of identity among American Jews. Nonetheless, the constant use of terms like *evolve* obscures the vibrancy of Judaism and replaces it with a much duller picture, one that is reflected in the sermons and Sunday school lessons of thousands of American Jewish congregations today. For instance, I have mentioned that the Babylonian exile was a transformative era for the Jewish people that began with major social upheaval and national trauma in 586 BCE. Many of the central practices and institutions of Judaism were created during that critical period. Historian Paul Johnson provides a dramatic account of this important time. Tracing the origin of several major Jewish practices to the Babylonian exile, he explains: "It was during the exile that ordinary Jews were first disciplined into the regular practice of their religion. . . . In exile the Jews, deprived of a state, became a nomocracy—voluntarily submitting to rule by a Law which could only be enforced by consent. Nothing like this had occurred before in history. The Exile was short in the sense that it lasted only half a century after the final fall of Judah. Yet its creative force was overwhelming. . . . From this point forward, therefore, we note the existence of an Exile and a Diaspora mentality among the Jews."[23] Although Johnson, as an historian, has no apparent need to promote Judaism, his account presents a dynamic picture. One would expect a denominational publication to portray Jewish history in similarly exciting ways. Unfortunately, this has not always been the case. The following example shows how a popular mid-twentieth-century Reform textbook presents Jewish history. Although the author recounts the same essential facts as does Johnson and describes the same period in Jewish history, he conveys an impression very different from Johnson's "overwhelming force": "Ideas grow, change, evolve; and we should expect this to be true also of religious ideas. . . . The religion of Israel has gone through a long process of evolution. Its ideas, attitudes, and practices have often been modified; only by degrees have they reached their full magnificence."[24] This text totally overlooks the important developments that took place during the Babylonian exile. By applying the lens of continuity, the author actually distorts Jewish history. Unfortunately, such language is all too typical of denominational materials. The study of Jewish history can be fascinating; such spiritless products serve only to harm American Judaism. The mild-mannered image books like this create cannot capture the imagination of new generations of Jews.

JEWISH–CHRISTIAN RELATIONS

The myth that Judaism is four thousand years old affects more than the Jewish community's own self-concept; it impedes understanding between the Jewish and Christian communities. The religion that Jews and gentiles call Judaism today has more in common with Christianity than many Jews acknowledge. Like Judaism, Christianity draws on Old Testament traditions. In varying ways, Judaism and Christianity were influenced by Greco-Roman culture. Both communities were traumatized by the ruthlessness of Roman military domination. Though their paths diverged from a common origin in Judea two thousand years ago, modern Judaism and Christianity both developed in response to the demise of priestly Judaism and the ascendancy of rabbinic Judaism. Elements borrowed from the Temple in Jerusalem and its priestly rituals can be found in both churches and synagogues today. To a large extent, the early church and rabbinic Judaism were competing sides of a debate about the meaning of the Covenant, the Torah, the oral law and the messiah.

Prior to the Christian era, Judaism was a religion of centralized worship. Though there were rabbis and synagogues, the important rites consisted of animal sacrifices conducted by priests, an exclusive bloodline of men consecrated to serve in the Temple in Jerusalem. That form of Judaism has been gone for two thousand years. What Jews and gentiles around the world think of as Judaism today is Diaspora Judaism, a two-thousand-year-old religion of decentralized worship whose important rituals are conducted in homes and in synagogues. What Jews and gentiles in America recognize as Judaism—a religion of Orthodox, Conservative, Reconstructionist and Reform denominations and their themes of survival, continuity and authenticity—is a hundred years old.

Normative Diaspora Judaism is no older than Christianity. Both emerged during the same time period as expressions of post–Second Temple Judaism; they are siblings. Not only is American Judaism a new form of Judaism, its denominational structure and its rabbinate are borrowed from Christianity.

Meaningful dialogue occurs among peers; the parties must accept each other as equals. All perceived differences of rank, from physical power to social status, interfere with mutual understanding. Clearly, Christianity is two thousand years old. While it may be less clear that what people recognize as Judaism is also two thousand years old, any claim that it is exactly twice the age of Christianity creates a significant psychological distance.

Obviously, organized religion is powerful force both in America and in the world. What has become increasingly apparent in recent years is that religious beliefs and practices are an inextricable part of the political processes of nations and the international community. When any one religious community takes offense at the actions of another, there is the potential for turmoil. It is vital for every society to understand as much as possible about the various religious sentiments of its members because no society can risk a misunderstanding. American Jews want their gentile neighbors to understand their needs and sensitivities as a minority group. It is no less important that American Jewry appreciate the issues that affect Christians, Muslims and the other religious groups that live in their communities. Candid, respectful and profound communication among religious groups is essential. Unfounded claims about American Judaism's venerable old age can only be a barrier to meaningful discourse, a discourse that is becoming more crucial every day. Moving beyond the myth of a Judaism that is four thousand years old opens up new opportunities for the religious communities in America to support each other as spiritual resources for a troubled world.

MOVING FORWARD FROM THE MYTH

An accurate understanding of Jewish history is essential to the appreciation of Judaism. The story of Jewish people—the many different places through which the Jews have passed and the many different places that have passed through Judaism—is liberating to Jewish civilization and empowering to new generations of American Jews. The various stories of Judaism—from its religious practices to its geopolitical realities—read very well without the denominational overlay of continuity. Clearing away the twentieth-century American themes of cultural evolution and social progress reveals the Jewish people as a resilient and wide-ranging civilization.

It does no dishonor to the memory of early forebears to move away from the myth of Jewish antiquity and acknowledge that subsequent generations have made their own contributions to Jewish civilization. Elements added a hundred years ago are no less valuable to Judaism than a legacy of four thousand years. What this means for Jews in America today is that the experiences and ideas of this generation are also gifts to Jewish civilization. It makes little difference whether the beliefs and practices of contemporary American Jewry differ from those of their parents: they are fully valid as the ongoing expression of Jewish identity in the midst of a tumultuous world.

Even though the whole of American Judaism is not as old as many teachers claim, its reverence for ancestral experiences, historically accurate or not, means that every Jew today is important not only as a descendant but also as an heir. American Judaism's emphasis on its continuity with its past leads to concern about its future and the fear that its descendants will not maintain their identity as Jews. In the next chapter, I examine how the theme of survival has created a powerful myth about the fate of the Jewish community in America.

3

FATE, SURVIVAL AND CONFIDENCE

The American Jewish population has grown from 1 million to 6 million during the twentieth century, supported by one of the most substantial networks of institutions, both secular and religious, in the history of the Jewish people. More than two thousand synagogues have been built in America since the beginning of the 1900s, and nearly half of the Jews living in America today belong to a Jewish congregation of one kind or another.[1] In spite of these verifiable facts, predictions of doom have been a constant feature of the past hundred years. Secular Jewish leaders have constantly warned of the approaching extinction of the Jewish population in America, while American rabbis have lamented the imminent demise of the Jewish religion. Often those who sound the alarm offer their own agency or denomination as the source of salvation.

Fear about loss of identity is a predictable psychological reaction for an immigrant population; it arises from the primordial human anxiety about death. The founders of American Judaism may have been genuinely worried that centuries of Jewish civilization would be lost to assimilation, but they also sincerely believed they knew how to construct a mechanism of survival. Ironically, the theme of survival in the face of assimilation became so much a part of the identity of American Judaism that few leaders today are willing to give it up. The myth that Judaism and Jewish identity are endangered in America was born from the trauma of cultural dislocation a century ago. The myth lives on in part because Jewish institutions believe they are essential to the preservation of Judaism in America; and the greater the peril, the more important their role.

When Jewish speakers discuss the preservation of Judaism, they are referring to two things: the number of children being born to Jewish parents and the number of those children who grow up retaining their Jewish identity. Judaism dies out in America if the number of Jews being born is too low to replace the Jews who have passed away, and Judaism dies out if Jewish offspring do not pass on Jewish identity to their own children. Jewish thinkers may disagree about what it means to live a Jewish life, but all acknowledge that the existence of Jewish civilization depends on the existence of people who can be recognized as Jews. Even though a low birth rate would be no less a threat than the loss of Jewish identity, most leaders tend to see assimilation as the enemy.

In the century following Conservative leader Solomon Schechter's warning that "traditional Judaism will not survive another generation in this country," approximately 750 Conservative congregations have been formed in North America. A new denomination, the Reconstructionist movement, developed from the Conservative movement and now consists of about 100 congregations. The Reform movement has grown to 900 congregations. Thriving new Orthodox enclaves are spreading across the country, and there is an active Orthodox presence on nearly every university campus. Even though Jewish religious life in America is thriving, the founder of the Orthodox National Jewish Outreach Program predicts that traditional Judaism will "likely cease to exist in the new millennium."[2] In fact, throughout the twentieth century, generation after generation of American Jewish leaders predicted the inevitable demise of Judaism—despite the lack of any concrete evidence.

In 1964, the weekly news photo magazine *Look* published a cover story titled "The Vanishing American Jew," claiming that the Jewish community was being lost to assimilation. The story said: "Young Jewish men and women are threatening the future of Judaism with their ever-increasing tendency to marry and raise their children outside the faith. And, slowly, imperceptibly, the American Jew is vanishing. . . . The Jewish share of the total [U.S. population] in the year 2000 will have fallen away from 2.9 percent to 1.6 percent. And if this happens . . . wouldn't the American Jewish community become increasingly vulnerable to assimilation—perhaps to the point of extinction?"[3] The story cited studies of Jewish intermarriage in several U.S. cities and quoted prominent Jewish leaders. *Look* magazine, with a circulation of 7 million—enormous for the time—was a very influential source of information for American households. "The Vanishing American Jew" made an impact, with the Jewish press relaying the news from city to city. Rabbis across the country repeated the prophecy from their pulpits. Even though the American Jewish population actually had quadrupled from the beginning of the twentieth century until the publication of the article in 1964, the specter of doom seemed very real to American Jews.

In spite of the Jewish community's fears, within a mere ten years of *Look*'s article, the three established branches of Judaism grew to four. Hundreds of new congregations, day schools and summer camps were established. The Havurah movement of local fellowship groups was beginning to take hold. In fact, there was every indication that a Jewish renaissance was taking place in America. Yet, although *Look* magazine had ceased publication by that point, the specter of the vanishing American Jew lived on. In 1973 the American Jewish Committee convened a task force on the future of the Jewish community in America. Its panel of prominent scholars produced a volume of essays on a range of topics from synagogue structure to youth culture. Intimations of impending disaster were woven through its pages. For instance, discussing the topic of identity and affiliation, Professor Charles Liebman of the Orthodox Yeshiva University said how "pessimistic one is likely to be regarding the prospects of Jewish survival in the United States. . . . Jews now represent about 2.6 percent of the American population, and their numbers are declining."[4]

Professor Liebman did not specify a source for his statement about a decline. In fact, the numbers were *not* declining; the population reports published by the American Jewish Committee each year since 1899 showed that they were increasing.[5] Not only that, there was evidence that Jewish identity among young Americans was stronger than ever. A groundbreaking book, *The Jewish Catalogue*,[6] appeared the very same year as the task force report and immediately became a national best-seller. *The Jewish Catalog* is a trendy guide to Jewish religious observance, packaged to capture the joyous spirit of 1970s youth culture. The fact that it is has sold more copies than any other Jewish book aside from the Bible is a clear indication of burgeoning interest in Jewish tradition among new generations of American Jews.[7]

Unfortunately, the facts of Judaism's resilience could not dispel the fiction that was continuing to spread about Judaism's endangerment. The Reform movement issued an official statement in 1976 alerting the community that "the survival of the Jewish People is of the highest priority."[8] Over the next twenty years, the reawakening of Jewish religious spirit in America increased. Various new, small congregations and fellowships could be found in every major city in America. A new progressive movement called Jewish Renewal emerged as an alternative to the established Jewish denominations. The Hasidic movement, Chabad, established missions on college campuses across the country. Nevertheless, even as the statistics showed a steady increase decade by decade, American Jews still believed their population was falling.[9] Secular leaders as well as rabbis issued cries of alarm and prophecies of doom. When Harvard professor Alan Dershowitz published *The Vanishing American Jew* in 1997, he meant the title to be taken literally.[10] Drawing on a few studies of Jewish population trends, the book is filled with portentous announcements of the "bad news" that "American Jews—as a people—have never been in greater danger of disappearing" and that "Jewish life is in danger of disappearing." Dershowitz blames assimilation and intermarriage for the supposed decline; however, he does mention low birthrate as a contributing factor. He predicts that "if trends continue apace, American Jewry—indeed, Diaspora Jewry—may virtually vanish by the third quarter of the twenty-first century." [11]

What is significant about the pessimistic speculations of so many American rabbis and secular leaders is how global their assessments are. Rather than smaller numbers, what they foresee is extinction. Their predictions take on mythic proportions. How did the fear of impending doom become part of the worldview of American Judaism? The answer can be found within the powerful historical forces that came into play at the beginning of the twentieth century.

THE ORIGINS OF A MYTH

When Catherine the Great of Russia "annexed" the eastern half of Poland in the 1790s, she inherited Poland's one million Jews. Not Polish, Russian or Christian, the Jews were an oppressed minority, never allowed to leave the conquered territory and cross into the rest of Russia. Their condition became more perilous after the assassination of Czar Alexander II in 1881. Bands of marauders rode through Jewish towns wielding swords, pillaging, raping, burning, beating, killing. The Yiddish word was *pogrom*, from the Russian for "devastation." A year later, the new czar forced those Jews residing in the larger cities to abandon their homes and businesses and relocate to impoverished Jewish villages within what was called the Pale of Settlement. As the czarist regime came under increasing criticism for its autocracy at the beginning of the twentieth century, it sought to divert the hostility of the populace from itself and onto the Jews. So the government arranged for new waves of pogroms. The rest of the world was shocked by news of the

Kishinev pogrom in 1903. After all, czarist Russia was considered one of the most enlightened nations in the world, a country of ballet and symphony and great literature; the Russian aristocracy spoke French as a matter of course, while among the French aristocracy the most elegant dinners were served *à la Russe*—in the Russian style. Newspapers expressed outrage at the ethnic persecution; heads of state wrote formal protests to the Russian government calling for an end to the violence.

Even though the pogroms were horrible, only a relatively small percentage of Russia's several million Jews were directly affected. The infamous Kishinev pogrom claimed fifty lives and injured five hundred,[12] far from the worst carnage that had already befallen the Jewish people and nothing like the horror that would overtake them a generation later. But the effect on the psyche of Russian Jewry was traumatic. Government-sanctioned violence meant that no Jew could ever feel safe on Russian soil. The anxiety compounded the severe economic and social oppression they had been suffering under for years.

Conditions were not much better for Jews living in other Eastern European countries at the turn of the twentieth century. Five thousand miles to the west, a new land promised freedom, opportunity and safety. As if summoned by the blasts of a ram's horn, millions of Jews fled Eastern Europe and sailed to America. The immigration laws of the time granted almost all of them entry. The passage to the New World was the largest population movement in Jewish history, and America promised the greatest freedom Jews had ever known throughout two thousand years of Diaspora.

Jewishness was not a matter of choice in Russia and other Eastern European countries. Jews were not granted the rights of citizenship in these countries, but instead were segregated as a distinct national group. They had no access to schools or other public institutions. They were not permitted to freely engage in commerce with non-Jews; they were barred from the trades and the professions. They therefore spoke their own language, the Hebraic form of German called Yiddish; they educated their children in Jewish religious schools; they cared for their own sick and indigent. Jews administered their own affairs, and to a large extent they managed their own judicial procedures according to traditional Jewish law.

Jewish isolation in Eastern Europe went beyond the far-reaching legal and economic restrictions that ghettoized them. By the twentieth century, several generations had grown up within the isolated world of Eastern European Jewry. Their status as aliens and as victims of persecution had become part of their very identity as Jews. Although they could barely envision any other way of life, in America they immediately saw one. In spite of the fact that they were newcomers, and in spite of the fact that they encountered prejudice, the millions of Jewish immigrants found vast new opportunities in the New World, opportunities for a life they never even imagined in the Old. The immigrant Jews had never encountered anything like American society. In America, they were not aliens or victims, as they had been for so many years in Russia and Poland. If those aspects of their Jewish world could vanish so quickly, would other features of their culture be lost as well?

The founders of denominational Judaism were no less worried that Jewish civilization would be lost in America. As Rabbi Schechter said, "What I understand by assimilation is loss of identity . . . that the so-called emancipation of the Jews must inevitably lead to the extinction of Judaism. . . . It is this kind of assimilation, with the terrible consequences indicated, that I dread most; even more than pogroms."[13] This anxiety was built into the basic structures of the institutions of American Judaism, and the theme of survival became a focus of denominational competition. When Schechter presided over the inauguration of the Jewish Theological Seminary of America in 1902, he outlined his plan for American Judaism: loyalty to tradition combined with scientific methods of study. His inspiring and visionary speech to the new generation of scholars and rabbis was nonetheless punctuated by striking portents of doom: the "tragedy" of an ancient people "losing thousands every day . . . doomed to oblivion. . . . The Jewish soul wasting away."[14] Generation after generation of rabbis have seen their respective movements as the heroes that would rescue America's Jews from the brink of annihilation, convincing themselves that "Judaism of the next generation will be saved by us. . . . It can be saved by no other group."[15] The theme of survival, and the belief that assimilation is the number-one threat to that survival, exerts enormous influence over the policies of American Judaism today.

THE PERSISTENCE OF THE MYTH

The fear of nonexistence is a very powerful emotion. It tends to remain active within the psyche long after the danger itself, whether real or imagined, has subsided. More facilities for religion, learning and community service have been built in one century in America than in any other period of Jewish history. Yet religious and secular leaders alike believe that American Judaism is about to die out. The shawl of impending dissolution has been draped over the shoulders of American Judaism since the beginning of the twentieth century.

Just as American Judaism holds on to the myth of the vanishing Jew, its holds on to the belief that assimilation and intermarriage, and no other cause, is bringing annihilation. In contrast to their concerns about the vulnerability of their *cultural* identity in America, the Jewish community has tended to enjoy a sense of physical safety here. This was certainly true for the immigrant generation. Unlike Russia, the United States was not ruled by a dynasty with a history of cruelty. Jews in America were not segregated and persecuted as an ethnicity. Nor was America on the brink of revolution and class warfare. Jews did not expect the American government to turn against them with violence. They could, however, imagine assimilation as the agent of their destruction.

Following World War II, as American Jews gradually comprehended the enormity of the Holocaust, the theme of survival was reinforced as the highest priority for American Judaism. It might be expected that the post-Holocaust generation would be less vigilant about assimilation as the enemy and look for signs of danger elsewhere, but that is not what happened. True, there were discussions of the fact that, prior to the Holocaust, Jews were well integrated into German society and did not foresee how social conditions would change so radically; their circumstances were not all that different from the situation of American Jewry. Nevertheless, it was the fear of assimilation that produced the American Jewish theme of survival; once it became part of American Judaism's worldview, even the murder of six million Jews could not dislodge it. The Holocaust has entered the permanent iconography of Judaism. But when rabbis preach about the destruction of American Jewry, assimilation, not anti-Semitism, is the agent of doom.

Curiously, American Jews have had an ambivalent relationship with anti-Semitism. For if social acceptance leads to assimilation, as many Jewish leaders have suggested, then anti-Semitism would be Judaism's ally. In other words, if American society were unfriendly to Jews, then Jews in America would be more likely to remain a distinct separate ethnic group. If they could not socialize with gentiles, and certainly not marry them, Jews would have little choice but to be loyal to their own community. If gentiles in America were actually hostile to Jews, the argument goes, Jews would identify even more strongly with their own people. In fact, the proposition that anti-Semitism preserves Judaism is a major premise of Dershowitz's book. Dershowitz warns that the current absence of anti-Jewish sentiment spells doom for American Jews and that "these good times may mark the beginning of the end of Jewish life in America as we know it." Tolling American Judaism's death knell, he blames social acceptance for the end of Jewish life, telling the reader that "the projected disappearance, or at least significant shrinkage, of the Jewish presence in America is largely a function of the improving status of the Jew in the world today."[16]

DEPENDENCE ON THE MYTH

Pervasive anxiety is not the only reason American Judaism has faithfully preserved the myth of impending disappearance. The myth survives today because influential religious and secular institutions have become dependent on it. Jewish leaders have assumed responsibility for saving Judaism from assimilation for so long that many of their skills and resources are oriented toward the goal of preserving Jewish civilization. The result is that American Judaism focuses on a particular narrow premise. Through its preaching, its publications and its programs, American Judaism teaches that one of the primary purposes of practicing Judaism is to perpetuate the practice of Judaism.

As thin as it is, this proposition constitutes a major ideological premise of American Judaism today. Its circular reasoning is a twentieth-century American creation and was never part of Jewish thinking in previous eras. Throughout their history, the Jewish people have developed a variety of religious philosophies, and each system provides a different understanding for the purpose of Jewish practice. One of Judaism's oldest belief systems, covenant theology, is derived from the Torah. God established a contract with Israel through the patriarch Abraham: The Jewish people will follow God's laws, and God in turn will make them a great nation. In covenant theology, the purpose of Jewish practice is to maintain the ancestors' commitment to God. Jews practice Judaism to keep the ancient flame burning eternally, motivated not by fear of doom but by veneration for their ancestors. Each generation is honor-bound to swear the next generation to renew the original commitment to God. A variation of this philosophy might be called commandment theology: God dictated to Moses specific laws for Israel, which Moses wrote down in the Torah and which the Israelites accepted. Their acceptance was also a covenant, and all Jews today are obligated to obey those laws. In commandment theology, the purpose of Jewish practice is the fulfillment of God's commandments.

Whereas both of these theologies point to the origins of Jewish faith, another philosophical outlook, prophetic Judaism, points to the future: The meaning of life is found in the struggle for the eventual perfection of human society. Prophetic theology derives from the literary prophets of the Hebrew Bible, roughly 2,500 years ago, and is based on their vision of a world of peace and justice. The purpose of Jewish practice is to bring about the messianic age, when all humanity will abide by God's will.

Kabbalah—Jewish mysticism—offers a different approach entirely. There are several schools of Kabbalah, dating as far back as the fifteenth century, but in one way or another they teach that the laws, the prayers and the rituals are pathways to personal knowledge of God. The essential purpose of Jewish observance is *dveykut*, joining with God. For some Kabbalists, the practices of Judaism are all part of an eternal cosmic wedding ceremony between God and His people, Israel.

As I have said, American Judaism espouses an entirely new and different ideology: The reason to live a Jewish life is to preserve the Jewish people. The twentieth-century theme of survival is found throughout denominational Judaism today, sometimes eclipsing the classic Jewish elements of God, Torah, Jewish law and Israel. For example, one of the major arms of the Reform movement is its teen organization, the North American Federation of Temple Youth (NFTY). NFTY's constitution enumerates ten principles of American Judaism. God and Torah are each mentioned once. The phrase "survival of the Jewish people," however, appears three times.[17]

Prior to the twentieth century, the theme of survival was not a formal ingredient of the Reform movement. In fact, none of the themes of American Judaism can be found in the historical *1885 Declaration of Principles*, also known as the Pittsburgh Platform. The concept of preserving Judaism entered the Reform movement's 1937 Columbus Platform and became a major feature of the movement's 1976 *Centenary Perspective*, which lays out six key principles of Reform ideology.[18] The first four are the familiar pillars of classic Judaism: God, Torah, the Jewish people and Jewish observance; the fifth, support for the State of Israel, is, of course, a product of the last half of the twentieth century. However, the document adds a sixth principle, "Our

Obligations: Survival and Service," and concludes that "Jewish survival is warrant for human hope." Thus the theme of survival pervades American Judaism today.

Certain voices within classical Jewish literature—primarily in the prophetic writings—speak about the loss of Jewish identity *following from* disregard of God's laws. The twentieth century idea that the primary purpose of Judaism is to forestall Jewish disappearance is dysfunctional to the extent that it is negativistic and creates a spirit of fear. When people focus on keeping the age-old flame burning eternally, they are engaging in an affirming process. Their efforts promise happiness and fulfillment. When people focus on averting the danger just around the corner, however, the process is defensive. All it can promise is a temporary respite from a relentless enemy. The persistent myth that American Jewry is about to vanish has produced a stilted form of Judaism that cannot capture the imagination of newer generations of Jews who are unlikely to embrace a system based on anxiety and guilt.

By making religious practice into a life-or-death struggle, American Judaism sometimes overlooks the religion's inherent liveliness. The Festival of Purim is a perfect example of Judaism's playful side. The celebration centers around the biblical Book of Esther, a colorful—and rather bawdy—story of a voluptuous Persian queen, a drunken king, an evil vizier, a pair of spies, the virtuous Jew (Mordecai) and his heroic niece (Esther). Mordecai learns of a plot to kill all the Jews of the realm, but Esther saves them. The Book of Esther is read from a Hebrew scroll in the synagogue, accompanied by cheering, booing and noisemakers. Children and adults alike come in masks and costumes; there is singing, dancing and indulging in sweets. In traditional settings there may even be some drinking; a little bit of drunkenness is acceptable in the synagogue during Purim, which takes place at the end of winter and resembles Mardi Gras and carnivals of other cultures.

Unfortunately, within denominational Judaism, even Purim can take on a serious role as a reminder of the constant struggle to preserve Judaism. The current website of the Union for Reform

Judaism devotes a couple of paragraphs to Purim. The authors do acknowledge that it is "typically a rowdy affair," but then conclude their description with the obligatory coda of impending doom. Alluding to "the Jewish historical experience" of persecution, the authors explain that Purim "has become a thankful and joyous affirmation of Jewish survival against all odds."[19] It would have been perfectly accurate to describe Purim as nothing more than an occasion for fun. And from the perspective of group mental health, it would be beneficial to remind people to make a place for joy in their lives. Instead, the entrenched denominational theme of survival compels these Reform authorities to attach a soberly didactic significance to the holiday.

In the same vein, educator and author Joel Grishaver produced a clever textbook for Jewish parents that provides practical advice for incorporating religious observance and education into family life. Grishaver's work is rich with wonderful ideas to make Judaism appealing to children. Unfortunately, the book's title, *40 Things You Can Do to Save the Jewish People*, and section headings like "Joel's Laws of Jewish Survival" imply that the joy of Judaism serves a most serious purpose.[20] There is nothing wrong with wanting to survive, and it is important to make learning fun for children. However, when Jewish educators adopt a defensive approach like Grishaver's, their underlying sense of apprehension gets in the way. The statement that Jewish life is a perpetual struggle for survival is not an appealing message for any child.

THE PERVASIVENESS OF THE MYTH

The myth of the vanishing Jew is not limited to the religious denominations. Secular organizations are just as likely to spread the alarm and just as likely to propose their own institutions as the solution. The United Jewish Communities (UJC) is the umbrella organization for the Jewish Federation and other non-synagogue communities in America. The Jewish Federation is the major source of funding for the American Jewish community. The UJC spent millions of dollars to take the pulse of American Jewry in 1990 and again in 2000. The results of each National Jewish Population Survey (NJPS) were widely publicized and highly influential, with numerous articles and books based on their findings. The 1990 survey reported the population had declined from nearly 6 million in 1980 to 5.5 million.[21] The authors of the 2000 survey reported a further decrease to 5.2 million.[22] Neither claim was correct, however. The survey report itself acknowledges that "NJPS 2000–01 may have undercounted the Jewish population," explaining that "many researchers believe that the methodologies of survey research may yield undercounts of the Jewish population."[23]

In 2003, J. J. Goldberg, editor-in-chief of the *Jewish Forward*, the oldest Jewish periodical in America, interviewed the authors of the 2000 survey and reported in the *New York Times* that the alarms were false.[24] The survey authors acknowledged that the population totals for 1990 and 2000 should not have been compared because they were reached by different methods. When Goldberg asked both the research director and project director if their data indicated a declining Jewish population, they told him that it definitely did not. According to Goldberg, other studies have estimated the American Jewish population as high as 6.7 million. As I mentioned, the American Jewish Committee has published its own Jewish population estimates since 1902. Volume 91 of the Committee's *American Jewish Yearbook* documented that the 1990 NJPS study undercounted Jews by 5 percent and corrected the figure to 5.8 million.[25] Subsequent editions of the *Yearbook* have reported the American Jewish population at a steady 6 million since the year 2000.[26]

The NJPS has had a powerful influence on the opinions of both Jews and Americans in general, and it has reinforced the myth that the Jewish population is disappearing. As I mentioned, the UJC, which sponsored the survey and published its findings, controls most of the Jewish community funding in America, serves as a voice for the entire Jewish community and holds considerable sway over the day-by-day policies and programs of many Jewish institutions around the world.

The very same year that Dershowitz's book appeared (1997), another prominent American Jew, former Assistant Secretary of State Elliott Abrams, relied heavily on the NJPS when he issued his own warning in *Faith or Fear*. Abrams begins by citing the 1990 NJPS report and goes on to talk about "a community in decline, facing in fact a demographic disaster." He predicts "a drop of anywhere from one million to over two million in the American Jewish population in the next two generations."[27] In a section of his book titled (like other works already discussed) "The Vanishing American Jew," Abrams announces that "the Jewish population is falling."[28] Nationally syndicated columnist Charles Krautheimer used population figures from both the 1990 and 2000 surveys to compose his own prediction of the disappearance of American Jewry in an article carried by newspapers around the world. According to Krautheimer, "America's Jewish population was about 5.5 million in 1990, dropped to about 5.2 million 10 years later and is in a precipitous decline that, because of low fertility rates and high levels of assimilations, will cut that number in half by mid-century."[29]

Whether the NJPS published misleading data or not, as the *Forward* editor and other experts have suggested, it is clear that the survey reflects a preoccupation with the role of traditional institutions. In particular, the 2000 survey report divides the American Jewish community into two camps:

> Traditionally, formal institutions have been vital to the Jewish community. The centrality of synagogues, JCCs [Jewish Community Centers] and other Jewish organizations is so profound that Jewish leadership frequently distinguishes between "affiliated" and "unaffiliated" members of the Jewish population. . . . The affiliated exhibit far higher rates of in-marriage, in-group friendship, ritual practice, cultural involvement, educational participation, ties to Israel, giving to Jewish causes and subjective commitment to being Jewish.[30]

At first glance, it might seem predictable that affiliated Jews would be more engaged with Jewish life than unaffiliated Jews.

However, when the NJPS report refers to "affiliation," it means formal association with traditional Jewish institutions, especially those associated with the UJC: community centers, schools, charitable organizations, Zionist organizations, and pro-Israel lobbyist groups. With regard to education, the survey questionnaire focused on attendance at "formal" Jewish education; the only informal education considered was reading books with Jewish content. By arbitrarily dividing American Jewry on the basis of formal affiliation, the UJC's survey is able to portray the traditional institutions as the heroes of an endangered people: American Jewry is being lost to assimilation, and affiliated Jews are assimilating less than others. The implication is that without traditional institutions, American Jewry will vanish. Indeed, the authors of the NJPS make it a point to indicate that they favor those Jews "who infuse Jewish communal institutions with significant resources."[31]

Many Jewish leaders have echoed the NJPS's conclusions that only the traditional, formal institutions can save Judaism in America. In *Faith or Fear*, Abrams insists that "in the face of demographic disaster," what is called for is the community financing of Jewish religious schools, stronger personal links to Israel and "bridging the gap between the lay organizations—above all, the Federations—and the community's religious institutions—its day schools and its synagogues." The major denominations are the only acceptable form of Judaism for Abrams. He recognizes the existence only of the Orthodox, Conservative and Reform approaches to Judaism. For some reason, he omits Reconstructionism entirely. Nor does even he mention independent congregations, fellowships or study groups.[32]

THE NEW MIGRATION OF AMERICAN JEWS

Just because a large number of American Jews are "unaffiliated" according to the standards of the NJPS does not mean that Jewish life in America has become weaker. The truth is that the Jewish life of many Americans simply has moved to other, less measurable venues. By restricting their investigation to traditional, formal institutions, the UJC overlooked a substantial segment of Jewish life and thereby produced a skewed assessment. For example, only one of the three hundred questions in the 2000 survey touched on the Internet as a source of Jewish information, although the authors did acknowledge its growing importance. This is an era when many Americans—especially younger generations—get information and make cultural connections through Internet resources. Underestimating the significance of the online world most certainly will give the false impression that Jewish life is declining in America.

It is understandable that the NJPS would use Jewish observance, attendance at synagogue, synagogue membership, charitable giving and *formal* education as benchmarks of Jewishness. After all, if attendance at denominational services is down, if enrollment in Jewish schools is down, if donations to Jewish agencies and Zionist organizations are down, whose survival is most immediately threatened? Web sites, blogs, bulletin boards, discussion groups, book clubs and other informal or online channels of engagement with Judaism do not directly support the brick-and-mortar institutions that comprise the UJC. Although American Jews may be disappearing from the radar screen of the UJC, they are not vanishing. The very opposite is true.

If, as the NJPS suggests, younger Jews are less affiliated with traditional institutions, that is because Jewishness is happening in new places that do not fit the old categories. There is nothing wrong with "informal" education. The online Jewish world is intense; its countless corridors extend deeply into the richest details of Judaism, from ancient Hebrew texts to modern bioethical problems. To date, no single publication—online or in print—catalogs all of the myriad "unaffiliated" and informal Jewish organizations that can be found everywhere in America today. The most cursory browsing of Internet-based resources shows that the storehouse of Jewish knowledge is richer than ever before. The proliferation of Web sites and the burgeoning of blogs devoted to Jewish issues reveal a vibrant and rapidly growing community of students of Judaism.

Not only is Judaism not dying out in America, elements of Jewish civilization that almost *did* die out are now being revived, largely due to the Internet's ability to link individuals who share common interests and the ability of digital media to reproduce cultural artifacts. One example is the five-hundred-year-old Hebrew-Spanish dialect, Ladino. Ladino was the daily of language of Jews living in Spanish-speaking countries (the name itself is a variant of *Latino*) as well as Turkey and Greece, but until recently it appeared to be on the verge of extinction. Ladino now lives on the Internet through the efforts of a virtual community called "Ladinokomunita," whose members around the world converse daily—exclusively in Ladino—by way of their keyboards and screens.[33]

Even though the religious denominations and other traditional institutions of American Judaism cling to the theme of survival and the myth of disappearance remains a part of American Judaism's worldview, there is considerable evidence that the reawakening of Judaism that began in the 1970s is expanding rapidly in the twenty-first century. Even forgotten and abandoned resources have come back to life in the new world of American Judaism. For instance, the *Jewish Encyclopedia*, published by Funk and Wagnalls in 1902, was an amazing compendium of Jewish scholarship. Many of its authors were Old World intellectuals who came to America in the wave of immigration. Long out of print, its erudite articles and one-of-a-kind graphic illustrations were available only in large libraries and antiquarian book stores. Now its thousands of articles are available online.[34] The *Jewish Encyclopedia* is just one example of a valuable Jewish source that has been revived through digital media. What is important is not just that the technology is there, but that the interest is there as well. Obviously, someone took the trouble to scan the encyclopedia's eight thousand pages, and people across the Internet are reading it again.

Attendance at Saturday synagogue Torah readings may have decreased, but the number of online discussions—both traditional and modernist—of the weekly Torah portions is proof that some Jews are actively involved in Torah study, even if they do not pay dues to any denomination. The gloomy prognostications of the NJPS and the writers who rely on it are not borne out by the pro-liferation of Internet resources for traditional Jewish practices. A dozen Web sites are devoted just to the technique of chanting the weekly Torah readings. As I discuss in chapter 6, numerous online communities are engaged in the study of classical Hebrew texts. The Hebrew Bible, the Mishnah and the Talmud—the Jerusalem as well as the Babylonian version—are available online.[35]

Jewish book and discussion groups may not be traditional edu-cation when compared to synagogue religious schools, but they are substantive. The number of books on Judaism in bookstores—both online and brick-and-mortar—has grown exponentially, and older works are being reissued as rapidly as modern publishing technol-ogy can manage. Clearly large numbers of people are fueling a new Jewish information industry. The UJC and some Jewish leaders may believe that Jewish education is in decline and that therefore American Judaism is in trouble, but many indicators have been pointing in the opposite direction for decades.

Just as the locus of Jewish *education* has shifted to different sources and different forums, Jewish meditation centers, klezmer music camps and numerous other nontraditional centers of Jewish *practice* can be found across the North American continent. There can be no doubt that there are large numbers of Americans who feel a personal connection to Judaism and are loyal to the Jewish way of life. They get their Jewish knowledge and make their Jewish connections in new ways that are invisible to the UJN population surveys. They are members of a new American Judaism.

Agencies affiliated with the UJC have been providing wide-ranging, invaluable social services for over a hundred years. The new Jewish community I have been talking about does not con-struct facilities to feed the poor, shelter the homeless or tend the sick. More traditional organizations may better meet the need for these essential human services. Nonetheless, many active Web sites do provide valuable information, comfort and networks of human support to those in need. For example, Atime.org is a valuable source of medical information and emotional support for the many observant Jewish families struggling with the pain of childlessness. Its discussion forums address the psychological suffering of women who cannot conceive and the impact on their families. It connects these couples with detailed medical information specific to issues of traditional Jewish law. In particular, Atime.org addresses questions of alternative insemination, such as sources of donor eggs, sources of donor sperm and methods whereby eggs are fertilized.

THE DYSFUNCTIONALITY OF THE MYTH

The responses of American Judaism to the perceived threat of disappearance are problematic because the struggle for survival can overshadow other sustaining motives for Jewish observance. Jews are told to keep the Sabbath and study the Torah not because God commands them to, not because it will bring joy to their lives, not because it will redeem the world, but rather because it will prevent the Jewish population from dying out. As long as American Judaism continues to tend the altar of survival, it will have difficulty bringing assimilated Jews back into the fold, and it will push marginal Jews farther away. In spite of the efforts and creativity of Jewish educators and rabbis, the more American Judaism concentrates on ensuring that its children will be Jews, the less appealing Judaism will be to those children; the subtext of survival can offer only guilt and anxiety. New generations of Jews can find greater inspiration and spiritual fulfillment by moving forward from the negativity and defensiveness of a survivalist approach to Jewish life.

When American Judaism cries that the population is declining, it points its finger of blame at intermarriage. The focus on intermarriage is also problematic because, as I will demonstrate, basic demographics show that intermarriage does not lead to a reduction in numbers for *any* group. Jewish leaders are so locked onto intermarriage and assimilation as the enemies of Jewish survival that they miss other real and tangible hazards, such as the proliferation through inbreeding of genetic diseases that affect Jews more than other groups, a topic I discuss in chapter 8. In addition, a host of preventable deaths has been eroding the American population in general. Although these sources of danger do not affect Jews more than they do other Americans, the preoccupation with intermarriage and assimilation has distracted the leaders of American Judaism to the point that they are doing less to protect their constituency than some other groups are. Poor diet, physical inactivity and alcohol and tobacco consumption are leading causes of death. How many Jewish lives could have been saved if the considerable resources of American Judaism concentrated more on promoting healthier modes of living and safer behavior and less on combating assimilation and intermarriage?

MOVING FORWARD

In many ways, American Judaism has been in the business of going out of business. Statements about the fragility of Judaism may have originated in the worry of the immigrant generation, but now they only serve to create worry in the minds of the American-born generations. In the beginning of the twentieth century, American rabbis believed that they were undertaking "a real work of heaven . . . on which . . . depends the continuance and survival of traditional Judaism in this country."[36] Many believe so now. However, by accepting the fact that the future of American Jewry is not imperiled, rabbis can move forward from their old role as the agents of Jewish survival and take on a greater role as prophetic voices for social justice and spiritual fulfillment.

So how many Jews are there in America these days? Is the population up or down? As I mentioned, the *American Jewish Yearbook* has posted annual demographic reports for the past hundred years. Its statistics show that there were about 1 million Jews in America in 1900. The numbers increased sharply to roughly 3.5 million by 1920. This precipitous rise was followed by a 60 percent increase to about 5.5 million in the middle of the century, and a further increase of 10 percent to 6 million by the beginning of the twenty-first century. The *rate* of growth appears to be slowing down in recent years, especially when contrasted with the unusually high rate of growth during the first half of the twentieth century. The American Jewish population may not be growing as rapidly as it once was, but it is not declining. It most certainly is not vanishing.

The myth of the vanishing Jew was born out of the emotional trauma that accompanied the mass migration of millions of Eastern European Jews to America at the beginning of the twentieth century. Although the preoccupation with survival has been part of the worldview of American Judaism for over a hundred years, the time has come for Jewish leaders to abandon an outdated Jewish ideology promulgated on the fear of extinction.

In spite of the reawakening of Jewish life that began in America in the 1970s and continues to expand and deepen, secular institutions and Jewish denominations alike perpetuate the myth of imminent doom in the mind of Americans, while at the same time claiming to be the source of salvation for the Jewish population in America. As long as Jewish authorities focus on major denominations and other traditional institutions, they will continue to discount the impact both of smaller, alternative groups and the virtual communities of the Internet. Population studies that overlook these expanding segments of the Jewish population will only gather misleading statistics that seem to indicate new generations of Jews are abandoning Judaism when in fact Jewish life is migrating to different kinds of institutions and new kinds of communities. Rather than vanishing, the American Jew is moving forward.

As I mentioned, the themes of survival and continuity became part of American Judaism with the wave of Old World Jewish immigration at the beginning of the previous century. The theme of authenticity, of course, was born at that time as well. However, it took on new life in the middle of the century with a wave of nostalgia for Eastern European Jewish life. In the next chapter, I look at why this sentimentality took hold of American Jews in the 1950s and the role it plays in American Judaism today.

4

AUTHENTICITY, SENTIMENT AND SOPHISTICATION

merican Judaism romanticizes the shtetl—the small town—beyond all reason, painting scenes of old Eastern European Jewish communities in colors so adoring that they can exist only in the imagination. Rabbis and Broadway producers alike reinforce the myth of the economically difficult but emotionally fulfilling life of the Old World Jew, set apart from the gentile world in a little Jewish town, where individual piety and community cohesiveness governed everyday life. According to the myth, Jews derived immense satisfaction from their religion, but were driven from their homes by the physical and economic oppression of the gentiles.

The beautiful portrait of a perfect Jewish world did not come to America with the immigrants themselves, nor was it created by them after they arrived. It was familiar to their children as a literary genre, but it became accepted as reality by their grandchildren.

No doubt the Jews who left Eastern Europe retained some nostalgia and regret for the past, but the immigrant generation itself never glorified the shtetl. The fact is that relatively few of the several million Jews in Eastern Europe lived in little Jewish towns, and those who did came to America because they wanted a better life for themselves and their children. Most of the immigrants lived in cities, some of which were predominantly Jewish, but most were not. In any case, the repressiveness of Eastern European Judaism itself was no less a motive for the exodus than were the poverty and the pogroms. Whatever was good and noble in the shtetl simply could not compete with the promise of freedom and opportunity in America.

THE LITERARY ORIGINS OF THE MYTH

What is now recognized as the world of the shtetl began as the work of a group of professional Yiddish writers around the late 1800s and early 1900s. Mendele Mokher Seforim wrote about the oppressiveness of shtetl life from the perspective of the poor; the short stories of Y. L. Peretz present a range of imagery, including the dark and the fantastical. Their portrayals were highly fictionalized. They tended to lump together different cities of varying sizes and compositions as "little towns." They often discounted the presence of gentiles in the towns, setting their stories and plays in the artistic equivalent of miniature Jewish kingdoms. Inevitably their descriptions were influenced by their personal visions of the shtetl as a besieged stronghold of Jewish authenticity and by their individual ideologies. Heightened sentimentality was a common feature of their writing style. The characters and scenes created by the Yiddish writer Sholem Aleichem (who came to the United States from Russia in the early 1900s) are the most familiar and the most popular. His work is best known to the world through the adaptation of his novel *Tevyeh's Daughters* into *Fiddler on the Roof*. This musical comedy first opened in 1964, and is one of the most successful Broadway plays ever produced. It is has been revived four times, and a film version was produced in 1971. *Fiddler on the Roof* preserves not only Sholem Aleichem's characters but also his appreciation for the psychological tensions that arise from stereotypes and social rigidity.

The musical brings in all the stock scenes and personalities that made up Sholem Aleichem's imaginary world. There is the Jewish village itself, so small and compact that everyone knows everyone else. The opening song, "Tradition," delineates four classes of people—fathers, mothers, sons and daughters—strictly defined by gender and generation. Each of the nuclear families loyally celebrates the Sabbath every Friday evening; the devoted mothers light candles while the stern but loving fathers bless their adoring children. Presumably not everyone in the village is part of a family, but there are no scenes that depict the private lives of widows, spinsters or bachelors. Everyone in the village dresses in accordance with Jewish law: the men wear hats and tallises; the women wear babushkas.

The fact that in varying degrees three of Tevyeh's daughters defy their traditional roles provides the dramatic tension of the play. Everyone else in the village is content with his lot in life. Tevyeh talks to God throughout the play and sings that his greatest desire would be to spend his day in prayer and study of Scripture. The only character with any awareness of the outside world is the educated young Jewish man who is passing through the village. Then there are the colorful individuals: the aged rabbi surrounded by his worshipful students, the scheming matchmaker, the wily beggar. Tevyeh the dairyman pretends to quote Scripture, the aged rabbi offers blessings and everyone is devoted to God and Judaism. A handful of gentiles lurk about the periphery of the village. The Jews are smarter, but the gentiles are stronger. Whenever any of the gentiles appears on stage, the Jews become nervous.

Although the village Jews are poor and oppressed by the government, they patiently accept their fate. Everyone minds everyone else's business while trying to be kind to one another. They are all content living in their little town, where the practice of Judaism is their greatest joy, and leave it only at the end, when they are forced from their homes by edict of the Czar.

Fiddler is a masterful production, witty and entertaining. Most everyone attending a performance or seeing the movie version can appreciate the elements of irony and satire woven throughout. However, even though the play is a work of fiction, the American Jewish community, from rabbis to university professors, treats it as historical fact. Hebrew school teachers and textbooks aimed at adults cite the play as an accurate depiction of the life of Eastern European Jewry a century ago. For example, Reform rabbi Ted Falcon writes that Eastern Europe's Jews "usually lived separated from the Christian neighbors, in small villages called shtetls."[1] Rabbi Falcon urges his readers to watch the DVD of *Fiddler on the Roof* as the best way to appreciate the culture of the shtetl.[2]

The myth of the shtetl did not begin with Fiddler on the Roof; it originated a few years before the play brought it to the attention of the world. In fact, the sentimental image of the little Jewish town is not found in nonfiction writing before the middle of the twentieth century in America. In the years following World War II, Jewish scholars and publishing houses begin treating fiction as if it were historical fact, and the colorful image of the Jewish village became an official feature of American Judaism. There really were shtetls in Eastern Europe, but it was the stock scenes and roles of shtetl *literature*, along with its ideological projections, that entered works on theology, history and religious observance. Unfortunately, much of the subtlety, ambiguity and irony of the literary art form was lost in the translation. The portrait of the shtetl as a miniature Jewish utopia was enshrined as an ideological icon.

In 1949 the noted theologian Abraham Joshua Heschel, a professor at the Jewish Theological Seminary, published a brief history of the communities of Eastern Europe. *The Earth Is the Lord's: The Inner World of the Jew in Eastern Europe* was one of the first works of shtetl nostalgia. The book glorifies Eastern European Judaism as "the golden period in Jewish history, in the history of the

Jewish soul. . . . Has there ever been more light in the souls of Jews in the last thousand years?"[3] Heschel invokes the shtetl in the reader's mind throughout his work: "Koretz, Karlin, Bratslav, Lubavich, Ger, Lublin—hundreds of little towns were like holy books. . . . The little Jewish communities in Eastern Europe were like sacred texts open before the eyes of God. . . . There were no concerts or operas in their little towns. . . . But even in the mud of their little towns there were pearling, tender flowers, and in the darkness, sparks smoldered waiting to be kindled."[4]

Heschel focuses on Eastern European Jewish spirituality, and he does so with both eloquence and sincere fervor. At the same time, he portrays his "little towns" as quaint expressions of an ideal Jewish life:

> But the Jews all sang: the student over the Talmud, the tailor while sewing a pair of trousers, the cobbler while mending tattered shoes, and the preacher while delivering a sermon. . . . The stomachs were empty, the houses were barren, but the minds were crammed with the riches of Torah. . . . Mothers at the cradle crooned: "My little child, close your eyes; if God will, you'll be a rabbi. . . ." Parents were ready to sell the pillow from under their heads to pay tuition for their children. . . . And when the melancholy, sweet chanting of Talmudic study . . . penetrated the neighboring streets, exhausted Jews on their pallets felt sweet delight."[5]

When Heschel talks about the spirituality of the Hasidim, the essence of his book, he depicts the faithful Jews in heroic terms. The heightened sentimentality of his poetic language places them above mere mortals: "Their spirit was . . . like a tremulous gleam of light, like the twinkle of cut gems. . . . The Jews patiently bore their lot and with superhuman ardor sacrificed themselves for their faith. . . . Supernatural splendor emanated from ordinary acts. . . . Such longing for the higher endowed them with an almost superhuman quality. . . . They did not write songs, they themselves were songs."[6] Of course, he is referring only to the men. Women were not students of Kabbala, but instead they "toiled day and night to enable their husbands to devote themselves to study."[7] Also, Heschel does not mention the fact that millions of Jews left Eastern Europe for America in the early 1900s.

The Earth Is the Lord's is not sociology but elegy; it comes from an address Heschel delivered in memory of the Jews who were murdered during World War II.[8] It is possible that references to "superhuman" Jews are intended as a defiant allusion to Nazism; however, the book itself does not discuss the Holocaust. Instead, Heschel draws on his own Hasidic background to project onto the shtetl his belief that human existence is a cosmic drama of God and humanity in search of each other. Heschel was one of the most influential Jewish thinkers of the twentieth century; all of his books have been widely read by rabbis and other serious students of Judaism. *The Earth Is the Lord's* is still in print and people are reading it.

By the time *The Earth Is the Lord's* first appeared in 1949, American Jews had begun to enjoy prosperity and social acceptance in America. The children of the immigrants had achieved the happy American family life. The Jews were fitting in well: They owned homes in decent neighborhoods, and their children attended good colleges. The Jews looked like the other middle-class suburban Americans. But because they looked so American, they also looked less Jewish in their own eyes. Indeed, the threat of assimilation alarmed the leaders of Judaism. At the same time, rabbis had no authentically Jewish model for the happy nuclear family to offer American Jews. Judaism's classic images of the nuclear family, the familiar stories in Genesis, were neither beautiful nor charming. Patriarchs had multiple wives who competed with each other for their husband's affection. Parents loved some of their children but rejected others. Sons betrayed fathers. Brothers fought violently; sisters plotted. American Jewry needed a popular literary image that would both reflect the ideal of the happy nuclear family and emphasize the practice of Judaism.

Just such a book came along in 1952, when a highly influential anthropological study adopted the shtetl literary genre and gave it scholarly credence. *Life Is with People: The Culture of the Shtetl* purportedly uses the voices and memories of American immigrants and their children to reconstruct personalities, values and day-by-day social interactions, painting a vivid and detailed image of a vanished Jewish society.[9] Like Heschel, authors Mark Zborowski and Elizabeth Herzog created a shtetl that previously could not be found in scholarly journals or historical studies, either American or European. *Life Is with People* is upbeat and easy to read. The Jewish community quickly adopted it as the definitive depiction of the world of Eastern European Jewry. Rabbis praised it in their sermons. *Life Is with People* remains one of the most influential books about the shtetl ever published.[10] It has been reissued several times and is still in print today.

The book is the product of an extensive project conducted by a team of Columbia University anthropologists and sociologists. The authors explain that their analysis is based on interviews with 138 people (128 immigrants and 10 children of immigrants) and on 50 biographies from the Yiddish Scientific Institute (YIVO).[11] However, far from presenting a scientific, impersonal study, *Life Is with People* is suffused with amplified nostalgia for the society it is documenting. The authors' own hyperbolic language and idealized descriptions, rather than the words of the immigrants themselves, comprise the bulk of the book: "Sabbath in the shtetl . . . is remembered as a time of ecstasy—father in a silken caftan and velvet skullcap, mother in black silk and pearls; the glow of candles, the waves of peace and joy, the glad sense that it is good to be a Jew, the distant pity for those who have been denied this foretaste of heaven."[12]

Zborowski and Herzog create a more affluent shtetl than does Heschel—silk dresses and pearls rather than pallets and mud. *Life Is with People* also projects a very different ideology onto the backdrop of the shtetl. Whereas Heschel tells the reader that the essence of Judaism is the spiritual enlightenment of the individual, for Zborowski and Herzog the essence of Judaism is the nuclear family. They explain that there can be no fulfillment of duties or pleasure as an isolated individual who is not part of a family. Being single is not only a shame, the authors declare, but also a "sin against the will of God."[13] Throughout their book, Zborowski and Herzog make it a point to categorize people by generation and by gender—everyone is either a father or a mother or a daughter or a son. They provide specific blueprints for each behavior. Mothers receive the most attention and the highest praise for having "pawned their pearls and gone hungry to give their sons education" or "trudged miles through snow." The ideal shtetl mother toils constantly for her family and is, in the authors' own words, "an eternal fountain of sacrifice, lamentation, and renewed effort."[14] The authors compose similar elaborate phrases to discuss the devotion of children for their parents: "All the sacrifice, all the suffering, all the solicitude pile up into a monument to parental love, the dimensions of which define the vastness of filial indebtedness."[15]

The authors promote the ideology of nuclear family throughout the book, including ominous condemnations for anyone who does not conform. They emphasize that no man can be "complete" without wife, just as no woman can be complete without a husband. They warn that to be a spinster is a "dreadful fate," because the shtetl does not provide a place for an old maid. Apparently there *were* unmarried women and widows in the shtetl, but according to *Life Is with People*, no one cared what happened to them. Zborowski and Herzog elaborate on the plight of the childless woman as a "source of guilt and bitter shame," who arouses not only pity but also suspicion that her condition is a punishment.[16] The absence of detail about the daily lives of unmarried or childless individuals is remarkable in a book that provides a great deal of detail about other aspects of community life.

Gender roles are so critical to *Life Is with People* that the authors go out of their way to contrast the sexes. The man's area is the synagogue; the woman's area is the home. Men are restrained, poised and "laconic"; women are expressive, ready with tears, laughter and "volubility." No doubt the gender roles Zborowski and Herzog report were real, but the authors' ideological stance compels them to select examples—presented in forceful language—that reinforce the stereotypes. What they do not report also reveals their bias. Surely there was an "old maid" or bachelor or single parent or childless couple among the 178 people whose lives they examined. If so, their voices have been erased from the record. They are consigned to a "dreadful fate" but they do not speak. *Life Is with People* has no place for anyone who is not part of its ideal nuclear family. Although the book focuses on gender roles and the nuclear family, the other familiar characters from Yiddish literature make their appearance as well. For example, there are colorful and detailed depictions of the stereotypical matchmaker, including quaint touches like the "little dog-eared book."[17]

The authors do refer briefly to the mass emigration of Jews in the early 1900s. According to them, economic necessity was the primary reason so many left for America.

By the time *Fiddler on the Roof* opened in the 1960s, many American Jews were already familiar with the sentimental image of the little Jewish town through *Life Is with People*. The musical provided a vivid three-dimensional image of the same utopia, where the customs and values described in American Jewish textbooks—study and religious observance—are acted out. Ten years later, in the 1970s, the nostalgic image of Old World Jewish life was further reinforced by another major Jewish publication. People do not usually think of *The Jewish Catalog*, which I mentioned in chapter 3, as a work of shtetl nostalgia, yet in many ways it is. Among the many pieces of artwork in the book, there are a hundred photographs of people. About a third depict scenes of 1970s Jewish fellowship (Havurah) life and other images of youth culture in America. Interestingly, more than half portray Eastern European Jewish life, early 1900s Jewish immigrant life or contemporary Orthodox life. There are no scenes of typical contemporary American synagogue life. Old men with beards and young men with beards, the visual impact is powerful: the pairing of twentieth-century American youth culture with nineteenth-century Eastern European Judaism. Curiously, the sexism of the other shtetl nostalgia books—where the men study Torah in the synagogue while the women are hard at work at home—seems to have carried over: only a handful of the photos in *The Jewish Catalog* show women.

Jewish leaders continue to treat the literary images in *Fiddler on the Roof* as the real world of Eastern European Jewry. Benjamin Blech, an Orthodox rabbi and professor of Talmud at Yeshiva University, uses "Fiddler on the Roof" as the title of a section of his popular textbook on Jewish history. Blech writes that the play "vividly re-created much of the reality of the life of the Jews in those days." Ignoring the social conflicts highlighted in the play itself, Professor Blech praises it for demonstrating the "comfort of a close-knit community, of people sharing and caring, of a social life that welded the community together through synagogue prayer and study."[18] *Fiddler on the Roof* does not actually depict synagogue prayer and study. In fact, the village rabbi and his students are portrayed as rather foolish. No doubt prayer and study are of paramount importance to Blech. Citing *Fiddler on the Roof* in another textbook, he tells his readers that in the shtetl, "little children spent most of their days mastering legal texts that in other cultures would be considered difficult for aspiring lawyers."[19]

DISASSEMBLING THE MYTH

A theological treatise, an anthropological study, a Broadway musical, a guide to Jewish observance, a history text—these different works all feature the same sentimental image of the little Eastern European Jewish town whose pious inhabitants lived contented lives of joyous devotion to God and Judaism. It is to be expected that a musical comedy would make use of imaginary people and places. However, serious works produced by reputable authorities have fictionalized the shtetl far more than many people are aware.

For instance, not all of the towns Heschel lists as "little Jewish communities" were actually little, nor were they all Jewish. Karlin, a major center of Hasidism in the midst of rationalistic Lithuania in the 1700s, was a suburb of the large city of Pinsk, but the Hasidim moved elsewhere in the 1800s.[20] Lublin was one of Poland's largest cities; just prior to the period of Jewish emigration, its population of 50,000 was less than half Jewish.[21] Bratslav was indeed small but not predominantly Jewish; at the end of the nineteenth century, Jews comprised approximately one-third of its 6,300 inhabitants.[22]

Zborowski and Herzog acknowledge their extensive use of fictional sources in *Life Is with People*. They explain that literary sources were of "indispensable help," and they reveal that the work of writers such as Sholem Aleichem "contributed more than the academic discussions." *Life Is with People* reads like *Fiddler on the Roof* because Zborowski and Herzog borrow heavily from the same literature as the Broadway musical: "Even the least learned love to quote, and their speech is rich in allusions and references, often twisted, misquoted or manufactured. Sholem Aleichem's famous character Tevyeh is typical in his mangling of learned authorities."[23]

Writers who idealize the shtetl are highly selective in what they talk about. Their descriptions of the devout husbands and their devoted, long-suffering wives are amplified by intense nostalgia, in contrast to their silence about the other Jews who lived in the shtetl. Rather than delineate a real society, they declaim about Jewish values. *Life Is with People*, for instance, is organized around classic themes of Judaism—Sabbath observance, study of Scripture, performance of good deeds and marriage—and describes only the happier citizens of the shtetl. As mentioned, it alludes to widows and old maids, and hints that there might have been other such unhappy inhabitants, but it never provides any details about their lives. And for good reason. To do so would tarnish the image of an ideal Jewish world, where practicing Judaism brings joy and contentment to everyone.

The most glaring omission of most writers who perpetuate the myth of the shtetl has to do with why millions of Jews left Eastern Europe. The authors of *Life Is with People* devote a single paragraph to "the great waves of emigration," which, as I mentioned, they blame on poverty. They go on to explain that it was mostly the "underprivileged" who abandoned the shtetl.[24] However, they do not actually discuss poverty and unemployment. The book provides many details about the more affluent residents; but although they refer in passing to poor people, the authors never portray the lives of shtetl Jews who did not own pearls. Nor do they discuss the class tensions that are an inevitable feature of societies were some people have considerably more than others. And while they suggest that the fear of military conscription and pogroms were minor factors for emigration, the authors never mention the possibility that religious and social traditions may have played a role. In fact, none of the works I have discussed so far even hints at the possibility that some aspects of Eastern European Judaism may have caused many Jews to seek a happier life outside the community.

THE SOCIOLOGICAL BACKGROUND OF THE MYTH

It was not until after World War II that serious books set out to teach American Jewry how noble the shtetl was and to inspire them with descriptions of "authentic" Jewish community life. Up to that time, scholarly accounts of shtetl life did not show it to be a world of peace and happiness, nor even exclusively Jewish. The most extensive historical account of Jewish life in Eastern Europe prior to the Holocaust is the classic work by Simon Dubnow, *History of the Jews in Russia and Poland*, originally written in Russian and completed in 1918. Dubnow was close to his material, both in time and place. None of the colorful characters and beloved scenes made popular by the Yiddish story writers can be found in Dubnow's three-volume textbook. More important, it provides no evidence of the American Jewish ideological themes found in shtetl mythology: devotion to religion and learning, charity and caring, community cohesiveness, contentment and personal fulfillment. The same is true of other nonfiction works prior to the middle of the twentieth century.

However, Dubnow's comprehensive text does include a great deal of information about Eastern European Jewish life that more nostalgic books leave out. For example, parents arranged marriages between children as young as thirteen, with the result that teenage girls often became wives and mothers, and boys often became husbands and fathers while continuing to attend religious school. The strictness of Old World Judaism, combined with the responsibilities of family life under impoverished conditions, was not a pleasant life for young Jews: "The growing generation knew not the sweetness of being young. Their youth withered under the weight of family chains, the pressure of want. . . . The spirit of protest, the striving for rejuvenation, which asserted itself in some youthful souls, was crushed in the vise of a time-honored discipline, the product of long ages. The slightest deviation from a custom, a rite, or old habits of thought met with severe punishment."[25]

In recent years, new scholarship confirms that life in the shtetl was not as idyllic as it is often portrayed. As in every culture, social conditions were complex. Because of poverty, interpersonal relations were affected by stratifications of class, status and education. A profound disdain for physical labor went along with the high esteem for Jewish learning. The large families were intimate, the community was caring and the neighbors pitched in when needed; at the same time, the frequency and intensity of these forms of social intervention stifled individual privacy and freedom. "Beneath the popular images was the real shtetl, which was fraught with tension, discontent, and frustrated energies. Only thus can the massive emigration from the shtetls to the farthest corners of the globe in the nineteenth and twentieth centuries be explained."[26]

Why would reputable scholars abandon fact for elegy, mistake fiction for history, perpetuate stereotypes and portray ordinary men and women in superhuman terms? Shtetl nostalgia is ideologically driven and related to the cultural trauma of mass migration. American Judaism was anxious about authenticity in America.

In the Old World, identity was never a question for Jews because it was imposed from without. Jews had no choice but to be a separate and distinct people. The political and economic oppression also served as a kind of shield, ensuring the preservation of Judaism. America provided no such safeguard. After the Old World Jews stepped out onto the main street of western civilization, their Jewish identity gradually became a more personal—and less visible—matter. The New World provided Caucasian immigrants the unprecedented opportunity to adopt new identities as they emerged from the steerage of ships into the light and air. In fact, those who tried hard enough could lose their identity as Jews entirely. This alarming prospect for the leaders of Judaism made their task more complicated. The influence of the modernist movements would have to compete with the outside culture. Their constituency would soon spread throughout American society rather than being concentrated by locale or by political status. By contrast, the shtetl symbolized a Jewish life that was not compromised by external social influences.

In America, multiple identities and degrees of identity are possible. If there are degrees of Jewishness, it has to do with how much the individual's or the group's beliefs and behaviors derive from Jewish civilization and how much they derive from general society. One of the stated goals of denominational Judaism (across the spectrum of the movements) is that the individual be primarily—if not wholly—identified as a Jew. With this in mind, Jewish educators developed curricula aimed at establishing a sense of strong Jewish identity. The trauma of the Holocaust and the flourishing of the Jewish state (especially the impact of the Six-Day War) solidified identity as the core of all Jewish preaching and teaching. Over the twentieth century, all branches of Judaism increasingly struggled to enhance the religious identity of American Jews: "Participating in a majority culture whose patterns and rhythms often undermine our own, we are forced to live in two worlds. . . . In spite of the conditions of modern life, we must labor zealously to cultivate wholeness in Jewish personalities . . . to refract all aspects of life through the prism of one's own Jewishness."[27]

This quest for authenticity and undiluted Jewish identity is closely connected to the anxiety about the survival of Judaism itself, the fear that Jewish civilization will be lost to the forces of assimilation. Many Jews believe that adopting non-Jewish practices automatically weakens Jewish identity: The greater the intrusion of the surrounding culture, the greater the potential for assimilation. The denominations believe that promoting authentic Jewish practices over non-Jewish practices inoculates the community against assimilation. Orthodox rabbi Hayim Donin provides a very characteristic statement of this mentality and of American Judaism's themes of survival and authenticity: "Since the dangers confronting the Jewish people in their struggle to assure physical and spiritual survival must not be underestimated, it is essential that more of Jewish intellect, energy, skill and sacrificial idealism be redirected toward the strengthening of what is authentically Jewish."[28]

Whether from fear of assimilation or desire for influence, it is only natural that Jewish leaders would seek to make clear distinctions between those aspects of people's lives that are particularly Jewish and those aspects that are generally American; and it is only natural that they would confer approval on what they see as Jewish while expressing caution over what they see as non-Jewish. At the same time, the fact that American Jewish leaders themselves had modified Judaism by inventing new institutions in light of new social conditions caused them to question their own authenticity. They looked to other times and other places as examples of Jewishness. Most teachers, preachers and writers seem to assume that prior to the twentieth century, external influences did not compromise the cultural integrity of the Jewish community. This misconception results from the defensiveness many Jews feel about the high degree of integration they enjoy in America: Emancipation brings more opportunities for assimilation. The concern is that if

Jews are free to participate in American society on an equal basis with gentiles, they will become gentiles themselves. From this perspective, it is easy to imagine the past as a time when Jews, because they were less emancipated, were therefore less influenced by the surrounding culture. In other words, because they were excluded from gentile society—and were less familiar with it as well—they had neither the desire nor the opportunity to adopt gentile ways. This theory leads to the belief that somehow Judaism was more authentic prior to the experience of twentieth-century America.

The romantic appeal of bygone eras has long been popular for both Jews and non-Jews; and it makes sense that the world of Eastern European Jewry would be highly revered in America, since the majority of American Jews are the descendants of Eastern European immigrants. It is easy to forget that the European émigrés themselves were *not* nostalgic for the life they consciously sought to leave behind. Many were all too glad to have escaped not only the persecution and the poverty, but also the repressive and restrictive aspects of Jewish village life itself—its insularity, its intolerance of heterogeneity, its oppression of women. While the immigrant generation looked forward to America, and the American-born generation looked forward to prosperity, the next generation tried to grasp the ends of ribbons unspooling from the departing ship of a vanishing era. The grandchildren enshrined what the grandparents left behind.

During the 1970s, many young American Jews experienced a new interest in Eastern European culture and the traditions of their grandparents. This return to ethnic roots was fueled by the desire for a greater sense of authenticity than mainstream synagogue life provided them. The younger leaders rejected what they saw as borrowings from gentile practice and replaced them with resurrected Old World cultural trappings, which resonated with them as more vibrant, more emotional, more instinctual and more spiritual. This yearning for ethnicity and intensity was very much part of the general American zeitgeist of the 1970s and of that generation's distaste for social pretension.

The publication of *The Jewish Catalog* is emblematic of this phenomenon. *The Jewish Catalog* is not a catalog in the usual sense, but rather a do-it-yourself guide to ritual observance in the home. The idea was based on *The Whole Earth Catalog*, an avatar of 1960s youth culture that spawned an array of other catalogs. *The Jewish Catalog* was attractively produced with illustrations and numerous photographs of people engaged in Jewish religious life. It was funded by the Jewish establishment and heavily promoted by the mainstream Jewish Publication Society, which wanted to reach the younger generation of Jews. Adopting the friendly and inviting approach of the other catalogs, *The Jewish Catalog* encouraged individual Jews to bring into their lives a level of ritual observance that had become relegated to the synagogues.

The quest for cultural authenticity was powerful for the generation of Jews that founded the Havurah movement and produced *The Jewish Catalog*. They could not actually recall the Old World Judaism of their grandparents because they had not witnessed it, but they could learn about it and attempt to re-create it. Eastern European worship modes, folk customs and even superstitions held enormous appeal for young Jews who saw their parents' synagogue life as devoid of ethnic intensity. For example, *The Jewish Catalog* gives specific instructions for swinging a live chicken over one's head as a way to ensure a long life, including the exact words to recite while performing the rite.

The elaborate photo montage in *The Jewish Catalog* is a manifestation of shtetl nostalgia driven by the ideology of Jewish authenticity. Ironically, as much as the *Catalog* represents the quest for Jewish authenticity, it is also assimilationist. Its conscious imitation of *The Whole Earth Catalog* and other artifacts of popular culture are what made it a staple of Judaism in America. Even though the book emphasizes traditional Jewish observance, it was carefully designed with a contemporary American format. The romance of self-sufficient communal life and youth culture is as much a part of the book's appeal as is its enthusiasm for Judaism. The fact that this book—in its multiple editions—remains an effective resource that has introduced Jewish observance to a wide audience shows that is not necessary for American Judaism to engage in a battle for cultural authenticity. Indeed, the success of *The Jewish Catalog* demonstrates that Judaism can consciously copy aspects of the surrounding culture in order to preserve and celebrate its own. In many instances, adopting practices or ideas from the outside can enhance, rather than dilute, Judaism.

While *The Earth Is the Lord's* projected the spiritual life onto the backdrop of the shtetl and *Life Is with People* projected the nuclear family, the ideological projection of *The Jewish Catalog* is authenticity, which is reflected in the choice of photos: 1970s youth culture as modeled by the members of the Boston Havurat Shalom community and Old World Jewish life. After all, how are scenes of the shtetl and Lower East Side relevant to contemporary Jewish observance? The ideology is actually reflected in the scenes that were not included. The thousands of American Jewish congregations or institutions, including the very synagogues and schools that educated the members of the Havurah, do not appear in *The Jewish Catalog*. The absence of photos of contemporary American Jewish life outside of the Havurah community is a statement that Jewish authenticity could not be found within mainstream American Judaism. The Old World photos represented authentic Judaism to the younger generation. The visual statement of *The Jewish Catalog* is that grassroots Jewish observance will be a pathway into Jewish authenticity. Although the ghettos of the Lower East Side and the shtetls of Eastern Europe certainly were insularly Jewish, the concern about authenticity is a twentieth-century American Jewish theme. In the eyes of a generation of young Jews in search of authenticity, the insularity of the shtetl protected it from the pollution of assimilation, ensuring that it would be pure. The image of the self-contained Jewish world also represented another important ideal: community. The Havurah concept of peer community—where all the members are committed to Jewish learning and observance—promised a Jewish life not compromised by gentile values.

The myth of the shtetl met the individual needs of young Jews in search of ethnic authenticity; it served a different need for the leaders of American Judaism who were seeking new models for Jewish observance and family life.

As much as it would make sense to use the stories in the Bible as the examples of Jewish family life, the Torah contains almost no Jewish observances. As remarkable as this may seem to some people, Sarah, Rebecca, Rachael and Leah did not light Shabbat candles; Abraham, Isaac and Jacob did not recite kiddush, the blessing over wine that inaugurates the Sabbath on Friday night. The Torah has no beautiful scenes of papas and mamas and sons and daughters celebrating holidays together, no wise rabbi who can produce a blessing for everything. Also, as mentioned, the Torah's depiction of the nuclear family actually is at odds with American Jewish values. The image of the observant Jewish family—adult father standing at the head of the dinner table, adult mother at his side, a school-age son or two, a daughter—is not found in the Hebrew Bible.

Since Scripture provides no scenes of Jewish families walking to synagogue on the Sabbath, celebrating bar mitzvahs, or observing any kind of family life that resembles the ideals of American Judaism, rabbis and teachers had to draw on another source. *Fiddler on the Roof* and the myth of the shtetl as a small Jewish world provided a dramatic tool to promote congregational membership and traditional religious observance. The American public, both Jewish and gentile, was already enamored of the heartwarming image of the little Jewish town in the Old World. It was only natural for Jewish authorities to promote the popular literature as an illustration of authentic Jewish life and thereby perpetuate the myth of the shtetl.

Aside from the fact that the American Jewish portrait of Old World Jewry is idealized, the pursuit of ethnic authenticity is illusory. No time or place or community of Jews has ever been free of the cultural influence of gentiles. For example, the Hasidic communities in America today appear to have preserved Eastern European

Jewish practices and could be viewed as contemporary representations of shtetl communities. The Hasidim are clearly distinguished by their Old World dress and their use of Yiddish. Even though how they look and how they sound—essential elements of Old World Jewish life brought to the New World—set the Hasidim aside as a unique culture today, both are actually the result of assimilation.

The *shtreimel* and *kapota* (fur hat and long black coat) of the Hasidim are so widely recognized that they are used in popular visual arts as an icon to represent Jewishness. They have an interesting history. Each Hasidic group maintains its own particular clothing style for its males (female members dress relatively the same across the groups). Each combination—style of hat, cut of coat, length of pants, color of stockings—was established in the Old World by the founding rabbi of the particular sect. These early Hasidic masters made it a point to copy the fashionable garb of the well-to-do gentiles in their various locales and time periods. Their aim was to demonstrate to the world the exuberance of their relationship with the Holy; they showed their devotion to the religious life in general by wearing their holiday best every day. Each sect faithfully replicated its particular style throughout subsequent generations, even as the prevailing fashions changed. What began as the conscious emulation of popular culture is now a distinguishing uniform of an insular Jewish community. What was in fact gentile in the Old World has become Jewish in the New World.

The same is true of Yiddish. During the Middle Ages, Jews in German-speaking lands developed a dialect of German that incorporated some Hebrew words and used the Hebrew alphabet. The grammar and most of the vocabulary of Yiddish (the word means "Jewish") is German; it is written using letters from the Hebrew alphabet, but with a different vocalization system. The other name for this dialect, Iwre-Teutsch, means "Hebrew German," and conveys its bicultural origins just as the term "Yiddish" claims it for Judaism. Diaspora Jews no longer spoke Hebrew as a daily language but instead adopted local languages, a sign of their partial assimilation. In fact, during the 1890s, advocates of reviving Hebrew as the language of the Jewish people disparaged Yiddish as inauthentic. Adapting German to Jewish use resulted in the creation of a unique dialect. As Jews migrated westward from Germanic lands into Poland, they continued to use Yiddish, supplementing it with Slavic words. By the nineteenth century, there existed a vast body of Yiddish literature: theater, poetry, fiction, music, philosophy and liturgy. In the early 1900s, Yiddish came to America, where it flourished as the language of the immigrant generation. There were Yiddish newspapers, theaters, radio stations and even movies. What began as a linguistic intermarriage and a sign of assimilation had become unique and defining feature of Jewish civilization.

THE IMPACT OF THE MYTH

No matter how beautiful or how harsh life may have been in the shtetl, no town or society is ever totally free from the forces of history, the random events of daily life on earth or the conflicts that are an unavoidable feature of the human condition. Unfortunately, the excessive sentimentalization of the shtetl can be a barrier to serious historical understanding about an important aspect of Jewish civilization and obscures the fact that many of the religious and cultural values of Old World Jewry were problematic. Since the middle of the twentieth century, American Judaism has depended on a sweetened memory of family life among the Jews of Eastern Europe. Yet the values that many people believe to be the hallmark of authentic Jewish life are not unique to Judaism. Images of self-sacrificing mothers, strong, silent fathers, obedient daughters and smart sons exist among gentiles as well. Moreover, these cherished ideals were not as deeply engrained in the souls of Eastern Europe Jews as *Fiddler on the Roof* and other works of shtetl nostalgia would have the world believe. In fact, there is evidence that traditional Jewish values did not always hold up well to the trauma of relocation in America.

The *Jewish Daily Forward*, the Yiddish newspaper of the immigrant community, ran an advice column for immigrant families called "Bintel Brief." Letters published describe abused wives and families destroyed by alcoholism and gambling. Many people would be surprised to learn that Jewish families had a much higher rate of deserted or widowed women than did other immigrant groups. In fact, desertion reached extremely high rates during the early 1900s and took up a large part of Jewish social service agency budgets.[29] The *Forward* printed a regular feature that posted the names and photos of husbands who had deserted their families, and Jewish social services agencies created a special department to help find fleeing husbands.[30]

This picture is far removed from the ideal families portrayed in books and plays. Did the lustrous fabric of shtetl life disintegrate under the culture shock of life in America and difficult conditions? Were the conditions in the immigrant neighborhoods worse than the oppression that had forced the Jews out of Poland and Russia? Where there no alcoholics in the shtetl, no compulsive gamblers? Not one single man who abused his wife or children? Not one instance of marital infidelity? Or were these problems always a part of family life for Jews in the shtetl, as they likely are for people everywhere? Certainly some shtetl inhabitants experienced lives of shame and humiliation, and many Jewish women were forced into unhappy marriages. In fact, many individuals could not enjoy the cultural riches of Eastern European Jewish life: gays and lesbians, the mentally ill, the disfigured, the impotent.

Perpetuating the myth of the shtetl distracts the American Jewish community from confronting some of the pressing moral and social issues Judaism faces today, such as human sexuality and the meaning of gender. First of all, the nostalgic image of shtetl life is not respectful of women. Instead, the myth reinforces the concept of a patriarchal society. Women are seen as dutiful wives and self-sacrificing mothers. They may hold jobs or run businesses to help their families survive, but they have neither educations nor careers. In *Fiddler on the Roof*, the young women think only about getting married. No doubt at the time most women wanted to find husbands, if only for their own survival, but the image ascribes a very narrow mentality to them.

The romanticized image of shtetl family life also makes a statement about people who, for whatever reason, are not married. Widows and spinsters are to be pitied. The possibility that someone may be single by choice is never considered. As for gay men and lesbian women—it is as if they do not exist. It is a reassuring and comforting image for traditional Jewish families today, but a menacing rejection of anyone who does not fit in: single adult Jews, lesbian and gay Jews, disabled Jews, divorced Jews, childless Jews, Jewish mothers pursuing careers, Jewish fathers caring for children at home.

Contemporary American Judaism cannot afford to perpetuate a worldview that ignores sexual minorities and alternative families, marginalizes single people and demeans women. As it moves forward from the myth of the shtetl, the American Jewish community is learning to embrace the full diversity of its membership, and by so doing it enhances its power as a moral voice in contemporary society.

Moving beyond the myth of the shtetl will also have a positive impact on Jewish-gentile relations in American. *Fiddler on the Roof* projects a powerful image of the Jews as an ethnic minority wanting to be loved, and especially wanting to be seen as nonthreatening. Broadway comedy mixes with the literary genre of the shtetl to produce characters that are all colorful, quaint or charming. There may be hints of courage and moments of poignancy, but everyone is somehow likable and no individual is ever far from the joke and the song. The pervasiveness of the image of the little Jewish village influences how gentiles in America perceive Jews, and no minority group can attain power in any country by portraying itself as harmless. By ceasing to package a sentimental view of Jewish life and present it to the public, American Jewry will increase its own political clout.

Just as the myth of the shtetl influences how gentiles perceive Jews, it also affects how Jews perceive gentiles. *Fiddler on the Roof* suggests that non-Jews are evil. There is one decent gentile, the kind Russian boy who falls in love with Tevyeh's daughter, but the play makes it a point that he is not like the others. The others are loutish, prone to drunkenness and violence. Granted, the Polish peasantry living in the Russia Pale may not have been kind to their Jewish neighbors, but in the microcosm of the little Jewish town there are Jews, who are basically good, and there are non-Jews, who are basically bad. Moving forward from this simplistic us–them worldview will do a great deal to help the American Jewish community effectively navigate the waters of social acceptance and ethnic authenticity. It can open up important new possibilities of dialogue in a world that is being torn apart by religious and ethnic differences.

Finally, the myth also influences how Jews in America perceive Judaism. Even though rabbis cite *Fiddler on the Roof* as an example of the ideal Jewish life, where everyone practices Judaism and preserves its traditions, the play in fact demeans Jewish religion rather than esteems it. The rabbinical students are portrayed as pedants devoid of worldly experience or philosophical sophistication, slavishly devoted to a not-very-bright rabbi. Jewish ritual observance is seen as sweet and beautiful, but also naïve and quaint. Even God is reduced to a personality: a loving father figure, but hardly a redeeming force.

The time has come for rabbis and textbooks to stop presenting the lost world of the shtetl as the standard of Jewish authenticity. Whether it ever existed in reality as it does in the modern American imagination or not, the shtetl is a world that cannot be recreated. It is beautiful to imagine, but it no longer exists. Nor can it offer inviting role models for twenty-first-century Jews. *Fiddler on the Roof* is delightful entertainment, but who can take it seriously? What American Jewish girl or boy aspires to be Tevyeh or Goldeh? As American Jewry moves beyond the image of shtetl life to embrace a contemporary Jewish religion that is intelligent, sophisticated and forceful, American rabbis have much more to offer than *deedle-daidle-dum* Judaism.

———

The theme of authenticity that inspired American Jewish leaders to project their own sentimentality onto the world of Eastern European Jewry also motivated them to project their modern rationality onto the world of ancient Judaism. In the next chapter, I explore how denominational Judaism suppressed significant facts about the beliefs and practices of earlier eras.

5

IDENTITY, REASON AND SELF-ACCEPTANCE

The rabbis who created American Judaism in the beginning of the twentieth century were rational men who respected scientific truth. Embracing the spirit of the age, they made reason and historical perspective cornerstones of the religious movements they founded, and rabbis today apply contemporary insights to the study of classic Jewish texts. Jewish thinkers have placed so much emphasis on the rationality of Judaism that teachers and textbooks today insist that the Jewish religion was based on reason even in its earliest days. Just as Jewish authorities have inserted contemporary images of a utopian Jewish community into the historical record of Eastern European Judaism, some rabbis have preferred to forget other aspects of Judaism's past. The fact that certain supernatural beliefs existed in previous eras challenges the notion that Judaism was always a religion of reason. The Torah describes divination and trials by ordeal. The sages of the Talmud routinely discussed Heaven and Hell. The traditional Hebrew prayer book mentions Satan. The Talmud records a claim that Rabbi Shimon ben Shetach hanged eighty women for witchcraft on one day (Sanhedrin 45b), and the seventeenth-century Italian philosopher Moses Hayyim Luzzatto was forced to flee to Amsterdam when the rabbis of Padua raided his home and accused him of sorcery.[1]

Paradise as reward for the righteous, Hell as the place of fiery punishment for sinners, Satan as a supernatural being, divination, trial by ordeal—these concepts are no longer part of normative Judaism, but the fact that they once were the subjects of discussion is problematic for American Jewish leaders. As a result, throughout the twentieth century, rabbis and scholars have insisted that these supernatural beliefs were never part of Judaism.

THE MYTH THAT JUDAISM IS BASED ON REASON

In his popular book *Jewish Literacy*, Orthodox Rabbi Joseph Telushkin tells his readers: "Afterlife is rarely discussed in Jewish life, be it among Reform, Conservative, or Orthodox Jews. . . . Jewish teachings on the subject of afterlife are sparse."[2] He then goes on to observe that "afterlife has always played a critical role in Islamic teachings [and in] Christianity." Another popular guide to Judaism, *What is a Jew?*, by Conservative rabbi Morris Kertzer, makes a similar claim that Hell is not a Jewish concept: "There is almost no speculation about the nature of hell. Jewish literature knows no equivalent to Dante's Inferno. The form of punishment to be meted out to the wicked never exercised Jewish imagination or folklore."[3]

As I mentioned earlier, the Reform movement published a formal statement of its principles in 1885; it also states categorically that Heaven and Hell were never Jewish concepts: "We reject as ideas not rooted in Judaism the beliefs both in bodily resurrection and in Gehenna and Eden (Hell and Paradise) as abodes for everlasting punishment or reward."[4] Although assertions that Heaven and Hell are not part of Judaism today may be true, claims that Heaven and Hell *never* were part of Judaism are completely false.

Indeed, there is near-universal denial in modern Judaism about an entire constellation of beliefs that comprise a significant portion of Jewish tradition. For example, nowhere in *The World of the Talmud* does author Morris Adler mention Hell, Heaven, divination, magic or any of their synonyms.[5] The same thing is true of Adin Steinsaltz's classic *The Essential Talmud* and Hayyim Donin's *To Be a Jew*.[6] Not all contemporary writers mislead readers about these traditional Jewish beliefs. In *The Jewish Book of Why*, Rabbi Alfred Kolatch makes it clear that "the belief was prevalent in talmudic times that the wicked are consigned to hell (gehenna or gehinnom) and are subject to punishment for a maximum of twelve months." He does not discuss the traditional beliefs about Satan, but he does cite a few references to Satan in rabbinic and folk literature.[7] Unfortunately, popular books like *Judaism for Dummies* mostly reinforce the myth that Judaism has always been scientific and reasonable: "While some faiths imagine an evil being, a 'Satan,' with whom God contends, this idea never really developed within Judaism."[8] The idea may not have developed in *modern* Judaism, but there was indeed a time when Jews imagined Satan as an evil being contending with God.

Why would knowledgeable writers mislead their readers by creating the impression that these beliefs were never a major part of Judaism? What harm could possibly result from American Jewry knowing that these ideas were actually quite prevalent among the Jews in the past and were seriously considered by the rabbis of earlier times? The reason has to do with the fact that the founders of denominational Judaism were highly educated men who applied scientific methods to Jewish studies and aspired to a rational understanding of the universe. At the same time, they wanted their teachings to be seen as authentic in the eyes of Old World Jews, so they made it a point to link them all to sources in the Hebrew Bible, the Talmud and the Midrash (these sacred texts are defined in the appendix). Yet there were certain old concepts about supernatural forces, supernatural beings and supernatural realms—all with sources in the same Bible, Talmud and Midrash—that they very much wanted to leave behind. In the theology of denominational Judaism, there would be one and only one supernatural being: God. Everything else would be reasonable and conform to modern knowledge. The founder of Reconstructionist Judaism, Mordecai Kaplan, even went so far as to define God in his writings in nonsupernatural terms, as "the power that makes for salvation." Other supernatural entities—demons, angels—would not be part of Jewish cosmology. Heaven and Hell would not exist as real places in the real world of modern Judaism. Magic and divination would not be part of the enlightened Jewish community of the New World; American rabbis would not be fashioning amulets or exorcising evil spirits, as they had in the Old World.

Yet as I mentioned earlier, American Judaism maintains that its body of concepts and practices evolved from the ancestral religion recorded in the Torah. Denominational Judaism's dependence on the theme of continuity generates another assertion: that the Judaism of earlier times has been faithfully preserved. In fact, however, much of ancient Judaism—such as the sacrificial system and the priesthood, as well as the beliefs I have been discussing—has been discarded.

The founders of denominational Judaism faced a philosophical dilemma: How could they claim to be preserving Judaism while at the same time disposing of its undesirable elements? One option would be to avoid mentioning these elements in sermons, lectures or textbooks; new generations of Jews would not learn about outdated concepts that were no longer relevant to Jewish life. Consistent with denominational Judaism's policy of presenting its innovations as the continuation of ancient Judaism, these pioneering American Jewish philosophers taught that Judaism has always been a religion of reason.

In spite of the reluctance of Jewish leaders to talk about the subject, it is obvious from both the Hebrew Bible and the rabbinic literature I cite later that the founders of Judaism believed that divination is a way to induce God to reveal hidden information, Satan is a supernatural power of evil, Heaven is a reward for the righteous and Hell is a place of punishment for sinners. A century of silence has been so effective that the American Jewish community today associates Satan, Heaven, Purgatory and Hell with Islam and Christianity; it cannot imagine resorting to magical oracles to reveal truth. Americans—Jewish and gentile—have never stopped asking about supernatural beliefs in Judaism, and American rabbis have been giving the same evasive answers for a hundred years.

People often speculate about what happens after we die, and the leaders of many organized religions have been quite vocal when it comes to the afterlife. American rabbis, however, usually talk around the topic of life after death. For example, they might note that in the Torah, God rewards and punishes people during their lives on earth and then explain that in postbiblical Judaism, the reward for a good life is the satisfaction of living a good life and the penalty for misdeeds is a troubled conscience. Any speculation about life after death, they claim, is part of Judaism's faith in the future of human society, when God's truth will prevail over the earth. American Jewish writers typically discuss two classical Jewish concepts: *olam habah* and *michayei hametim*, the future age of perfection and the resurrection that will be part of it. Although the denominations differ somewhat in their understanding of these two traditional concepts, when it comes to the belief in Heaven and Hell as realms where people's souls go upon their deaths, they either say nothing at all or claim that it is a Christian concept.

In recent years, though, a new generation of scholars has broken American Judaism's reticence to talk about life after death. For instance, *The Death of Death* by Jewish Theological Seminary professor Neil Gillman discusses classic Jewish teachings about *olam haba* and *michayei hametim*.[9] According to this concept, God has promised that there will be a future age of perfection, the messianic era. At that time the dead will be revived, and the entire world will be united as the kingdom of God. Heaven and Hell are a somewhat different concept in Jewish tradition: They are realms that exist in the present, where each individual soul goes upon death to await the world to come.

Although Heaven and Hell are no longer a part of normative Judaism in the way that the world-to-come and resurrection are, they still have a place. The familiar Hebrew Prayer for the Dead, *El Molei Rachamim*, is chanted at every traditional Jewish funeral service; it is part of the Yizkor memorial service in synagogue on major holidays. Here is my own literal translation:

> God full of compassion, dwelling on high, grant perfect rest beneath the wings of the Divine Presence, amid the high places of the holy and the pure, who shine as the brightness of the sky, to the soul of _____, who has gone to his world. Because charity has been pledged to the memory of his soul, may his rest be in Heaven. Therefore, Master of Mercy, hide him in the shelter of your wings forever. May his soul be bound up in the bonds of life. God is his legacy, and may he lie on his resting place in peace.

These words mean that when people die, their souls immediately go to another realm called Heaven or Paradise (*gan eden* in Hebrew) and reside there eternally.

Although none of the denominations teaches about Heaven and Hell in this literal way today, the Prayer for the Dead is still problematic for the Conservative and Orthodox denominations, which preserve the traditional Hebrew liturgy. Because most American Jews do not know enough Hebrew to understand the service, most modern Jewish prayer books are bilingual: The Hebrew prayers are printed alongside their English translations. The official prayer book of the Conservative movement, of course, keeps the Hebrew text of the Prayer for the Dead, including the reference to Paradise.[10] The English translation of the prayer, however, omits the sentence about the deceased's soul dwelling in Heaven. Thus the denominational authorities who compiled the prayer book are practicing a kind of ideological censorship because the average worshipper has no way to know that the passage has been left out.

By consciously withholding problematic information in this way, American rabbis end up misleading their membership about Jewish tradition. Orthodox rabbi Maurice Lamm takes a similar approach in *The Jewish Way in Death and Mourning*, which for many years has been a standard text for lay people on Jewish funeral practices and beliefs. Lamm includes a brief section on the afterlife but never mentions "Heaven" or "Hell." In the middle of an elaborate discussion of contemporary Jewish teachings about the afterlife, he sandwiches a brief remark in parentheses: "Concepts such as Gehinnom and Gan Eden are too complicated for discussion in this work."[11] Lamm does not inform his readers that Gehinnom and Gan Eden mean Hell and Heaven. He does, however, go on to discuss immortality of the soul, the world-to-come, bodily resurrection and messianism (not exactly uncomplicated topics). In these examples and in many others, American rabbis have restricted rather than expanded the public's knowledge of Jewish tradition.

HEAVEN AND HELL
IN JEWISH TRADITION

Both the Talmud and the Midrash contain specific references to Heaven as a place of reward when a righteous person dies and Hell as a place of punishment when a sinner dies. This passage from of the Talmud (Eruvin 19a), which I have translated literally, is typical of classical Jewish discourse about Heaven and Hell:

> Master of the Universe, well have you judged, well have you rewarded, well have you punished; and well have you prepared Hell for the wicked, Heaven for the righteous. . . . All the sinners descend to Hell, but the patriarch Abraham comes and brings out the Israelites (who are circumcised). . . . Rabbi Jerimiah ben

Elazar said Hell has three entrances: one in the desert, one in the sea and one in Jerusalem. . . . According to the school of Rabbi Ishmael, [the biblical passage] "His fire is in Zion" refers to Hell, and "His furnace is in Jerusalem" refers to the entrance to Hell. . . . But there are more [entrances], for Rabbi Meryon has said that there are two palm trees in the Valley of Ben Hinnom, with smoke rising between them, and this is an entrance of Hell. Rabbi Yehoshua ben Levi said there seven names for Hell: Sheol, Abyss, Pit of Destruction, Pit of Desolation, Slime of Suffering, Shadow of Death and Underworld. . . . Resh Lakish said that if Heaven is in the Land of Israel, its entrance is Bet Shean; if it is in Arabia, its entrance is Bet Gerem; and if it is between the rivers, its entrance is in Dumaskanin.

The matter-of-fact way these famous rabbinic authorities discuss the specifics of Heaven and Hell indicates they took it for granted that such realms existed as physical entities.

Elsewhere the Talmud is quite specific that Heaven exists as a place of reward and Hell as a place of punishment: "Master of the Universe, You created Gan Eden and you created Gehinnom; you created the righteous and you created the wicked" (Sota 22a). In total, Gehinnom—Hell—is mentioned sixty-eight times in the Talumd. Gan Eden—Heaven or Paradise—appears in thirteen different passages. Heaven and Hell also appear in the Midrash and other allegorical rabbinic works. In fact, the first chapter of the Midrash (Bereshit Rabbah 9:5) explicitly states that "*takantah gehinnom lirashaim gan eden litzadikim*—God created Hell for the wicked and Heaven for the righteous." The Midrash talks about Heaven and Hell in several other places, and there are dozens of similar references in other classic rabbinic texts.

Although American Jewish textbooks intended for general readership mostly avoid these problematic topics, one scholarly study, *Legends of the Jews* by Louis Ginzberg, meticulously documents the numerous references to Heaven, Hell and Satan in ancient Jewish sources. Originally written in German, this multivolume work reproduces rabbinic texts which explain that Hell is located in the center of the earth, that it has seven divisions, that each division has seven compartments, that each compartment has seven rivers of fire and seven rivers of hail and that the height, width and depth of each compartment of Hell would take three hundred years to walk across.[12]

The *Pesikta Rabbati* (a book of rabbinic allegories compiled in the 700s, about two centuries after the final redaction of the Talmud) presents a lengthy and elaborate description of Moses visiting the different realms of Heaven and Hell. He finds Hell is filled with fire and consists of several realms where sinners are tortured horribly. In the first realm, Moses sees men hanging by their eyes as punishment for looking with lust on other men's wives, by their ears for listening to vain speech, by their tongues for speaking slander, by their feet for not going to synagogue and by their hands for robbing and murdering. Women hang by their hair and breasts for seducing young men. In the second realm, people hang upside down while giant black worms crawl over their bodies as punishment for lying, violating the Sabbath, insulting their neighbors and being disrespectful of the rabbis. In the third realm of Hell, people are stung by seventy-headed scorpions whose poison causes their eyes to melt in their sockets; they had betrayed their fellow Israelites, refused to accept the authority of the Torah or denied the Creator. In the fourth realm, Jews who ate on Yom Kippur, made amulets for gentiles or tasted nonkosher food are standing up to their waists in mud while devils whip them with chains and smash their teeth with flaming rocks; their teeth grow back each day. In the last realm, people are half buried in snow while the rest of their bodies are eaten by worms, burned by fire and whipped by devils; these are sinners who committed incest and idolatry.

Pesikta Rabbati also has a lot to say about Heaven. After traveling through Hell, Moses then goes to Paradise, which has seven heavens. The first is filled with flowing streams and is made entirely of windows; in the second heaven, multitudes of angels made of fire and water sing praises to God; in the third heaven, there is an angel of infinite height, with seventy heads, each head with seventy mouths and each mouth with seventy tongues extolling God; in the fourth heaven, Moses sees a temple made of red fire, white fire, green fire, carbuncles and rubies; the fifth heaven is filled with angels whose upper bodies are fire and lower bodies, snow; the sixth consists of multitudes of angels made of ice; and the seventh heaven is guarded by a an immense angel covered from head to toe with glaring eyes.[13] Because these passages appear in a source that—unlike the Talmud—is almost entirely poetic and allegorical, they are not necessarily intended to be taken literally. Nonetheless they show that speculation about supernatural realms and supernatural beings did occupy an important place in rabbinic Judaism.

Some rabbis take pains to keep people in the dark about Jewish traditions of Heaven and Hell. For example, a popular guide to Jewish belief, *Nine Questions People Ask About Judaism*, tells readers that "the notion of a hell where sinners suffer eternally is foreign to Judaism and entered the Western world's religious consciousness through the New Testament."[14] Its authors, Orthodox rabbis Dennis Prager and Joseph Telushkin, have chosen their words carefully. Talmudic discussions about Hell do indeed agree that the average sinner remains in Hell for a limited period of time (typically either eleven or twelve months) before going to Heaven. However, some Talmud sages taught that other sinners remain in Hell forever. So while it may be true that the Talmud teaches that *in general* sinners are not punished *eternally*, Prager and Telushkin misinform their readers when they claim the notion is "foreign to Judaism." The notion is not at all foreign to Judaism, even if it is not part of mainstream Judaism today. Like many rabbis, they want to draw clear distinctions between Judaism and Christianity. As a result, they are very reluctant to acknowledge that at one time Judaism embraced beliefs that are characteristic of Christianity.

SATAN IN JEWISH TRADITION

Rabbis are even more uncomfortable about the references to Satan in traditional Jewish literature than they are about Hell, even though the Talmud explains that Satan is the Prince of Hell. In fact, descriptions of Satan as a supernatural being intent on sowing discord between God and humanity are found throughout the Talmud. One passage (Sanhedrin 95a) tells that when David was fleeing Saul, Satan appeared to him in the form of a deer; David kept trying to shoot the deer with arrows but could not, and thus he was led into enemy territory. A little farther on, the Talmud says that Satan appeared to David in the form of a bird and ultimately led him to behold the beautiful Bathsheba combing her hair. The Talmud (Sanhedrin 89b) also provides a story of Satan as tempter and foe of God. Here is my translation:

> When Abraham made a great feast on the day Isaac was weaned, Satan said to the Almighty, "Master of the Universe, this elderly man whom you have graced with offspring at the age of one hundred years did not sacrifice before You a single dove or a single pigeon out of this entire feast he has made. The only thing he has made is for his son." [God replied:] "If I were to say to him sacrifice your son before me, he would sacrifice him immediately." Immediately, God tested Abraham and said, "Take your only son [and sacrifice him before me]."

Although Abraham passes God's test of faith, in this allegory Satan is shown having at least some influence over God.

The Talmud talks a great deal about Satan seducing rabbis. Another passage (Kiddushin 81a), which I have also translated literally here, says: "Rabbi Meir used to make fun of people who committed sins. One day Satan appeared to him as a woman on the other side of a river. There being no ferry, he crossed over by holding onto a rope. When he reached the middle of the rope, [Satan] left him. He said, 'If the firmament had not proclaimed to be careful with Rabbi Meir and his Torah, I would have destroyed your life.'" The passage goes on to tell of similar confrontations between Satan and other Talmudic sages. Many other sections of the Talmud mention Satan, and references to him can be found in numerous other rabbinic texts.

Satan is even named in the traditional Jewish prayer service. Part of a familiar blessing known as *Hashkivenu* asks God to "keep Satan from before us and behind us." However, this particular phrase is never translated directly into English. Different denominations substitute other words for Satan, such as "adversary" or "evil forces." Although the original Hebrew words for *Hashkivenu* have been set to music and are sung as a part of every evening prayer service, the literal meaning of the passage is hidden from the average worshipper. Orthodox rabbi Hayim Donin explains this omission by denying that "Satan" refers to an actual being:

> The word we translate as "adversary" is rendered in the Hebrew text by the word "satan." In the Hebraic idiom, this word does not mean a "Satan" who fights against God. Judaism recognizes no independent spiritual power other than God. "Satan" refers to the evil impulses within man that prevent him from following his good inclinations and thus lead him astray. The verse might therefore also be translated as "Remove every evil impulse from before us and from behind us."[15]

The Conservative prayer book avoids raising any eyebrows by rendering the troublesome phrase as "Shield us from enemies."[16]

Numerous Jewish authorities throughout the twentieth century point to one specific sentence in the Talmud as proof that whenever the Hebrew Bible and other classical sources refer to Satan, they mean nothing more than the personification of evil within people. Reform pioneer Kaufman Kohler, Conservative writer Louis Jacobs, Talmudic scholar Abraham Cohen and many others cite this phrase (Baba Batra 16a) as evidence that Satan was never a part of Judaism.[17] As much as modern Jewish authorities seize on this famous passage, its meaning is open to interpretation. I have translated it so you can draw your own conclusions. The sages are discussing a verse in the Bible where God says that Satan incited him against Job to destroy him for no good reason: "Rabbi Yochanan said . . . in this verse [God] is like a human being who when people incite Him is influenced. The Mishnah teaches: [Satan] goes down and tempts, and he goes up and accuses; he gets permission and takes a soul. Resh Lekish said: He is Satan; he is the Evil Impulse; he is the Angel of Death." Regardless of how these sentences are interpreted, they show that the ancient rabbis considered the possibility that Satan is a supernatural being with the power to manipulate God. In fact, Satan is mentioned in sixteen other places in the Talmud as well as numerous places in the Midrash.

SORCERY IN JEWISH TRADITION

In classical Judaism, supernatural power was not limited to Satan and God or the realms of Heaven and Hell. Belief in divination and magic was part of the daily world of the Jewish people. The Torah contains specific examples of ancient Israelite divination and trial by ordeal. American educators and rabbis usually omit these parts of the Torah when they publish textbooks, teach classes or deliver sermons. Since the amount of material in the Talmud and Midrash is enormous, and anthologies of rabbinic literature therefore are forced to be selective, it is an easy matter to translate the inspiring passages while ignoring the problematic ones. What preacher would not prefer to talk about loving one's fellow and similar precepts in Kedoshim (the "holiness" portion of Leviticus) rather than, for instance, the gruesome trial by ordeal in Sotah (the "adulteress" portion of Numbers):

> Any man whose wife has been unfaithful to him . . . shall bring his wife to the priest. . . . The priest shall take holy water in an earthen vessel, and the priest shall take some dust from the floor of the Tabernacle and put it in the water. The priest shall bare the woman's head . . . and say to the woman: "May the Lord make you a curse and an example among your people by causing your loin to drop and your womb to swell. . . . The priest shall write these curses on a scroll and swirl it into the bitter water. He shall make the woman drink the bitter water that brings the curse. . . . If she had defiled herself and been unfaithful to her husband . . . her womb will swell and her loin will drop. But if the woman has

not defiled herself and is pure, she will be unharmed and able to conceive (Numbers 5:11–28; my translation).[18]

Divination is the term for ritual procedures that induce God to reveal something that could not be found out by natural means, and this passage from the Bible clearly is an example. Modern rabbis usually select some more enlightening passage to speak about when this particular section of the Torah is read in the synagogue.

Bible scholar Richard Elliot Friedman's *Commentary on the Torah* is an English translation accompanied by detailed interpretations for each of the weekly portions in the cycle of Torah readings. When he comes to the problematic Sotah section, Friedman acknowledges in passing that "the traditional Talmudic belief is that a miracle is expected to occur through this procedure."[19] In other words, it is divination: Truth is made known by supernatural means. Friedman mingles this fact in a single sentence with several other hypotheses about the trial by ordeal and points out that the procedure eventually was abandoned.

The Reform movement has produced its own annotated translation for use during Sabbath services: *The Torah: A Modern Commentary.* Its author, Gunther Plaut, is more forthright about the supernatural basis of the ordeal and its place in Jewish tradition: "Mishnah and Talmud treated of the ordeal extensively in the tractate Sotah (faithless wife). One major problem inherent in the law of the ordeal is the underlying assumption that by invoking the procedure a husband could force God to make the truth known. No other Torah law is dependent on such a divine manifestation. According to the Rabbis, an immediate response was expected to the test." Having stated the fact, however, Plaut quickly moves on to conclude that "the law of the ordeal implies that fidelity is an essential element in marriage and that jealousy is a legitimate sentiment, for trust is the foundation of the marital covenant."[20] Nowhere in his commentary does he address the question of whether "divine manifestation" has a place in Judaism, now or in the past.

Other oracular ceremonies prescribed by the Torah include the well-known example of divination by the Urim and Tummim, jewels set into the breastplate of the high priest that could be consulted to determine guilt or innocence: "You shall set the Urim and the Tummim in the breastplate of judgment, which shall be on Aaron's chest when he goes before the Lord. Thus shall Aaron carry the judgment of the children of Israel on his chest before the Lord at all times" (Exodus 28:29–30). "Joshua shall stand before Eleazar the priest, who shall ask the Urim for judgment of him before the Lord" (Numbers 27:21). According to the Talmud (Yoma 73b) certain jewels would glow, thus revealing the answer to the inquiry.

The Talmud has a great deal to say about magic in all its forms, and Rabbi Yochanan, the head of Sanhedrin, the highest rabbinic court in ancient Judea, even established a requirement that no sage could sit on the Sanhedrin unless he was well-versed in magic (Sanhedrin 17a). Numerous passages supply colorful details about the practice of sorcery in ancient Judea. For example, according to Sanhedrin 67a, carrying a grasshopper egg is a charm to ward off earaches; a tooth from a live fox will induce sleep, while a tooth from a dead fox will ward off sleep; and reciting a formula based on the names of angels will cure skin disease. In Sanhedrin 67b, the Talmud tells of a sage named Yannai who went into an inn and asked the serving woman for water. As he began to drink, he noticed her lips moving and became suspicious. When Yannai poured out some of the water, it turned into snakes. He made the woman drink the water, and she was transformed into an ass. He then rode the ass to the marketplace, where one of the woman's companions broke the spell and transformed the ass back into a woman. He was then seen to be riding on a woman in the marketplace. Some rabbis also believed that drinking water at night made a person vulnerable to the power of Shavriri, the Demon of Blindness; according to Avodah Zarah 12b, the incantation to protect against Shavriri is "shavriri avriri riri rir ri."

Descriptions of sorcery are found in many places in the Talmud. For example, Rabbi Yochanan learned the language of angels and demons so that he could use the words for incantations (Baba Batra 134a). Rabba created a man out of dust and sent him to Rabbi Zira. Rabbi Chaninnah and Rab created a calf and then ate it (Sanhedrin 65b).

Not only did the sages of the Talmud believe in sorcery and witchcraft, they feared its power. According to the Talmud, Jewish women frequently practiced witchcraft and burned incense for purposes of sorcery (Eruvin 64b, Berachot 53a). Rabbi Ameimar learned from the leader of the witches that he could protect himself from their power by reciting the words "May a pot of boiling excrement be stuffed into your mouths, vile witches. May the hair you use for magic be torn from your heads. May the crumbs you use for divination be scattered by the wind. May the spices you hold in your hands for sorcery be blown away" (Pesachim 110a, b).

The practice of magic and divination was common among the Jews during the centuries following the rabbinic period and continued until modern times. One form of divination, known as Princes of Glass or Princes of Oil, and based on procedures described in the Talmud, was employed by Jews in the Middle Ages. In the traditional procedure, some sort of shining surface was prepared from water, crystal, wax, oil or metal. A young child would be made to gaze on the shimmering light reflections while the practitioner pronounced the words of a spell, posed a question and commanded the "prince" to respond. The child would have visions of supernatural beings that revealed the answer to the question being posed.[21] The ability to fashion a golem (a human figure) and bring it to life by using one of the secret names of God was considered part of the repertoire of Kabbalist rabbis around the 1600s.[22]

Beliefs about secret names for God—vestiges of divination and magic—persist in Jewish tradition, just as remnants of old beliefs about Heaven and Satan are found here and there in Hebrew liturgy. Perhaps the most prominent example is the ancient concept of the supernatural power of the personal name of God. In Jewish law, the Bible's four-letter Hebrew name for God (called the Tetragrammaton, the Unpronounceable Name or the Ineffable Name) may never be said aloud. In fact, no one today knows how to pronounce it. The Hebrew alphabet does not have vowels like English does; the vocalization of words is determined by grammar and context. Vocalization marks (sometimes called "vowels") are added in printed editions of Hebrew Bibles and prayer books, but no vocalization was ever provided for the four-letter name of God. The universal custom among Ashkenazi Jews for centuries has been to substitute the Hebrew word for Lord, *adonai*; so the vocalization for *adonai* is printed along with the four-letter name. Non-Jews who learned to read the Bible in Hebrew but did not know the custom about the vocalization marks mistakenly assumed that the Bible's name for God is "Jehovah." Jews have many names for God, but Jehovah is not one of them; it is a misunderstanding.

Jewish law also states that the four-letter name of God may never be written, except in copies of the Bible, the parchments contained in *mezzuzot* and *tefillin*, or in prayer books. It may never be erased or destroyed; when documents containing *shemot* (God's name) wear out, they must be kept in storage or buried in a grave in a consecrated cemetery. There is nothing scientific or rational about these laws. They were enacted during a period of history when people believed that divine names had supernatural power as well as sanctity.

Jewish tradition today continues to treat the name of God with considerable awe. Some Jews even write the name in English as "G-d." Contemporary Jewish veneration for the name of God is a sign of respect for a sacred symbol, but the mystique surrounding the word itself still holds sway.

AMERICAN JUDAISM AND
THE SUPERNATURAL

Ideas about magic and divination, Heaven and Hell and Satan are found throughout the full range of Judaism's sacred literature—the Bible, the Talmud, the Midrash and other classic rabbinic texts spanning more than a thousand years. Not only is this material extensive, it is quite consistent in its viewpoint. Some may have been intended as allegory or poetry, but those that are part of legal discussions in the Talmud were meant in earnest. The sheer volume of discussion of these topics indicates that classical Judaism had clearly defined beliefs about them. These beliefs can be summarized this way:

- God created a physical realm called Gan Eden (Heaven) as a paradise where righteous people go after they die.
- God created a physical realm call Gehennah (Gehinom, Hell) as a place of torture where sinners go after they die; for some sinners the punishment is temporary while for others it is eternal.
- God ordained specific mechanisms in the Torah that people could use to solve mysteries, although these rituals may no longer be employed.
- Certain objects, procedures and words have the power to change the form of living beings and objects, ward off diseases, protect against evil forces, bring inanimate objects to life or reveal secrets.
- Satan exists as a supernatural being independent of God, and he has the ability to corrupt human beings and interfere adversely in the relationship between God and people.

Nonetheless, when American rabbis created denominational Judaism, they wanted to establish reason and modern ways of thinking as its pillars. Because of their concerns about whether Jews in America would accept the authenticity of this new form of Judaism and the authority of its leaders, these rabbis were careful to present New World Judaism as the continuation of ancient heritage. Since neither the authority nor the authenticity of denominational Judaism is in question today, it is time to move forward and acknowledge that the intellectual enlightenment of American Judaism is itself a product of the modern age.

Whether there ever was a need for rabbis and teachers to insulate American Jews from the supernatural beliefs of previous eras, there certainly is no need to do so now. The Jewish people are not likely to be either confused or disillusioned by the knowledge that Jews in ancient times were not scientific people. Whatever its perceived power in earlier times, the four-letter name of God is not really viewed as magic today; the customs surrounding it are seen as symbols of respect for God. The same will hold true for the references to Paradise and Satan in Jewish liturgy, and prayer books do not have to skip over them on the English side of the page. American Jews can move forward from myths about Jewish rationality and make their own determinations about Jewish authenticity, without the mediation of denominational authority. Learning about old rabbinic beliefs regarding supernatural forces will not diminish the world's respect for the Jewish people today. In fact, it well might add new layers of human interest to the story of a contemporary civilization with ancient roots. With this in mind, it would be a simple matter for any writer, rabbi or teacher to set the record straight by making these points:

- Jews used to believe in Heaven and Hell, but they no longer do.
- Jews used to believe in Satan, but they no longer do.
- Jews used to believe in magic and divination, but they no longer do.
- American Judaism prefers to understand the world rationally and scientifically.

The denominational themes of continuity, survival and authenticity have been central to American Judaism for over a century, and denominationalism dominates the Jewish religion in America today. In fact, as I discuss in the next chapter, it is difficult for many people to imagine American Judaism any other way.

6

DENOMINATIONS, AUTHORITY AND INDEPENDENCE

It is no surprise that a steadily increasing number of people connect to Judaism through a variety of independent, local communities. Fellowships, called *havurot* in Hebrew, function as close-knit congregations; *minyans*—literally, small groups that meet for prayer—are similar. Book discussion groups and other kinds of grassroots organizations meet for study, celebration, ritual observance and spiritual support. Some Jews affiliate with congregations outside of the four major denominations of Reform, Conservative, Orthodox and Reconstructionist Judaism. The Society for Humanistic Judaism consists of about thirty congregations in America, and the Jewish Renewal movement boats almost forty member congregations.[1] Other Jews belong to any of a wide range of independent congregations that are not affiliated with any formal movement or denomination. Nonetheless, most people take it for granted that the four denominations represent all the branches of Judaism or that the Jewish religion spans a continuum from Reform to Orthodox.

By their very nature, independent congregations and fellowships are hard to count, since there is no system for registering them. Because small fellowships both form and dissolve more rapidly than larger congregations, demographically they are a moving target. Currently there are about thirty independent congregations and *havurot* in the Washington, D.C., region; they range in size from a handful of individuals up to a couple hundred families.[2] Extrapolating from this figure, it seems likely that the nationwide number of independent communities is somewhere in the hundreds. One umbrella group, the National Havurah Committee, serves well over one hundred congregations.[3] It would be quite useful to the American Jewish community to know just how many Jews are affiliated with fellowships or independent congregations. Although the United Jewish Communities did collect these data as part of their National Jewish Population Survey 2000–2001 (NJPS), the numbers were not published in the official report. In addition to tallying the membership of the four denominations, the *Survey* workers counted individuals who identified their congregational affiliation as "traditional, Sephardic, Jewish Renewal, Humanist, Havurah, nonaffiliated, Messianic, don't know, can't say or refused."[4] The NJPS then reported that 46 percent of American Jews belong to congregations, of which 38 percent are Reform, 33 percent Conservative, 22 percent Orthodox and 2 percent Reconstructionist. The other 5 percent are all simply lumped together as "other."[5] It may be that the numbers were too small to calculate accurately from the sample population, but clearly the nondenominational group—comprising well over 100,000 religiously affiliated American Jews[6]—is more than twice as large as the Reconstructionist denomination, whose numbers were reported. Even so, considering that denominational Judaism accounts for 95 percent of religiously affiliated Jews in America, it is not surprising that the NJPS report did not even mention the word *havurah*.

The equation of Judaism with denominationalism is so entrenched that many people find it impossible to think in any other terms. The independent website Myjewishlearning.com says that it is "transdenominational," by which it means either that multiple viewpoints are represented or merely that the viewpoints are unbiased. Other information sources make it a point to provide an Orthodox, Conservative and Reform voice in order to cover all the bases; occasionally they include the newer Reconstructionist Movement in the pantheon. In any case, the presumption is reinforced that denominational Judaism is the default perspective. "Postdenominational" is, of course, a loaded term, implying the obsolescence of the denominations and the transcendence of the speaker's approach. It is virtually impossible to find examples of such simple expressions as "neutral," "unbiased," "independent" or "eclectic" in reference to any aspect of contemporary Judaism.

That the four denominations encompass the range of possibilities within Judaism is a complex myth that came about as each movement established its claim to be the continuation of Old World Judaism. Many people have the impression that the Conservative, Reconstructionist and Reform movements are liberalizations of Judaism and that Orthodoxy is Judaism unchanged. In fact, as I have explained, American Judaism in all its flavors is a twentieth-century invention. The denominations resemble each other far more than any one of them represents the Judaism of the Old World. The reality is that the movements are competing versions of a new product—denominational Judaism. None of the movements was founded on any assumption that there are four different but equally valid approaches to Judaism. Rather, each one claimed to be the authentic and authoritative voice of Judaism, and each intended to become the central body of the Jewish religion in America. Rabbi Mordecai Waxman, discussing the history of his own Conservative movement, reveals the fierce competition that underlies American Judaism, as each denomination claims to be the voice of Jewish tradition in America: "The founders of Conservative Judaism . . . did not even pretend to be modern Judaism. . . .

The Conservative movement has always clung to the position that it is not a denomination in the Jewish fold. It holds that it is Judaism. It is the Jewish tradition continuing along its path in time and space with its characteristic dynamism."[7]

Each denomination was organized specifically to establish its authority on the common themes of survival, continuity and authenticity. Each of the modernist denominations, and to a large extent the Orthodox community as well, was built on the same institutional structure. Around the beginning of the twentieth century, American rabbis recast Judaism following the pattern that had already proved successful for the Protestant denominations in America. Based on the precedent set by mid-nineteenth-century German Reform Judaism, they created Jewish denominations. In many ways resembling national corporations, the Jewish denominations fulfilled the role of employment agencies and fundraisers, franchisers and property managers, printers of documents and issuers of credentials. Scholars also became organizers. Preachers also became managers.

American synagogues, the rabbis that lead them and the denominational structure itself have as much in common with their Christian counterparts in the New World as they do with the Judaism of the Old World. The Jewish denominations resemble Protestant organizations. There is a central governing body on the national level; then there are regional and local branches. The cleric is credentialed by the central body and either assigned to the local congregation or hired by it through a central placement agency. The cleric becomes the organization's local representative, a kind of congregational supervisor.

As I mentioned previously, all of the denominations were built on a three-part structure consisting of an association of congregations, a school for the training of rabbis and an association of rabbis. The Reform movement was first; its Union of American Hebrew Congregations (UAHC) was founded in 1875. Every Reform congregation is a member of the UAHC and abides by its standards; individuals can affiliate with the Reform movement only by joining a member congregation. Hebrew Union College was established in Cincinnati in 1877 to train and credential rabbis, cantors and teachers for Reform congregations. Every Reform rabbi is a member of the Central Conference of American Rabbis (CCAR), which was organized in 1889, and abides by its standards. A Reform rabbi does not have to be a graduate of Hebrew Union College in order to join the CCAR, although most are.

The Conservative movement followed the same three-part model. The Jewish Theological Seminary was founded in New York City in 1886 to train the movement's rabbis, cantors and teachers. The Rabbinical Assembly was organized in 1901. Most, if not all, Conservative rabbis are graduates of the Jewish Theological Seminary, but every Conservative rabbi belongs to the Rabbinical Assembly and follows its laws and standards. The United Synagogue of America was established in 1913 and later renamed the United Synagogue for Conservative Judaism. Individual Jews belong to the Conservative movement through its affiliated congregations.

American Orthodox Jews established a modern denomination as well. The Union of Orthodox Congregations (whose O-U symbol has become a familiar mark on food packaging) was organized in 1898 as an affiliate of the Jewish Theological Seminary.[8] A separate Orthodox rabbinical school, the Rabbi Isaac Elchanan Theological Seminary, was established as part of Yeshiva University in New York City in 1915, and the Rabbinical Council of America was formed in 1935. A different Orthodox association of congregations, the National Council of Young Israel, was formed in 1912. Young Israel has its own rabbinical training program and its own association of rabbis. There are now several different Orthodox rabbinical schools, rabbinical federations and congregational alliances in America.

The youngest of the major denominations, Reconstructionism, began as a philosophy within Conservative Judaism.[9] Its body of congregations, the Jewish Reconstructionist Federation, was organized in 1955, but at first it was served by Conservative rabbis.

Reconstructionism did not become a completely separate denomination until 1968, when both the Reconstructionist Rabbinical College and the Reconstructionist Rabbinical Council were established in Philadelphia. The membership policies for individuals and rabbis are the same as those of the Reform and Conservative movements.

Later, additional national associations were formed within the denominations. The Reform Movement set up the North American Federation of Temple Sisterhoods (now the Women of Reform Judaism), the North American Federation of Temple Brotherhoods and the North American Federation of Temple Youth (NFTY). The Conservative camp created the Women's League (now the Women's League for Conservative Judaism),[10] the Federation of Jewish Men's Clubs and United Synagogue Youth. There are also the Jewish Reconstructionist Federation Youth Programming Network and the Orthodox National Conference of Synagogue Youth. Similar federations now exist for denominational cantors, educators and synagogue administrators.

The historical records of the various movements do not acknowledge that denominational Judaism is patterned after Protestant institutions. Instead, the founders of the denominations emphasized that they were perpetuating the ancient rabbinic governing institutions, which were by their nature quite authoritarian. At one time, these rabbinic courts and academies were very powerful in Diaspora Judaism, but their influence had dissolved by the Middle Ages. The leaders of the modernist movements in America, consciously or unconsciously, sought for themselves the same authority to direct Diaspora Judaism today that the rabbinic tribunals of Judea and Babylonia once wielded.

DENOMINATIONAL AUTHORITY

Although in theory all the movements respect the autonomy of the rabbis and acknowledge the independence of the congregations, in fact denominational Judaism holds considerable influence over both the rabbinate and the laity. The various organizations within each movement are conduits for the extensive and valuable resources of the denomination. National women's clubs, men's clubs and youth clubs provide riches beyond anything a typical temple or synagogue could manage on its own: national conferences, books, videos, magazines, summer programs and speakers. The Conservative movement, for example, runs several Hebrew summer camps, while NFTY hosts a summer youth program in Israel. In addition to training educators, each denomination produces textbooks and curriculum materials for its congregations' schools.

Multiple layers of lay organization serve to increase the central body's influence over the congregations' members. As I mentioned, upon joining an affiliated congregation, every individual automatically becomes a member of the denomination. In addition, however, individual members are encouraged to join national organizations within the movement. These constituent organizations offer regional and national conferences and retreats where members learn about the movement's principles and are trained as congregational lay leaders. The national organizations provide additional channels for the denominations to communicate directly with individual members and distribute denominational publications and policy statements.

The rabbis are just as dependent as the laity on the central organizations. In fact, the Reform, Conservative and Reconstructionist denominations (and to a lesser degree some of the Orthodox bodies) wield enormous power over the rabbis through their job placement systems. Every Conservative, Reform and Reconstructionist rabbi is obligated to go through the denomination's placement system in order to obtain a position with one of the denomination's congregations. A rabbi who bypasses the placement system can be subject to disciplinary action. The standard procedure is that a congregation seeking a rabbi applies to the denomination's headquarters, and the denomination notifies qualified member rabbis of the opening. The congregation interviews rabbis who present themselves for the position, and once an agreement is reached, a contract is signed between the congregation and the rabbi; the rabbi is employed by the individual congregation directly. Congregations are free to hire rabbis from outside the denomination, but member rabbis themselves are dependent on the denomination for placement. This means a denominational rabbi must abide by the policies of the denomination or risk being out of a job. For example, the Conservative movement's Rabbinical Assembly will expel a rabbi for performing mixed marriages. Although an individual Conservative rabbi might believe that officiating at interfaith weddings is a wise policy, he or she dares not act on that belief.

In varying degrees, each of the denominations claims that its particular interpretation of Judaism is best for every Jew in America and seeks to win the allegiance of the entire community. Each denomination tries to gather even assimilated Jews into its realm and believes that it is fully capable of serving all of American Jewry. None of the denominations condones unaffiliated Jews. None would mourn the disappearance of the other branches.

Even though their differences in interpretation of God, Torah, *Halachah* (Jewish law) and Israel are well understood and agreed on, in practice each denomination claims that its ideology provides *continuity* with ancient Jewish heritage. Each movement is careful to defend its approach to Judaism as *authentic*. The traditionalist and liberal camps make the identical claim that their movement best promotes the *survival* of Judaism.

Denominational leaders often speak in triumphant terms about their particular movements. In 1976, the Reform Movement convened to celebrate its hundredth anniversary and made the rather sweeping claim that "most modern Jews, within their various movements, are embracing Reform Jewish perspectives. We see this past century as having confirmed the essential wisdom of our movement."[11] Conservative rabbi Max Routtenberg used language that is much more victorious in an address to the Rabbinical Assembly in 1960: "I am convinced that 'the future belongs to us.' We ... are part of a movement that is destined to win over the substantial mass of Jews in this country and to have a powerful effect on the religious life of those who stay outside our camp. The tide of Conservative Judaism is still running strongly and will yet increase in the next generation or two. It meets the needs of American Jews better than Reform or Orthodoxy."[12] These rabbis could not conceive of Jews leading Jewish lives independently of denominational affiliation.

The tone of the Reconstructionist leadership has tended to be far more modest and respectful than the other movements. Nonetheless, Reconstructionism may also believe in its heart that it has invented the ideal formula for American Judaism. Rabbis Rebecca Alpert and Jacob Staub, for example, talk about their "faith that enables us to continue our struggle to reconstruct Judaism. That reconstructed Judaism is the necessary condition for Jewish vitality in our time."[13]

Orthodox competitiveness is so strident that not only does the denomination refuse to recognize the *validity* of the other movements, it sometimes does not even recognize their very *existence*. Rabbi Hayim Donin, for instance, describes American Orthodoxy in denominational terms. In his book *To Be a Jew*, he outlines the familiar institutional elements of the established Jewish movements, just barely hinting that Orthodoxy may not be the only branch.[14] However, "Orthodox" is the only denomination he actually names. The words *Reform* or *Conservative* do not appear in his book, nor do the actual names of any of their respective schools or organizations.

Even though the denominations have been successful and highly effective organizations, denominational leadership sometimes downplays its own centrality. For example, according to the website of Young Israel (a federation of Orthodox congregations): "The National Council of Young Israel is a grass roots organization which takes its direction from its lay leadership" (www.young-israel.org). And on the Conservative side: "The United Synagogue is a grass-roots organization, with the base consisting of its 760 Conservative congregations" (www.uscj.org). The term "grass roots" implies the opposite of centralized or hierarchical authority. It is hard to see how this applies to the Conservative movement. No one can affiliate with the United Synagogue as an individual, and everyone who joins a Conservative congregation automatically supports the central organization through dues payments. The constituent organizations within all the movements were established by the same group of founders at the beginning of the twentieth century, and successive generations of Conservative leaders—like all denominational authorities—remain committed to exerting the influence of their movement over the Jewish community. As Herbert Rosenblum, author of *Conservative Judaism*, states: "Conservative Judaism will depend upon its ability to persuade large masses of Jews that tradition and change is a workable symbiosis, and that it is the only viable key to success in the American Jewish effort to combine authentic Jewish loyalties with honest, forward-looking modernism."[15] Persuading "large masses" is an authoritarian, rather than a grass roots, mentality. Lest there be any doubt about the movement's concept of an official, central voice, the former chancellor of the Jewish Theological Seminary, Gershon Cohen, set the record straight: "Some sociologists and theological critics have chosen to study Conservative Judaism in the mass and, accordingly, have seized upon its ideologically weakest points on which to focus. This is odd, to say the least, for one does not appraise the theology of a religious group from the confusions or unauthorized statements of individuals."[16]

The fact that Judaism in America has been based on a denominational structure for so long means that many Jews are dependent on the denominations for their connection to Jewish life. Rabbinic services, Jewish education and life-cycle ceremonies often are tied to denominational affiliation because in many communities there is no alternative. Any Jewish family that wants the services of a rabbi or a formal Jewish education for their children must join a congregation and financially support both the local synagogue and the central denomination by paying annual dues, school tuition and sometimes a building fund assessment. Typically, congregational rabbis visit only their own members in the hospital. Some congregational rabbis do not perform weddings or conduct funerals for nonmembers. Religious school classes are open only to the children of member families. Usually anyone may attend services, except for Rosh Hashanah and Yom Kippur services, which have unusually high attendance levels. In a few cases only members are admitted to these High Holy Day services, although most congregations will sell tickets to nonmembers.

THE CREATION OF THE
AMERICAN BAR MITZVAH

Through its rabbis and synagogues, denominational Judaism has established its hegemony over what has become one of the most important events in the life of American Jews—the bar mitzvah. The phenomenon of the American bar mitzvah has an interesting history and to a large extent is the creation of denominational Judaism itself. The concept originated with the age of majority under Jewish law, which used to be linked to the onset of puberty and therefore varied from person to person. Over time, a standardized age was adopted: thirteen for boys, twelve and a half for girls. Under Jewish law the term *bar mitzvah* (*bat mitzvah* for women) means a member of the class of individuals who are fully subject to the commandments of God. Every individual automatically attains the status of bar or bat mitzvah at the set age. No rabbi need officially grant it, and there are no prerequisites beyond age and basic mental competency.

Traditionally, coming of age also meant that a young man could participate in important synagogue rituals. The most valued of these was the *aliyah*—being called up to recite one of the sets of blessings during the ceremony of reading the Torah. The Torah is read during services on Monday, Thursday and Saturday mornings, Saturday afternoons and festivals. Accordingly, an occasion for celebration would arise when a young man would receive an *aliyah* on the first Torah reading after his thirteenth birthday.

Sometimes he would read from the Torah or chant a section from the Prophets, called a *haftarah*. Women did not participate in synagogue rituals, and there was no celebration to mark the age of majority for young women.

The early Reform practice did not recognize coming of age at the beginning of the teenage years. Instead, the movement created a confirmation ceremony for boys and girls at the end of high school education. The Conservative movement, however, emphasized the traditional coming-of-age as an important family event. Rabbis created elaborate ceremonies surrounding the *aliyah;* bar mitzvahs were no longer held on the first weekday service after the birthday, but instead were scheduled during the Torah service on Saturday mornings. Eventually, the Reform movement adopted the practice of the observing the bar mitzvah as a major family event. In recognition of the equality of women in Jewish life, the Reform, Conservative and Reconstructionist congregations now conduct bat mitzvah ceremonies for girls on Saturday mornings.

Acknowledging that American children could not really be adults at age thirteen, the rabbis of the modernist movements wanted to make the bar mitzvah more meaningful. They modified it into a kind of graduation ceremony to mark the conclusion of elementary Jewish education. Today, students have to go through the congregation's Hebrew school, typically attending for two hours on Sundays and for two hours one or two days a week after regular school, beginning in the third grade. Depending on the congregation, students will lead parts of the service and will deliver a speech, in addition to their *aliyah*. Bar mitzvah in America became an achievement for the student to be proud of rather than a mere fact of Jewish law. It also attained extraordinary social importance for American Jewish families, who began to celebrate it on a par with weddings.

The twentieth-century American institution of the formal synagogue bar mitzvah ceremony is the bread and butter of denominational Judaism. As much as some rabbis lament about how overblown the American bar mitzvah has become—often pointing out how simple it was in the Old World—both individual congregations and denominations depend upon the bar mitzvah to populate their membership roles and finance their operations. There is no way to know for certain how many people join synagogues or temples primarily to obtain bar mitzvah ceremonies for their children, but all rabbis, religious school principals and synagogue officers recognize a common cycle: Many families join a congregation (and therefore the denomination) when the oldest child reaches age eight and quit after the youngest child reaches age thirteen. Congregational finances usually are structured with this in mind.

The cost of membership in a Jewish congregation can be considerable. Annual membership dues for denominationally-affiliated congregations in metropolitan areas average around $1,000–2,000 per household. Building funds assessments are common; they can cost an additional $2,000 and must be completed by the time of a child's bar mitzvah. Annual religious school tuition is approximately $1,000 per child; most congregations also charge a bar mitzvah preparation fee of several hundred dollars. This means that a family might have to pay $20,000–40,000 for their children to have bar and bat mitzvahs. If American Jews actually followed the rabbis' call for a return to the traditional weekday low-key bar mitzvah, the denominations would have to find new ways to finance their operations.

THE KASHRUT INDUSTRY

In spite of their competitiveness, all of the denominations agree that Orthodoxy is the most traditional expression of Judaism. This perception has given the Orthodox rabbinate its own particular hegemony over another important area of Jewish religious life: the dietary laws, or *kashrut*. The Union of Orthodox Congregations has built a multimillion-dollar industry providing kosher certifications for packaged foods through its O-U Laboratories.

Many people are unaware that many of the products which bear the O-U symbol could never have been nonkosher in the first place. This is because the Jewish dietary laws, based on commandments in the Torah, are concerned only with the use of animals for food.[17] Certain classes of animals may not be eaten; animals must be slaughtered by prescribed methods and blood drained from the meat; meat and dairy products may not be consumed at the same meal. Kosher inspection has nothing to with modern science; for instance, a rabbi would have no way of knowing if meat were contaminated by salmonella bacteria. However, with the advent of mass-produced packaged foods, Jews who observe the dietary laws have a concern that chemical additives derived from nonkosher animal sources might be used in the manufacturing process. Even though this is highly unlikely in the case of uncomplicated products, such as whole coffee beans or bottled water, companies are willing to pay the fees for kosher inspection because the O-U label boosts sales. Observant Jews prefer the reassurance, and many people—both Jewish and gentile—are under the misconception that kosher products somehow are cleaner or safer. As a result, kosher inspection, which in the Old World was the province of the local rabbi, in twentieth-century America became a global denominational industry.

It may be true that Orthodoxy is committed to the strict observance of Jewish law, but that does not mean that modern Orthodox Judaism has not introduced numerous innovations of its own. As mentioned earlier, Orthodoxy does not allow the liberalization of traditional laws, but it does permit the creation of new laws that are more *stringent*. As a result, Orthodox rabbis have enacted hundreds of new rulings and procedures. For example, recently some Orthodox rabbis have required that the wigs worn by very observant women (who cut their hair after marriage) must be made from synthetic material rather than from the natural hair of gentiles. Other Orthodox rabbis introduced the requirement of *halav yisrael:* Jews may purchase milk only from Jewish producers. New World Orthodoxy is no more a continuation of Old World Judaism than are the other denominations. In fact, one of America's leading Orthodox rabbis, Haym Soloveitchik, lamented that "the Orthodoxy in which I and other people my age were raised scarcely exists anymore . . . [due to] the swing to the right . . . [and] the new rigor in religious observance now current among the younger community."[18]

NEW WORLD JUDAISM

Despite any remaining doctrinal differences, the denominations as a group are a manifestation of a new Jewish religion in America. American Judaism is denominational Judaism, and the differences between the movements are less significant than the differences between denominational Judaism and earlier forms of Judaism. Old World Judaism did not branch out in America in the twentieth century; it was replaced by New World—denominational—Judaism. As a matter of fact, rather than diverging over time, the denominations have tended to coalesce. Indeed, the history of the denominations over the past century is evidence that social trends determine their practices more than do the doctrines on which they were founded. In recent years, all four have shifted to the right. The three modernist movements are now so similar in their tilt toward the traditionalist side that the casual observer of a Saturday morning service would be hard pressed to tell them apart.

Although the denominations came into being with distinguishing ideologies, they shared a common desire for institutional dominance. As the dynamics of the competition have changed, the denominations have moved beyond their own foundational ideologies. The immigrant generation is gone, and few of their children are left. Because newer generations of members prefer more Hebrew and more traditional rituals during services, all the denominations have moved to accommodate them. A century ago, the movements could be distinguished by their textual sources. Orthodoxy emphasized the *Shulchan Aruch*, the Code of Jewish Law, as the basis of practice, while Conservative Judaism drew on the Talmud. Reform Judaism was inspired by the great literary prophets in the Hebrew Bible, who emphasized ethical values over ritual observance. Now the Conservative and Reform movements echo the Orthodox in proclaiming their loyalty to the Torah.

Nonetheless, the essential nature of denominationalism is constant. Large organizations do not shrink voluntarily, and powerful institutions do not deliberately dissolve themselves. The concepts and practices of denominational Judaism will continue to change over time, but its drive to survive as an institution will remain, as will the ardent rivalry that has always existed among the denominations.

INDEPENDENT JUDAISM

Americans who seek a life within Judaism that is free of denominational concerns and biases will need to find resources to replace the valuable services the denominations now offer to their members. The first of these benefits is connection to the Jewish community through a congregation. As I have discussed, many Jews form their own local communities outside of any denomination. However, by their very nature, national denominations offer a greater sense of participation in the worldwide Jewish community than any local group can provide on its own. An independent congregation can compensate by networking with similar communities, such as the National Havurah Committee, and by being active in its local Jewish community council, but by itself cannot compete with a denominational congregation in this regard.

No denomination or national federation, however, can compete with the immediacy or breadth of the Internet. There is considerable evidence that the Internet now functions as a kind of international "house of assembly" for many practicing Jews, and there is every reason to assume that online Jewish life will continue to expand. Some of the most traditional expressions of Jewish observance are finding electronic homes. For example, there is even web-based support for the tradition of *daf yomi* (daily page). The regular study of the Talmud in its original languages is a lifetime pursuit for observant Jews, and *daf yomi* refers to a personal commitment to learn one two-sided page of the Talmud in its original Hebrew and Aramaic each day, completing the entire work in about seven years. The more than twenty *daf yomi* websites reveal the extent to which electronic resources are now a part of Jewish civilization. For instance, Dafyomi.org, the most popular Internet resource for Talmud study, provides daily audio broadcasts along with on-screen discussions and interpretations. Ouradio.org offers daily Talmud study podcasts. Obviously, some of the most traditional Jews in America today are connecting to Judaism in some of the trendiest ways.

Another example of how the Internet provides connections for Jewish observance is the fact that there is now a web log (blog) for synagogue Torah readers: onchanting.blogspot.com. It is a centuries-old tradition to chant the weekly Torah portion in Hebrew during synagogue services. This is a rather specialized skill, requiring good memorization abilities. Some students manage to learn to chant a small passage for their bar mitzvah service, but few Jews can even pronounce the Hebrew words from the Torah scroll, much less chant them. Now a dozen or two websites teach people exactly how to do just that, using audio clips to supplement the on-screen instructions.[19] The Internet is rapidly expanding as a vast resource for Jewish civilization on a par with the more traditional denominational institutions.

Education is another important benefit of denominational Judaism. Since their inception, the denominations have provided most of the religious education for Jewish children in America. Of those Jews who have any Jewish training, the majority attended congregational schools (often referred to as Hebrew schools) until the age of bar mitzvah. A relatively small number of Jewish children receive more extensive educations, such as day schools, Hebrew summer camps and post-bar mitzvah programs in synagogues. An even smaller number of American Jews attend adult education classes. Unfortunately, many intermarried parents cannot use the services of their local denominational school, even if they find the idea of denominational membership appealing, because in many cases the denominations do not accept their children as Jews. Yet it is not easy for parents to find any Jewish education for their children outside of a congregation, and, as discussed, the majority of American congregations are affiliated with one of the denominations. Because most Jewish day schools in America are either Orthodox or Conservative, a lot of children from intermarried households are barred from their classrooms.

This leaves two routes to Jewish education for families who cannot—or who choose not to—use denominational schools for their children. One is to find a nondenominational equivalent of a congregational school. Some independent congregations run their own religious schools, and a handful of unaffiliated schools can be found in major metropolitan areas. These groups generally do not discriminate against intermarried families. Unfortunately, it is difficult for small communities to organize substantive educational programs for their children.

Fortunately, religious schools are not the only educational source available. A wide range of secular Jewish organizations offer worthwhile programs. For example, educational summer camps are an excellent way for parents to provide Jewish backgrounds for their children. Many Jewish community centers run day camps during the summer; their programs almost always offer Jewish content. Many Zionist organizations, such as Habonim (www.habonimdror.org), have educational summer camps with intensive and stimulating programs, both in the United States and Israel. In addition, secular groups like B'nai B'rith Youth (www.bbyo.org) have branches in most metropolitan areas. Usually geared toward teens, secular youth groups offer quality Jewish content through regional and national conferences. As a rule, these institutions do not discriminate against intermarried families or partial Jews (children of intermarriage who consider themselves both Jewish and gentile).

While denominational schools are the primary source of religious education for Jewish children, there are many more options for adult education. Most independent communities offer some kind of classes or study groups. Indeed, often they were founded for this express purpose. Every major city has a Jewish community center, which usually offers adult classes in Judaism. However, even though intermarried families and partial Jews are welcome at these centers, in many cases Judaism classes are taught by congregational rabbis who bring their denominational biases with them. Many colleges and universities also offer adult courses of interest to Jews. In addition, the National Havurah Committee convenes an institute every summer, as do other organizations.

There are many avenues of informal Jewish education as well. Adults can educate themselves, either privately or as part of a group of friends, by taking advantage of the vast array of print and online media available. And it is an easy matter for Jewish parents to harness those same resources to tutor their children. Recent advances in publishing technology make it affordable to reissue Judaica texts that have been out of print and feasible to issue new works in limited numbers. The result is that more books of Jewish interest are in print than ever before, and the large online stores effectively bring them to the attention of potential readers and make them easily available.[20] A wide variety of online resources now provide levels of access to Jewish knowledge that used to be the province of national denominations. For example, Greatjewishmusic.com has an extensive selection of files that can be played online or downloaded, and Digital.library.upenn.edu/freedman is a collection of 25,000 Jewish songs in English, Hebrew and Yiddish. There are thousands of Internet sources for every imaginable Jewish topic.

And while denominational Judaism is very uncomfortable with partial Jews and dual identities, the World Wide Web not only accepts multiple identities, it fosters them. Observant Jews participate in Internet-based affinity groups along with partial Jews and even gentiles when they share interests that do not conflict with Jewish tradition. In the online world there are no pure identities, Jewish or otherwise. This makes the Internet a nonjudgmental resource for those partial Jews who seek engagement with Judaism and who find suspicion and rejection within the established houses of denominational Judaism.

———

The third essential resource the denominations provide is rabbis. I have more to say about the modern American rabbinate, and the mystique with which it has surrounded itself, in chapter 7.

7

RABBIS, KNOWLEDGE AND SELF-RELIANCE

American rabbis are a new kind of cleric: part Talmudic scholar, part priest, part minister. As preservers of rabbinic literature, teachers of Torah and experts in matters of Jewish law, we are like the rabbis of the Old World. When we conduct ceremonies and perform rituals, we assume the role of priests. To the extent that we are denominational representatives, congregational leaders and pastors, American rabbis function like the ministers of Christian churches. Even though the particular combination of roles that delineates the denominational rabbinate is a modern invention, we rabbis see ourselves as the direct descendants of the ancient line of Judaism's leaders.

Prospective rabbinical students searching the website of Reform Judaism's Hebrew Union College (www.huc.edu) are directed to this passage from the Mishnah, the primary code of rabbinic law: "Moses received the Torah [from Sinai] and transmitted it to

Joshua, and Joshua transmitted it to the elders, and the elders transmitted it to the prophets, and the prophets transmitted it to the members of the Great Assembly" (Avot 1:1). The Mishnah uses the term *Sinai* for God's revelation of His law, and the "Great Assembly" refers to the first rabbis. The Jewish Theological Seminary's website (www.jtsa.edu) tells prospective students that "Conservative rabbis devote their lives to a sacred mission: helping to ensure the continuity of the Jewish people as a vital spiritual force." By the time we are ordained after several years of intense study, American rabbis believe that we are the living repositories of religious teachings as old as the earliest ancestors of the Jewish people and that the preservation of Judaism rests on our shoulders.

This belief may contain some threads of truth, but many people do not realize that the institution of the America rabbinate is little more than a hundred years old and that much of it is based on Christian practice rather than Jewish tradition. Even some rabbis are not aware that classic rabbinic Judaism was based as much on Hellenism as on the Torah.

THE HISTORY OF THE RABBINATE

The rabbinate is a 2,500-year-old calling whose history represents the triumph of intellect over lineage. The rabbis of old spoke of three "crowns," but before rabbis entered into Jewish history there were only two.[1] The crown of priesthood was conferred by bloodline—only a direct descendant of the house of Aaron within the tribe of Levi could wear the priestly miter and perform the sacrificial rituals of Israel's religion. The crown of government passed by bloodline as well—Israel's throne belonged to the Davidic dynasty alone. According to the Bible, it was God who appointed Aaron and his line to be Israel's priests, and it was God who anointed David and his line to be the lawful kings. But there were no rabbis in the days of the Old Testament. Their role in Judaism did not begin until after the destruction of the First Temple in Jerusalem, after the Babylonian exile, after the last books of the Jewish Bible were set down. Over the next five hundred years a new crown was forged in Judea, the crown of Torah. With the destruction of the Second Temple in Jerusalem, the crowns of priesthood and government passed into oblivion, but the crown of Torah belonged to the rabbis.

By the time the first compilation of rabbinic teachings, the Mishnah, was completed in the year 200 CE, the rabbis had written themselves into biblical history: Moses received Torah at Sinai and bequeathed it to Joshua, Joshua to the elders, the elders to the prophets and the prophets to the first rabbis. So their crown had come from God as well, and henceforth they would be the government of the Jewish people. How did this class rise to power in Judea two millennia ago, and how has their leadership of Judaism survived into the third millennium?

In the sixth century before the common era, the Babylonian emperor Nebuchadnezzar learned to consolidate his power over the countries he conquered by transplanting the indigenous populations. Over the course of a generation, the people he ruled lost contact with their cultures of origin and became citizens of the empire. When Jerusalem fell to Nebuchadnezzar's armies in 586 BCE, Judea's middle and upper classes were exiled to a region in the middle of Babylonia. Somehow they held on to enough of their language and laws to invent a new form of Judaism that did not depend on the altar or the throne in Jerusalem. When the Persian emperor Cyrus assumed control of Babylonia fifty years later, many of the exiled Jews returned home. At the same time Jewish communities in Babylonia flourished. By the time a new Temple was built in Jerusalem, in 515 BCE, Judaism—both in homeland and in exile—had changed dramatically.

The reading of the scroll of the Torah became a permanent part of the Temple service around the 400s BCE. And even though there would continue to be only one holy altar, that in Jerusalem, the Torah could be copied. This fact meant that Jerusalem would no longer be the sole repository of Judaism's sacred artifacts. It also meant that the priesthood had a rival profession to contend with, a profession based on neither lineage nor sword, but on knowledge: the scribes. It was the *sofrim*, the scribes, who copied the scrolls of the Torah, and it was the scribes who read the Torah to the people. The scribes in effect possessed the sacred books of the Jewish religion, in particular the Book of Leviticus and other sections of the Torah that contain the codes of practice for the priestly rites. This gave them power on a par with the priesthood.

However, the scribes' technical skills—which could be acquired by any competent man regardless of social class—were not their only source of power. By the time of the Second Temple, much of the material in the Torah was obscure, so the scribes orally explicated the words they read. They also claimed to possess knowledge of the spirit of the Torah as well as its letters, and based on this understanding, the scribes eventually evolved into an ideological movement, the Pharisees. The Pharisees formulated the doctrine of the oral Torah: Along with the written Torah, God gave Moses an even more extensive body of law that was not written down but was preserved by the scribes.

The Pharisaic doctrine of the Oral Torah succeeded because the scribes' descendants had acquired a new skill. The technology of writing had given the scribes power, and the position of the Torah as the constitution of Judea increased their influence, but a very different kind of knowledge transformed them into sages. During the second century before the common era, Judea was conquered by Syria and thereby became part of the Hellenistic empire. Hellenism, the civilization of Greece, exerted a powerful influence on the Judeans. The Jewish scribes in particular were impressed by the Greek academies, their veneration for written texts and especially their hermeneutics, the principles of logical inference Greek scholars used to interpret classical literature. Jewish scholars adopted these formulations of logic and applied them to the Hebrew Scriptures. They used them to demonstrate how the Oral Torah is hidden within the written Torah, and they used them to derive new laws from old laws. Over time the scribes became rabbis—sages of Judaism and masters of Jewish law. In fact, the word *rabbi* means "master," and Judaism's religious leaders are known by this name today. The *shalosh esrei midot*, thirteen principles of textual interpretation, are codified in the Mishnah as the framework for all rabbinic discourse. To a large extent the rabbinate derived not from the Hebrew Bible or from old Judean customs, but from gentile influence, the Hellenism imposed by a conquering empire.

A competing political party, the Sadducees, represented the royal and the priestly classes. The Sadducees denied the validity of the Oral Law and challenged the authority of the Pharisees. At times the two factions clashed in violent civil war. Their rivalry was a source of vexation to the Roman Empire as it conquered the Hellenistic empire and relentlessly established dominion over Judea. The Babylonian destruction of the First Temple set off a chain of events that produced rabbinic Judaism, but it was the Roman destruction of the Second Temple that eventually established rabbinic Judaism as the normative religion of the Jewish people.

There is no way to determine how much of what we know about Rabbi Yochanan ben Zakkai is legend, but the fascinating story of his life contains the blueprint of how a network of scholars preserved Jewish civilization. Determined to crush the Jewish state once and for all, the Roman army laid siege to Jerusalem in the year 70 CE. Inside the city walls another political party, the Zealots, had taken control, guarding the city gates and vowing death before submission to Rome. After word went out that the renowned Rabbi Yochanan had died, his students carried his coffin past the Zealots, ostensibly to the burial ground outside the sacred precinct of Jerusalem. The students, however, did not carry the coffin to the cemetery; instead, they brought it before the Roman general Vespasian, who was camped outside the city. Rabbi Yochanan, who was not really dead, emerged from the coffin, knelt before the general and begged permission to set up a modest school with his students in a village on the Mediterranean coast. According to the story, Vespasian granted his request, for he failed to appreciate the fact that the civilization of Judea was contained within the minds of these humble scholars—they had committed it to memory. In the academy at Yavneh, Rabbi Yochanan and his students set about reconstructing Judaism. Rabbi Yochanan elected to survive, and because he survived Judaism survived. The throne of Judea was crushed, the Temple in Jerusalem destroyed, but the law and literature of Judaism passed through the wall that separated the old Jewish state from the Diaspora, carried inside a human being inside a wooden box and resuscitated in an academy in the hills of Judea.

The story of Rabbi Yochanan and his school encapsulates how the rabbis transformed Judaism from a monarchy and a religion of priests, to a religion of the mind and the People of the Book. There were many other academies, of course. The great rabbinic centers at Sura and Pumbeditha in Babylonia probably developed from the gatherings of Jews during the Babylonian exile. Houses of assembly, where the Torah was read and the Oral Law discussed, had existed in Judea and surrounding territories for some time. They were the prototype for the other great institution of post–Second Temple Judaism: the synagogue.

It is reasonable to assume that ancient Israel preserved oral traditions predating the Torah, and Bible scholars have found evidence of oral law within the Torah itself. The rabbinic doctrine goes far beyond that, however, for it asserts that the entire body of its literature was revealed at Sinai—explicitly and implicitly. Not only had Moses received truths from God in addition to the 613 Commandments of the Torah, which he told to Joshua and which finally reached the ears of the rabbis, but new and equally authoritative truths could be derived from the Hebrew Scripture by logical inference.

In the year 200 CE, Rabbi Judah the Patriarch produced a written compilation of rabbinic law, the Mishnah. The Mishnah records the three foundations of rabbinic Judaism: that an Oral Torah was transmitted from God to the rabbis, that the written Torah could be expanded by thirteen principles of textual interpretation and that knowledge of the Torah conferred authority on a par with the monarchy and the priesthood. Rabbinic law also ensured that the Judaism's previous sources of authority would not return to power. The rabbis declared that prophecy had ended with the last visionaries of the Hebrew Bible and the destruction of the First Temple in 586 BCE.[2] Specific ritual requirements would prevent the Temple from ever being rebuilt, and without the Temple, there was no role for the priests. Since the line of David was gone, there could be no king over Israel unless God Himself miraculously restored the throne. There were no longer three crowns—there was just one, and the rabbis wore it. Subsequent generations of scholars in academies in Judea and Babylonia elaborated on the Mishnah to produce the Talmud. The Babylonian Talmud was completed around the year 500 CE (see the Appendix), and the Midrash was redacted in the same century, finally committing to paper a thousand years of scholastic tradition that began with the scribes of the Torah.

As the Roman empire declined, so did the Jewish communities in Judea. The rabbinic academies eventually faded away as well, while new Jewish communities spread throughout Arabia and Asia Minor, along the Mediterranean and into Europe. Synagogues became centers for Jewish life in exile. The role of the rabbi also changed. He still wore the crown of the Torah as an authority for Jewish law and its judge among the people, but he was no longer the academic master discoursing with his fellow scholars and training new generations of rabbis. The Diaspora rabbi was the local teacher and authority on matters of Jewish law, independent from rabbinic colleagues just as the Diaspora communities became increasingly isolated—and increasingly independent.

As the Jews dispersed over a wider and wider area, the influence of the rabbis as a professional group declined. However, rabbis as individuals continued to hold real power in the various communities over which they had authority. Under monarchies and later under the feudal system, Jewish communities enjoyed a certain degree of autonomy. Typically the Jews were not a regular part of the feudal system; sometimes they were not subject to the rule of the local lord, but would be the "king's Jews" instead. They did not necessarily fall under church law either, but often governed themselves. The local Jewish communities administered daily commerce and managed their own institutions. The rabbis decided all matters of Jewish law; they controlled who could be married, who could be divorced, who could be buried in the cemetery and so forth. In many countries rabbis had the power to enforce Jewish law; they could punish criminals with fines or flogging, as prescribed by Judaism. Although the imposition of capital punishment, also part of Jewish law, was the province of the ruling powers, the rabbis could excommunicate recalcitrant individuals and expel them from the community. Because a Jew separated from the protection of the community was an easy target, excommunication could be tantamount to a death sentence. In different countries at different times, secular Jewish councils governed the members of their communities. But ordained rabbis had the final say about the application of Jewish law.

Some rabbis were spiritual leaders as well. Charismatic preachers and teachers held sway over the hearts and minds of Jews. Under the industrialized states of modern Europe, occasionally *landes-rabbiner*, state-appointed rabbis, derived income from taxes and enjoyed limited institutional authority under state law.

THE DEVELOPMENT OF THE AMERICAN RABBINATE

Of course, when the mass migration of Europe's Jews to the United States occurred in the early 1900s, Europe's rabbis migrated too. The passage to America completely changed the essential nature of the rabbinate. As soon as the rabbis boarded the boats to safety and freedom, they left behind the power and authority they had held for so long. In America, Jews would no longer be governed by the religious laws of the ghetto and the shtetl. In America, Jews would be full participants in the legal system of the cities and states. Rabbis were empowered by the states to legalize marriages, but no rabbi could dissolve a marriage; no rabbi could impose a fine or order a flogging to enforce Jewish law. No state appointed an official rabbi to preside over Jewish matters.

For this reason, when the Jewish religious leaders arrived in America, they had to reestablish their authority on different terms. Realizing that they could play a critical role in helping the transplanted Jews of Eastern Europe find new ways to live as Jews in a very different society, they undertook the task of re-creating themselves as the governing body of a new American Judaism. And they did it within a matter of a few years.

The founders of denominational Judaism never fully acknowledged that they were forming a new Jewish religion. As I mentioned before, Solomon Schechter and the other early leaders of the Conservative movement emphasized that they were preserving Jewish tradition in America. Nonetheless, denominational Judaism is not making a new claim when it insists that the American rabbinate it created is actually an ancestral institution. It is simply renewing the doctrine that the authority of the rabbis originated in the Torah. Whether that assertion is true or not, American rabbis did fulfill their age-old commitment to transmit Jewish tradition into new lands and new times. True to their principles, the first thing they did was build schools, rival centers of rabbinic learning that were the cores of competing denominations. The rabbinical schools would ensure that the chain of Jewish knowledge, having crossed the ocean, would be passed to future generations of rabbis and teachers. The denominational schools would assume the sacred responsibility for transmitting the Torah from rabbi to rabbi, but the rabbis themselves would have a different responsibility. They would convey not the techniques of interpreting Jewish law but the love of Judaism itself; their workplace would be the congregation, not the academy; their students would not be aspiring rabbis but the entire American Jewish community. American rabbis would be popular Hasidic masters rather than ivory-tower Talmudists, showing the people the joy of living a Jewish life.

Denominational Judaism's founders believed that unless Judaism adapted to America, it would disappear. Just as Rabbi

Yochanan ben Zakkai's generation modified Judaism so that it could live without a Temple or a king, and just as the rabbis of the diaspora reshaped Judaism so that it could live without a homeland, American rabbis reinvented Judaism so that it could live in the freedom of the New World. In so doing, they reinvented themselves.

CHRISTIAN PARALLELS

In the centuries following the destruction of the second Temple, Judaism and Christianity developed side by side, each community finding its own way to adapt the defunct sacrificial system of biblical religion. Christians re-created the Temple and reinstituted the sacrifices in their own churches. They created their own priests as well and invested them with divine power. Jews essentially did the same thing but with three exceptions. Jews brought into the synagogues representations of the Temple's Holy Ark (which according to tradition contained the tablets of the Ten Commandments), its raised platform (bimah) and its seven-branched candelabrum (menorah), transforming the house of study into the house of worship. The fire that burned perpetually on the Temple altar was also brought into the synagogue, but not the altar itself and not the water basin. Nor did Jews create a new priesthood. Instead, many of the former functions of the priesthood became ordinary home rituals: the washing of hands before meals, the sanctification of wine (kiddush) on the Sabbath and holy days, and the rituals of the Passover Seder. The *kohanim*, descendants of the priestly family, retained a few minor ritual functions, but the Jewish priesthood essentially had come to an end. The rabbis were teachers and judges, but they were not priests.

The rabbis were Judea's surviving institution of power. Their rivals—the priests, the kings, the prophets—were the centers of power in biblical Judaism, appointed, anointed or called by God. Rabbinic Judaism was a new religion, founded on the Hellenistic principles of logic and academic discourse. When the second Jewish State was destroyed, the rabbis became both the monarchy and the prophecy of Israel, judging the people and revealing God's teachings. In America, the rabbis became the priesthood as well.

Borrowing from Christian practice, nineteenth-century German Reform Judaism invented the formal worship service conducted by the rabbi. Rabbis in America continued the practice by establishing themselves as the celebrants of Judaism. They donned ecclesiastical vestments and stood before the people assembled for worship in the temples and synagogues. Rabbis and cantors began to wear academic robes like those of Protestant ministers. Jewish religious supply houses designed the "form-fitting" tallit in imitation of the stoles worn by Christian clerics.

Today every Jewish denomination assumes that each of its member congregations is led by one of the denomination's rabbis, and conversely, Americans assume that every rabbi has a congregation. Thus denominational congregations are "rabbi-centric." This is a radical departure from Old World Jewish practice where the rabbi was not necessarily associated with a congregation, and not every synagogue had a rabbi. The functions of the synagogue and the duties of the rabbi were independent of each other; communities had their rabbis, and communities had their synagogues.

Traditional Jewish synagogue practice is very different from church practice, and shows the extent to which the modern American rabbinate is based on Christian customs. Prior to the modern era, rabbis did not lead services, and they do not do so in Orthodox congregations in America today. Instead, a member of the congregation who knows the prayers leads the service while the others chant along with him. This prayer leader stands facing the east (in honor of Jerusalem as the historical center of Judaism), as does everyone else. In Jewish law people can pray anywhere; a synagogue is not required. Synagogues are oriented approximately toward Jerusalem, and a podium for the leader faces the front. This means that typically the leader has his back to the congregation. In some synagogues, the podium is placed in the center of the room, or occasionally at the back, to show that the person leading the prayers is acting from the midst of the congregation.[3] In a traditional service no pages are announced, and worshippers do not necessarily pray in unison. People are free to read through the set liturgy at their own pace, as long as they join in the responses to the leader. In fact, in traditional settings, people might use different editions of the prayer books—all with the same prayers in the same order, but not necessarily with the same arrangement of pages. People know how to follow along because the order of the service is standard.

Continuing the policies of European Reform Judaism, one of the first changes introduced by the Reform and Conservative denominations in America was to turn the podium to face the people. While this innovation meant that the person leading the services would no longer have his back to the congregation, it made the rabbi far more prominent. Further copying Christian practice, the modernist movements had everyone recite the prayers in unison, with the rabbi announcing the pages and telling the people when to stand and when to sit. The denominations composed English prayers for the rabbi to read responsively with the congregation.

In the modernist movements, many of the priestly functions—for example, performing the daily worship services—shifted from ordinary Jews in ordinary homes to the rabbi and the synagogue. American rabbis assumed the duties of burying the dead by creating formal funeral rites over which they presided. Very few Jews in America today can imagine burying their dead without the services of a Jewish cleric. As the professional practitioners of Judaism, rabbis took over the role of praying for the sick. They also invented new ceremonies to preside over: the unveiling of tombstones, the naming of babies, the conferring of bar mitzvah. If anything needed to be blessed or dedicated or memorialized, the rabbi would do it.

Christian clergy are primarily preachers, pastors and priests. The theological interpretation of their functions, as well as the emphasis, varies from denomination to denomination, but ministers and priests have three basic jobs: They bring the Word of God to the congregation and inspire them spiritually, they counsel their members and tend to their personal well-being and they perform official church ceremonies. Compared to a traditional rabbi, the typical Christian cleric is neither learned sage nor judge in matters of religious law.

American rabbis adopted not just the priestly role, but all three functions of their Christian counterparts. In the Old World, not all rabbis were preachers, and many of those who were reserved their words for their personal students. Once installed as the leaders of American congregations, however, denominational rabbis became preachers and teachers of the entire laity. They had to expound the Torah to every member, both to those who were knowledgeable and those who were not. In addition to new priestly functions and expanded preaching functions, the American rabbinate willingly accepted the other important job of the American Christian cleric. Rabbis became pastors to a far greater extent than they had ever been before, counseling troubled individuals, attending to families in crisis and visiting members in the hospital.

A rabbi reading from a small black book during a wedding or funeral or hospital visit is a familiar sight, but very few people have actually seen one of the volumes up close. They are not prayer books in the traditional sense. They go back to the middle of the twentieth century when the Reform, Conservative and Orthodox rabbinical organizations separately produced professional manuals for their members. These guidebooks instruct the rabbi how to preside at life-cycle ceremonies. No such practical handbooks for rabbis existed before the middle of the twentieth century in America because there was no need for them. Interestingly, the three manuals are nearly identical in size, color and shape; all three were designed to assist American rabbis in their new role as master-of-religious-ceremonies. They are emblematic of the fact that Orthodox, Conservative and Reform rabbis—despite their distinct doctrinal differences—essentially resemble each other in their function as ministers of Jewish religion.

One important aspect of the modern American rabbinate distinguishes us not only from the classic rabbinic period, but even from early Reform Judaism: the ordination of women. Even though the Reform and Conservative movements phased in the equal participation in services of women laity during the first half of the twentieth century, it took longer for women to be accepted as rabbis. The Reconstructionist rabbinical school was established with full gender inclusion in 1970 and graduated its first woman rabbi in 1977; the Reform denomination ordained the first woman rabbi in 1972; and the Conservative movement's seminary began ordaining women in the 1980s. To this day, Orthodox rabbinical schools do not admit women.

RABBINIC POWER

Consistent with our traditional role as judges, American rabbis preserved two outdated legal functions from ancient Judea: the marriage contract (*ketubah*) and the religious divorce (*get*). At one time these were lawful functions for rabbis, but they have little if any standing today because the state is sovereign in matters of marriage and divorce. Although the *ketubah* is merely symbolic, Orthodox and Conservative rabbis still require the old Aramaic document and preside over its signing. Other rabbis permit modernized wording for marriage certificates and conduct brief ceremonies when they are signed. What was once primarily a legal proceeding is now purely a religious ceremony performed by the rabbi. I will say more about both the *ketubah* and the *get* later.

Over the years, the increasing prominence of the rabbi in American Jewish religious practice has varied. In general, during the first half of the twentieth century, the Reform movement instituted formalized, rabbi-led worship at all its services, while the Conservatives tended to hold both rabbi-led and lay-led services. Orthodox Jews continued to pray according to traditional practice of lay-led services, although like their progressive colleagues, some Orthodox rabbis began to preside at life-cycle ceremonies. In the second half of the twentieth century, the modernist movements became enchanted with Old World Judaism. Some Conservative congregations moved away from the formal rabbi-led services, even going so far as to drop the very American-style late Friday evening services. While Reform congregations have introduced more and more traditional elements into their services, ironically it is the Reform rabbinate that has pressed for the changes and as a result remains prominent in the ritual life of the movement. Because Reconstructionist Judaism did not become a fully independent denomination until the 1970s,[4] its rabbinate has not had as long a history as the other movements. Many rabbis stopped wearing the clerical robe and the narrow tallit in the last half of the twentieth century, when there was a renewed interest in Jewish ethnicity and people realized how "goyish" that attire looked. However, many rabbis still like to wear a tallit when officiating, even in settings where other Jews are not wearing them. Although there is nothing in Jewish tradition about any kind of vestments for rabbis, many of us prefer to wear some kind of distinctive garb when we conduct ceremonies.[5] The Christian influence persists, and regardless of theological persuasion, rabbis are still seen as the official practitioners of American Judaism.

It is fair to say many American rabbis today are quite concerned about the historical authenticity of our profession. In fact, many rabbis would much prefer to be teachers of Torah rather than religious functionaries or enforcers of denominational policies, and have attempted to revive the ancient rabbinic academy in the form of regular study groups. Rabbis frequently commiserate with each other about how much time they spend driving from hospital to hospital and how little time they have left for course preparation or for personal study. Nonetheless, the priestly and pastoral roles of the modern rabbi are very valuable to the Jewish community and appreciated by its members. The average American rabbi performs these duties with such devotion and skill that it is easy to imagine that rabbis have been leading congregations and caring for congregants forever.

Most people are unaware how few of the functions of American rabbis are derived from Judaism and how much are borrowed from the precedent of Christian practice. Prior to the establishment of the modernist movements, congregational practice was governed by Jewish law, the *Halachah*. A review of traditional Jewish law concerning life cycle events might be enlightening.

Jewish parents bestow names on their newborn children and bless them. A boy's name may be recorded on the circumcision certificate issued by the mohel who performs the ritual, and a girl's name may be announced in synagogue, but no rabbi is needed to make it official.

As I mentioned earlier, at age twelve and a half every Jewish girl automatically ceases to be a minor under Jewish law and becomes a bat mitzvah. Boys attain their majority at age thirteen; they are bar mitzvah whether they have attended classes or not. No synagogue is obligated to grant them special honors, but any Jewish male who knows the blessings may participate in the Torah-reading rituals. If he is unable to recite the blessings, he may have other honors, such as rolling the Torah scroll.

According to Jewish law, if a Jewish man presents a ring to a Jewish woman in front of witnesses while reciting the nine words of the Hebrew marriage vow, and she accepts the ring, they are bound together in holy matrimony. It does not matter if a rabbi is present.

Two valid witnesses are all that are needed to sign a traditional Jewish marriage certificate, a *ketubah*. Neither bride, nor groom nor any rabbi signs it.

Any Jew may recite the prayers at a burial service. Grave markers are placed at the direction of the family; no rabbi is needed to dedicate them.

According to Jewish law, any observant male Jew who knows how may write a Torah scroll or the parchments that go into a mezzuzah or tefillin. Jewish women may consecrate the bread that is eaten at Sabbath and Holy Day meals.

Even though most of the rituals may be performed by ordinary worshippers, there are two areas of Jewish practice that require specialized training and rabbinic authorization: Brit Milah, the ritual circumcision of infants, and *shechitah*, the kosher slaughtering of animals. While many practitioners of ritual circumcision, mohalim, are rabbis, rabbinic ordination is not a requirement of Jewish law. The same is true for ritual slaughterers, *shochatim*. However both mohalim and *shochatim* must be certified by rabbinic authority. Only a rabbi may carry out two Jewish ritual procedures: conversion and religious divorce. Conversion to Judaism requires a rabbinic tribunal, and religious divorces are issued only by those rabbis who are expert in the details of this area of Jewish law.

Even though rabbis are not needed to conduct most ceremonies under Jewish law, our presence during such occasions often brings a depth of Jewish knowledge that few laypeople can match. It is customary for rabbis to use rituals as teaching opportunities by discussing the historical background of the ritual and offering an explanation of its significance. Most rabbis cite passages from classical Jewish literature when speaking at religious events and also discuss the contemporary relevance of ancient texts. By virtue of our extensive specialized education, rabbis draw on a wealth of Jewish knowledge and in this way are able to endow a religious ceremony with considerable meaning.

Unfortunately, not all Jews can take advantage of the connection to Judaism that rabbis bring to ritual events. Some are unable or unwilling to comply with the rabbi's requirements; others may be reluctant to accept the level of control rabbis often assume when presiding over events. In some communities, unaffiliated Jews have no access to the services of a rabbi. And of course many rabbis will not conduct ceremonies for partial Jews or intermarried families.

Fortunately, with some research and preparation, laypeople can move forward from American Judaism's dependence on rabbis and organize their own life-cycle ceremonies. Various popular books on Jewish practice describe the history and meaning of the ceremonies and present the exact step-by-step procedures to perform them.[6] Obviously the services of a trained professional would be needed for a circumcision, but a baby-naming in the home can be celebrated in numerous ways. Parents are free to devise their own ceremonies, whether simple or elaborate. Of course, it would be very difficult for a family to replicate a synagogue Torah service for a bar or bat mitzvah.

Wedding ceremonies are a different case entirely because marriage is a legal status conferred by the state, and each jurisdiction has its own regulations. It is illegal in every state to perform a wedding ceremony unless the couple has a license and the celebrant is authorized by the jurisdiction. Heterosexual couples who want a Jewish ceremony without a rabbi have a few options. (Same-gender couples do not enjoy equal benefits.) They can be married legally in the local courthouse during the week and then—assuming local laws permit it—observe whatever religious ceremony they want, with a friend or relative presiding. In some jurisdictions it is possible to arrange for a judge or other civil authority to preside over a civil ceremony in a home or other venue. The official co-celebrates with a family friend or relative who provides the Jewish content; or the official first performs a legal ceremony in private, and the friend or relative then celebrates a Jewish ceremony in front of all the guests. Some states also have a procedure whereby a friend or relative can obtain a one-time authorization to perform a wedding.

Funerals are an easier matter. Funeral directors and cemetery personnel will help the family arrange a lay-led service and then will stand by to guide the officiant through the procedure. Many of these professionals are knowledgeable about Jewish practices and routinely provide step-by-step assistance even when services are conducted by clergy.

The average layperson may not have the learned background a rabbi has, but with a little research anyone can prepare a brief address with some Jewish content. Today some rabbis actually encourage laypeople to conduct their own ceremonies and will provide instruction. Since all rabbis take it upon themselves to be sources of Jewish knowledge, a rabbi who for whatever reason declines to preside at a ceremony may nonetheless be willing to offer guidance.

Through our learning, today's American rabbis are heirs to authority dating back to the beginning of their profession. But our prominence as the practitioners of Judaism is entirely a twentieth-century phenomenon. Nonetheless, few rabbis are willing to give up whatever power we currently derive from our position as presiders over American Judaism. Of course, all rabbis will refuse to conduct a ceremony under circumstances that violate professional or personal principles. When some of us exercise our prerogatives to approve or disapprove of people's behavior, we are wielding power, whether we acknowledge doing it or not.

While no rabbi should be forced to do something that goes against his or her conscience, one who denies services based on the pretext of Jewish tradition is using the mystique of antiquity to defend precedents set by modern American gentile practices. Unfortunately, rabbis do just that on a regular basis. Some rabbis are quite subjective in deciding which rituals deserve their official presence. It is not at all uncommon for a rabbi to conduct the equivalent of a Jewish wedding ceremony for a same-gender couple when both partners are Jews, even though the Torah explicitly forbids homosexuality, but refuse to bless a Jewish–gentile couple.[7] The reason, of course, is that the more progressive leaders of American Judaism are supportive of gay and lesbian relationships, but all the denominations strongly disapprove of intermarriage.

Even though the modern American rabbinate does not function in a time or place where daily life is governed by Jewish law, many rabbis find ways to enforce their authority. For example, some Conservative and Orthodox rabbis hold the wedding as ransom for the *ketubah* and the *get*. A Jewish wedding is legally binding in America because the state authorizes members of the clergy to perform the ceremonies, but ancient Aramaic prenuptial agreements and divorce documents are not. The requirements of a Jewish religious divorce are arcane and have no legal standing in any jurisdiction in America. The couple is always civilly divorced anyway, so the idea of a Jewish divorce has no real legal standing. They only thing it affects is the right of the couple to be remarried by an Orthodox or Conservative rabbi. So some rabbis enforce the *get* by threatening to deny a marriage ceremony if the parties do not submit to the process, a procedure only rabbis can carry out. Many centuries ago the *ketubah* was a prenuptial agreement (written in Aramaic), which served a practical purpose: It provided a legally mandated minimum amount of financial security for the woman in case of divorce or widowhood. Conservative and Orthodox rabbis insist on carrying out all the original requirements of the *ketubah*, making sure that only valid witnesses sign (in Hebrew) the groom's pledge of money in ancient Judean coinage. The procedure, like the Jewish divorce, has no legal standing because the monetary provisions of the *ketubah* are never actually carried out. But for some rabbis, if there is no *ketubah*, there will be no marriage.

The detailed procedures of the *ketubah* and the *get* established in ancient Judea were a civil process with no theological or spiritual component. Carrying out those same procedures in America today does not fulfill the original intent of the Jewish prenuptial contract or the Jewish divorce. The most it can do is to honor the concept of the Jews as a nation; it can never be anything more than a pro forma reenactment. Nonetheless, the

Conservative and Orthodox branches of American Judaism expect their rabbis to carry out all the legal requirements of both ceremonies.

Orthodox and Conservative rabbis maintain their expertise in these areas almost to the point of secrecy. Although many textbooks describe the customs and the words that make up the Jewish wedding ceremony, full English translations of the traditional Aramaic *ketubah* are hard to find. Printed certificates (including the Conservative movement's official document) that contain both Hebrew and English columns use replacement language for the English rather than a literal translation. It is the rare groom or bride who has any idea what he or she is agreeing to in the religious document. The full Aramaic text of the *get* is also hard to find; it is virtually impossible to find an English translation. The only sources for these would be rabbi's manuals, which are not readily available to the general public.

BEYOND RABBINIC POWER

The time has come for American rabbis to move forward from our roles as authority figures. Rabbis who show their disapproval of intermarriage by withholding their services only create resentment and alienation in the face of the most challenging significant social phenomenon affecting the Jewish community at this time. Rabbis who refuse to perform mixed marriages may believe they are acting out of respect for Jewish law, but there is nothing in Jewish law that absolutely prevents rabbis from presiding over such ceremonies. Religious law may not recognize the relationship as sanctified within Judaism, but it is no sin for a man and woman to stand under a huppah while a rabbi chants a blessing and then signs a state marriage license. To be fully compliant with Jewish law, the rabbi will need to replace the three Hebrew words of the groom's vow to the bride that state that the contract is "according to the law of Moses and Israel," a modification rabbis routinely make when the bride gives a ring to the groom (or when there are two grooms or two brides). Orthodox rabbis are not likely to perform such ceremonies, and the Conservative movement's Rabbinical Assembly bars its members from performing mixed marriages. Reconstructionist and Reform rabbis are under no such ban, but relatively few preside at interfaith weddings. Rabbinic refusal to be part of Jewish–gentile weddings is arbitrary. Although rabbis who reject requests for mixed weddings may be acting out of deeply held beliefs, we preside over other ceremonies that are distasteful to us. What rabbi has refused to chant the Prayer for the Dead at the grave of a sinner? What rabbi has refused to pray at the hospital bedside of an adulterer or an embezzler? What rabbi has denied a bar or bat mitzvah to a student who learned to chant the Torah portion by memorizing it from a recording rather than faithfully learning the actual words and chant notations? Considering how much is at stake, and how much pain it causes, rabbis who deny their professional services to a Jew who falls in love with a gentile might want to reconsider their policies.

It is in the nature of institutionalized religion—and especially a religion that identifies itself as ancient—to anoint its representatives with the mystique of the ages. What harm, after all, is done when American rabbis put on the crown of the Torah and thereby lend an ancestral aura to our teachings? Why shouldn't the Hebrew Union College or the Jewish Theological Seminary tell the public that rabbinic tradition is as old as the Torah? The harm is that when rabbis—whether by intention or by instinct—make inaccurate claims about the historical facts of Jewish civilization, we undermine our own position in the community. For better or worse, the Jewish community has entrusted its rabbis to both acquire and convey the corpus of Jewish knowledge. Rabbis who present only certain facts of Judaism while allowing others to remain hidden, or who distort Jewish history, fail in their responsibility to the Jewish community. Ultimately they weaken our membership's connection to Judaism by placing a filter between the laity and their heritage.

In the new American Judaism, the rabbinate is a profession based on knowledge rather than authority, and our leadership should be determined by how much we know about Judaism, not by how much power we wield. In the twenty-first century, the knowledge gap between the rabbinate and the laity is narrowing. A hundred years ago, the rabbi was likely to be the only member of the congregation with a graduate education; obviously that is no longer case. Today anyone with a keyboard and an Internet connection has more extensive access to Jewish information than any seminary professor could provide. To the extent that rabbinic authority is based on inaccurate assumptions about biblical origins, that authority is at risk. The American Jewish community is highly educated and very well informed. The third millennium is an age of easy access to specialized knowledge of all sorts. Sooner or later, myths will be revealed as such. The American rabbinate's belief that our professional roots go back to the time of the Torah is no more factual at the beginning of the third millennium than it was when Rabbi Judah the Patriarch encoded the doctrine at the beginning of the first millennium.

The American rabbinate has succeeded in constructing a New World Judaism that is just as rich and vital as that in any other era of Jewish civilization. American rabbis are highly trained and possess a great deal of specialized information about Jewish tradition. We teach, counsel, provide pastoral care; we become part of our members' lives in unique ways that help individuals and families thrive. Our ability to serve new generations of American Jews requires us to give up our claims to ancient authority and to accept the fact that our professional role is a modern American creation.

The rabbinate has been at the center of one of the American Jewish community's greatest challenges: intermarriage. As I discuss in chapter 8, our continuing confusion and apprehension about this critical issue are part of the problem.

8

COMMUNITY, INTERMARRIAGE AND OPTIMISM

Virtually every Jew in America today—and probably most gentiles as well—knows that Jews are not supposed to marry non-Jews. Some rabbis teach that intermarriage is a modern aberration, the result of assimilation; other leaders depict it as a sign of disloyalty to Judaism. Official disapproval of intermarriage is so unyielding that no Orthodox or Conservative rabbi and relatively few Reform or Reconstructionist rabbis will preside at a mixed wedding ceremony.

The Jewish community has come to believe that intermarriage violates ancient Jewish tradition, that it weakens Judaism today and that it threatens the future of the Jewish people. None of these beliefs has any basis either in present-day fact or in Jewish history, yet none is questioned. Instead, American Jewish leaders view the current high rate of Jewish–gentile marriage in America as a kind of systemic disorder—and a potentially fatal one at that.

A column in the *Baltimore Jewish Times* exemplifies American Judaism's belief that Jews who intermarry betray their people and contribute toward its demise. Its author, a correspondent for the *Jerusalem Post*, exclaims that American Jewry is "disappearing before our eyes" through intermarriage because non-Jewish partners have "no reason to be concerned with the perpetuation of the Jewish people."[1] Conservative Jewish leader Jack Wertheimer writes of the "potentially subversive link" between intermarriage and religious assimilation and warns that the "intermarriage crisis is now propelling a massive transformation of American Jewish life."[2] Similarly, the American Jewish Committee, whose mission is to protect the Jewish community from anti-Semitism and other threats, issued an official statement on "Jewish Continuity" which warns that intermarriage "represents a serious risk to the vitality of the Jewish community, Jewish continuity, and identity" and emphasizes that Jews must marry other Jews.[3] Other rabbis go so far as to describe intermarriage as "the silent holocaust of assimilation" that has caused millions of Jews to "disappear."[4]

Although the rate of intermarriage in America is indeed high, intermarriage is not solely a modern American phenomenon. Nor are assimilation and weakening loyalty entirely to blame. Finally, there is no concrete evidence that intermarriage is a danger to the Jewish population in America, just as there is no proof that inmarriage increases Jewish population numbers.

DISASSEMBLING THE MYTH

Intermarriage is as old as the Jewish people. Of the 613 commandments in the Torah, the first five books of Scripture that form the core of Jewish law, no commandment categorically forbids a Jew to marry a gentile.[5] In fact, in Exodus 2:21, the Hebrew Bible recounts that Moses married the daughter of a Midianite priest. Even though she was of a different religion, their son, Gershon, was without question one of the Children of Israel. The Torah completely accepts the legitimacy of Moses' relationship with this non-Israelite woman and takes for granted the Israelite status of their offspring. A later passage in the Torah (Numbers

12:1) tells that Moses married an Ethiopian woman. Elsewhere (Ruth 4:10–17) the Bible describes the marriage between the Moabite woman Ruth and the Israelite man Boaz as an ordinary fact of daily life. The descendant of that mixed marriage, David, became the king of Israel.

Simply put, intermarriage was not a major issue during the biblical period because women and children automatically assumed the identity of the male head of the household. This meant that if a non-Israelite woman became the wife of an Israelite, she was considered to be an Israelite, and all children born to the couple would be Israelites. Similarly, an Israelite woman who married a gentile was lost to the nation of Israel, as were her children.

Jewish–gentile relationships did not become problematic for Judaism until the rabbinic period, around the time of the Second Temple. As society became more sophisticated, Jewish law became more complex. The rabbis replaced the biblical understanding of marriage as a business arrangement between the man and the woman's family with a new concept: marriage as a *legal contract* between the man and the woman. Then, because a gentile was not subject to Jewish law, the rabbis ruled that a relationship between a Jew and a gentile could not be sanctified by Judaism. Jewish–gentile relationships were not forbidden, but they could not be legitimized.

The legal status of their issue was a more complicated question because of another major change in Jewish law. The rabbis replaced the biblical policy of patrilineal descent, whereby Jewish identity was transmitted through the father, with matrilineal descent because of a purely practical necessity arising from legal situations in which the paternity of a child might be in doubt. The rabbinic courts decided to take a conservative approach: In questionable cases, the Jewishness of all children would be based on the identity of the mother, since of course it is easier to determine the mother of a child than the father. Basing the Jewish identity of the child on its mother rather than its father meant that children born to gentile mothers, even in families headed by Jews, were no longer counted as Israelites.[6] (Jewish law does, however, specify rituals whereby a Jewish father can convert an infant.)

Thus, the question of the ethnic identity of families, a simple matter during the biblical period, became complicated during the rabbinic period. The father was still the head of the household, but it was the mother who provided the Jewish or non-Jewish status, at least at birth. This major change in Jewish law set up a tension that would make intermarriage a problem in ways it had not been before. The rights of male heirs of Jewish men would be split: Property could pass from father to son in the traditional way, but religious rights might not. For example, if a man's wife were gentile, his sons could not inherit his Levitical or Kohanitic status—a status that still carries special ritual honors in many synagogues today—even if they were converted to Judaism as infants. And unless they were formally converted, they would not be required to recite the mourners' kaddish in the father's memory after he died. In fact, without the benefit of conversion by a rabbinic court, they would be barred from participation in much of the Jewish religious life, such as burial in the family plot in a Jewish cemetery. The requirement of formal conversion introduced a new dependency on the rabbinic courts. Religious rights that had been automatic for all Jewish offspring under biblical law would now be mediated by rabbinic authority.

Even though these radical changes instituted by rabbinic law made intermarriage more problematic, Jews did not stop marrying gentiles. Intermarriage was a feature of Jewish life in the Roman empire, medieval Europe and colonial America and was common among American Jews in the nineteenth century.[7] The Jews have been a Diaspora for two thousand years, migrating in large and small numbers to regions remote from the ancestral homeland. Often they settled in lands where there were no established Jewish communities and where it would be difficult to find other Jews to marry. It makes sense that they would marry the indigenous peoples and do their best to maintain their own Jewish identity and that of their children. Numerous old photographs show that some isolated Jewish communities were racially mixed: Jews from China look Chinese, while Jews from India look Indian.[8] This visual evidence indicates that intermarriage was common at various times throughout Jewish history. Traditionalists may believe that all these marriages were preceded by formal religious conversions of the gentile spouses, but more likely Jews simply took partners from among the non-Jewish people around them and raised their offspring as Jews. Conversion to Judaism would not have been an option for a gentile spouse in places where no rabbinic courts existed to authorize the procedure. By the same token, intermarriage had to have been common among the small number of Jews living in different parts of America in the seventeenth and eighteenth centuries. Even the venerated Jewish community of Eastern Europe was not immune from intermarriage. Statistics available for several European cities at the end of the nineteenth century show rates of Jewish intermarriage ranging from 2 percent to as high as 46 percent, with an overall rate of 15 percent.[9]

Thus, intermarriage is not an anomaly of modern America, but rather a normal part of the life of the Jewish people and other minority groups over time. In fact, the high rate of Jewish inmarriage in prior years was as much a result of prevailing social conditions as is the high rate of Jewish intermarriage today. During the first third of the twentieth century, American Jews lived within communities that were both well established and socially segregated; Jewish marriage partners were readily available, Jews had less social contact with gentiles than they do today, and gentiles were less likely to accept Jews as partners. Consequently, intermarriage was exceptionally low among American Jews during that period—less than 7 percent.[10] By the middle of the twentieth century, the intermarriage rate had risen to 13 percent.[11] Due to the very different sociological factors prevailing during the last third of the twentieth century, the rate of intermarriage soared to nearly 50 percent by the mid-1980s and has remained at that level.[12] The dramatic contrast of a period of unusually high intermarriage rates immediately following a period of unusually low intermarriage fueled a sense of alarm within the Jewish community.

How did this transformation come about, and what does it mean for Judaism in America today? Most Jewish authorities claim that the high rate of intermarriage is an unfortunate side effect of Jewish integration into American society. Greater gentile acceptance of Jews, the theory goes, results in more Jewish-gentile marriages: "[the] collapse of barriers has facilitated mobility, and mobility has facilitated intermarriage."[13] Certainly the Jews have been assimilated into American society, especially when compared to the isolation they experienced in Eastern Europe. Jews live in the same neighborhoods as gentiles. Their children are educated in the same school systems and universities. Jews are admitted into the professions, as well as civic and social organizations; they are part of the workforce and the government. Of course, American law enforces the inclusion of Jews and other minorities, but Jews have become very well integrated. They have been successful in politics. They socialize freely with gentiles in daily life and even enter into intimate relationships with them. Nonetheless, assimilation alone does not account for the high rate of intermarriage.

When American Judaism links intermarriage to assimilation, it is reacting to the old fear that freedom and acceptance for Jews in America will cause their disappearance. Pinning the blame on Jewish participation in American society is an oversimplification and only part of the explanation for the dramatic increase in the number of Jewish–gentile couples in America beginning in 1970s. Multiple sociological factors have produced today's high rate of intermarriage. During the last third of the twentieth century, three distinct trajectories of profound social change intersected: Americans were embracing new attitudes toward women's equality, new beliefs about ethnic diversity and new views about love. The impact on the Jewish community was profound.

By the 1970s, Jews and gentiles were socializing with each other much more than in the past. But just as important, *men* and *women* were socializing with each other to a much greater degree than ever before. New opportunities in American society meant that more women were attending postsecondary educational institutions, more women were entering the workplace, and women were beginning to pursue a wider range of professions. As women became more integrated into American life, American men and women had more opportunities to associate with each other on a daily basis. Men worked side by side with more women than in the past; they did business with more women and attended classes with more women than before. More Americans had women doctors, lawyers and professors than ever before. These changes also meant that fewer women of marriageable age lived under the daily authority of their parents. Not only would men and women be associating as peers, they would be meeting each other without the mediation of parents—or of congregations.

Now that social norms have changed, few Americans meet their future mates in the synagogue or church youth group; they do not find their spouses through their parents or neighbors. They tend to establish their serious social relationships after the high school years, when they are relatively independent of the households and communities of their youth. Marriageable men and women meet in the university, in the workplace, in peer social settings and online—all gender-integrated settings.

Along with increased male–female socialization beginning in the 1970s came greater acceptance of ethnic and religious differences, especially among whites. Although many Jews believe that the rising rate of intermarriage is the result of changing attitudes among Jews and a greater willingness to form relationships with gentiles, the opposite is just as true. One of the reasons Jews tended not to intermarry during earlier periods in America was that in many communities, a gentile would not consider dating a Jew.

During the period of expanding opportunities for women, other social barriers were being lowered. First of all, many in white gentile America were making a conscious effort to appreciate ethnicity. Discovering one's "roots" became a popular cultural theme by the late 1970s. In addition, ethnic differences in America had in fact diminished in the generations since the period of massive immigration, especially for whites. Over time, as gentiles became more familiar to Jews, Jews became less foreign to gentiles. Greater tolerance for differences, plus fewer actual differences, produced more Jewish–gentile relationships.

Finally, during the 1970s in American society, the notion of marriage also changed significantly. Relationships were no longer based on traditional gender roles; love and intimacy became more important. In earlier times the expectation was that men and women could not understand each other completely and could not be emotional partners. The genders were considered to be unfathomable mysteries to each other. Men formed platonic friendships with other men and women with other women, but husbands and wives did not expect to be friends with each other in the same way. These gender concepts began to fade as romantic couples came to view each other as "soul mates." Marriage vows began to include such phrases as "you are my best friend." Romantic love acquired far greater power than in previous generations. As ethnic distinctions became less important in America, romantic love became more important.

The combination of these three powerful sociological changes—the increased participation of women in American society, greater acceptance of ethnic differences and changing attitudes about the importance of romantic love—produced the high rate of Jewish–gentile intermarriage. Now that Jewish men and women were meeting far more gentile women and men on a daily basis than ever before, Jews who may have grown up intending to marry only other Jews did not refrain from casual socializing with gentiles. Now that Jews and gentiles were more accepting of each other, the likelihood of an intimate friendship developing became greater. Finally, because the point at which friendship shades into romance is not always discernible, Jews often found themselves falling in love with non-Jews. And because of the high value placed upon romantic love, even Jews who were taught that intermarriage is wrong maintained their relationships whether their partners were Jewish or not.

In fact, the desire for self-actualization through intimate partnership has become so important today that once a promising relationship begins to blossom, most couples will place loyalty to the relationship above loyalty to their religion. They will pursue the romance with the assumption that religious differences will have to be accommodated. What this means for the Jewish community in America is that Jewish–gentile intermarriage is now a fact of life. Few Jews will break up with a gentile partner because of the difference in religion, no matter how much rabbis condemn them. Jews and gentiles will continue to socialize with each other, and Jews will continue to form intimate friendships with gentiles, no matter how much Jewish leaders emphasize the importance of in-marriage.

There is further evidence of how sociological factors outweigh religious differences in the choice of partners. In spite of the fact that virtually all books and articles refer to Jewish–gentile intermarriage in general, a distinct trend is obvious to everyone who works with interfaith couples but is never talked about. Data I gathered from face-to-face and telephone interviews of approximately one thousand Jewish–gentile couples (dating, engaged and married) in the Washington, D.C., area between 1986 and 2006 revealed that slightly more than half of the non-Jewish partners were Catholic. It made no difference whether a man or a woman was the Jewish partner. As this is much greater than the proportion of Catholics in the general population in the region—23 percent—it indicates a trend toward Jewish–Catholic relationships. If roughly half of the Jews in the Washington area marry gentiles, and half of those who do marry Catholics, then a quarter of the Jews are marrying Catholics. I have heard clerics and social service workers from other regions describe a similar trend. So within the general phenomenon of Jewish–gentile intermarriage there may be a distinct sub-phenomenon of Jewish–Catholic intermarriage.

My interviews with these couples indicate that Jews and Catholics are not seeking each other out consciously; for some reason, Jews who date gentiles are more likely to fall in love with a Catholic than someone of another faith. Social and historical factors are playing a part. The majority of Jews in America today are the descendants of working-class European immigrants who fled persecution or poverty to settle in the northeastern maritime cities in the early years of the twentieth century. The same is true for the majority of Catholics in America, whereas most Protestants in America have a different history. These Catholic and Jewish immigrants came from similar socioeconomic backgrounds. They grew up in the same neighborhoods during the same period in American history and under the same social conditions; but they spoke different languages and married their own people. Today, due to freedom, integration and acceptance in America, their descendants speak the same language and are marrying each other.

If roughly one in every four marriageable Jews in the Washington, D.C., area—and probably other urban areas as well—is marrying a Catholic, then intermarriage cannot simply be chalked up to assimilation. Social affinity may be a contributing factor that makes Catholics and Jews attractive to each other. At least some Jews are being drawn to members of another minority group with a similar history rather than merely melting into the American majority. It is significant that the overwhelming majority of the Jewish–Catholic couples I interviewed face to face in the Washington study are remarkably well-matched regarding social class, educational level, values and interests—on a par with Jewish–Jewish couples and more than couples who are non-Catholic and Jewish.

THE IMPLICATIONS OF IN-MARRIAGE

Many people take it for granted that in-marriage preserves the Jewish population and that intermarriage decreases it, because a Jewish couple is more likely than a mixed couple to raise their children as Jews. Basic demographic analysis, however, shows that this assumption is not true. According to the in-marriage model, a Jewish woman marries a Jewish man. If they have two children, then all things being equal, they replace themselves: Two Jews produce two Jewish children. If instead the Jewish woman marries a gentile man, while the Jewish man marries a gentile woman, and each couple produces two children, then two Jews will have produced four children. Even if one couple raises their children as Jews and the other does not, the results are the same for both the in-marriage model and the intermarriage model: two Jews produce two Jewish children. Whatever the average size of families in America, inter-marriage produces twice as many offspring for Jews as does in-marriage. The overall Jewish population level, therefore, depends on what percentage of the children of intermarriage are counted as Jews. Here the picture actually is encouraging.

The National Jewish Population Survey of 2000–2001 (NJPS) reported that one-third of Jewish–gentile couples are raising their children exclusively as Jews. The NJPS did not release its findings about the number of children being raised exclusively in another religion and the number being raised as both Jewish and gentile. Based on the results of my Washington area study, which are comparable to the figures produced by the NJPS, less than one-fifth of Jewish–gentile couples raise their children exclu-sively as gentiles. Using the same criteria the survey employed when it counted the Jewish parents (any individual with one Jew-ish parent who is not exclusively a member of another monothe-istic religion), the *majority* of the children of intermarriage have to be counted as Jewish.

In reality, very few offspring of Jewish–gentile intermarriage grow up without any Jewish identity at all. It is rare for a child of intermarriage, even someone living a Christian life, not to identify as a Jew to some extent. The vast majority of children of mixed couples grow up with either an exclusively Jewish identity or a par-tial Jewish–gentile identity.

There is another reason why a high rate of intermarriage does not represent a one-way road to assimilation. In a society where Jews and gentiles intermarry on a regular basis, it is likely that some of the non-Jewish or partial Jewish offspring of intermarriage will grow up to marry Jews and subsequently raise *their* children exclusively as Jews. During periods of intermarriage, Jewish iden-tity weaves in as well as out.

The question remains why the Jewish population in America is not soaring, given the fact that intermarriage produces more Jewish offspring than does in-marriage. Basic science provides an answer, but few if any Jewish leaders want to consider it: in-marriage *reduces* the Jewish population. As I discuss later, generation after generation of inbreeding narrows an ethnic group's gene-pool and leads to the proliferation of genetic disorders, including any that affect fertility. There is evidence that this is precisely what is happening to the Jewish community in America.

In the year 2000, the overall birthrate for American Jewish women was 1.9, which is below the replacement rate of 2.1.[14] These figures mean that in order for the Jewish population to remain level, for every subpopulation of 100 Jewish men and 100 Jewish women, there must be 210 children born. Since only 190 children are being born, there is a 10 percent gap. In other words, the overall Jewish birthrate is actually 10 percent below the replacement rate. This is a very significant number for a group that is worried about its survival. NJPS correlated infertility in woman with increasing age and concluded that because Jewish women are on the average better educated than other American women and have children as later ages, they experience a higher than average rate of miscarriages and fertility problems. Nonetheless, even when compared with gentile women of similar age and educational levels, Jewish women still bear fewer children. The overall Jewish fertility rate is too low even to replace the Jewish population, let alone increase it.[15]

If Jews have higher levels of miscarriage and fertility problems than do gentiles in the same age brackets and levels of education, the implications are enormous. Mainstream Judaism insists that Jews should marry only other Jews, and for generations in-marriage has been the norm. Unfortunately, this practice has a negative genetic impact. When an ethnic group is as highly inbred as American Jews have been—at least until a generation or two ago—health problems are more likely to emerge than for groups that are more intermarried. In fact, the Centers for Disease Control reports that among Orthodox Jews, who have low intermarriage rates, the rate of ovarian cancer has risen to the point where it has begun to exceed that of the general population.[16] The impact on the Jewish population would be no less threatening if there are higher than average fertility problems among Jewish males. There is some evidence that this is the case, since Crohn's Disease (a serious disorder of the gastro-intestinal tract) occurs four to five times more frequently among Jewish men of Eastern European background than other men and is associated with reproductive complications.[17] Any biological basis for the low Jewish birthrate—whether the source is women, men or both—would mean that in-marriage *reduces* the Jewish population. This suggestion does not appeal to American Jewish leaders.

By insisting on the tradition of in-marriage as the standard for the community, American Judaism is advocating a practice that, while facilitating the survival of Jewish identity, works against the physical survival of the Jewish community. The fear of assimilation through intermarriage has blinded the community to the health dangers of in-marriage. It is no secret that certain diseases occur more frequently within certain ethnic groups, and the Jews are no exception. In fact, scientists have identified a group of genetic disorders and medical conditions that are unusually common among Jews of Eastern European descent, the majority of Jews in America. These diseases include cystic fibrosis, Gaucher disease, Tay-Sachs disease, breast cancer and colon cancer; they afflict Jews of Eastern European background from twenty to one hundred times more frequently than the general population. The elevated rate of occurrence of these diseases is attributed to the fact that because Jews have tended to marry within their group, the high frequency of the disease-bearing genes stayed within the community. Furthermore, not enough genes from outside the Jewish community have been introduced to reduce the frequency of these disorders.[18]

Basic arithmetic shows intermarriage by itself does not reduce the Jewish population, even if partial Jews are discounted. If partial Jews are counted—and the United Jewish Communities does indeed include them in its calculation of the number of Jews in America—then intermarriage actually *increases* the number of Jews. This assumption correlates with the fact that the Jewish population is not decreasing, even though the Jewish birthrate is 10 percent below the replacement rate. There are at least two reasons why Jewish numbers have remained steady in recent years despite the negative effects of in-marriage. Immigration is one factor: During the years between 1980 and 2000, over 300,000 Jews came to the United States, mostly from the former Soviet Union.[19] However, the wave of Soviet Jewish immigration is over, and those Jews have been found to have a lower-than-average birthrate themselves.[20] Intermarriage is the other dynamic offsetting attrition from the Jewish genetic disorders. If the American Jewish population is to remain constant, the support will have to come from intermarriage. Thus, when it comes to the physical continuity of the Jewish community, intermarriage is more helpful than in-marriage. Jews who marry outside the community are not contributing to a silent holocaust—they are, in fact, contributing to the survival of the Jewish people.

ORIGINS OF THE MYTH

The myth that intermarriage is an enemy destroying the Jewish people arose from the combined effect of the other six myths of American Judaism. Each contributed its own ingredient. The first myth, that the American Jewish community is in imminent danger of dying out, has placed intermarriage in the spotlight of an illusory struggle for survival. Sometimes intermarriage is portrayed as the *evidence* Judaism is disappearing in America. Other times intermarriage is portrayed as the *reason* Judaism is disappearing. In any case, American Judaism believes that intermarriage is bad news for the Jews. And if doom is just around the corner, then intermarriage must be very bad news indeed. Whereas the myth of Jewish disappearance created a sense of alarm about intermarriage, the myth that Judaism is a four-thousand-year-old religion produced the belief that intermarriage in America today is strictly a modern phenomenon. When viewed from the perspective of the twentieth-century American Jewish theme of historical evolution, intermarriage appears to disrupt the continuity of the Jewish people. It is seen as alien to Jewish tradition and a betrayal of its ancient origins.

The myth of Old World Judaism has made the Jewish community intolerant of its intermarried members. Nostalgia for the fictional world of the shtetl produced the image of a pure Jewish world unthreatened by any melting pot of assimilation. Eastern European Judaism represents an ideal for many American Jews, and it is true that intermarriage was uncommon within the Pale of Settlement. When the contrasting portraits of the shtetl and the New World are placed side by side, intermarriage pops out as a recent American phenomenon, even though it has always been part of Jewish life. At the same time, the myth that Jews have always been reasonable—and never believed in such supernatural concepts as Heaven, Hell, Satan or sorcery—produces a sense of Jewish uniformity and authenticity. As a result, American Judaism is highly intolerant of divergent concepts and unorthodox relationships. It rejects the religious expression of Jews who intermarry and is insensitive to the complex religious needs of their children. Partial Jews—those who consider themselves in varying degrees both Jewish and gentile—are seen as a contradiction of Judaism.

The myth that Jewish denominations in America are authoritative forms of Judaism has meant that intermarried Jews and their families suffer when Jewish religious institutions flex their muscles in an attempt to discourage intermarriage. Denominational Judaism penalizes Jews who do not conform by denying its services to them. In the name of taking a stand against intermarriage, the denominations sometimes deliberately block connections between interfaith families and the Jewish community, thereby increasing the separateness despite their claims of "outreach" to mixed families. Nonetheless, most people believe that the denominations speak for Judaism when they discriminate against interfaith families.

Finally, the myth that rabbis are the official leaders of Jewish congregations has given us considerable influence over the religious life of Jews in America. Interfaith households are no less affected because they often rely on the good graces of Jewish clergy for life-cycle ceremonies: the legalizing of their marriages, the blessing of their babies, the bar mitzvahs of their teens, the burying of their dead. Different rabbis have different rules for these situations, but in one way or another many rabbis treat interfaith families differently from families where both partners are Jewish. Even rabbis who are willing to conduct mixed marriages sometimes impose additional requirements on interfaith couples, such as extracting pledges to raise the children as Jews—a demand they do not make on Jewish couples. As much as mixed couples resent the discriminatory behavior of rabbis, they tend to understand that religious leaders are acting out of conscience and adherence to Jewish tradition. Rabbis who withhold their services from interfaith families are respected for adhering to their principles rather than being challenged for wielding power.

The leadership of the American Jewish community today works hard to underscore the presumed dangers of intermarriage. As I have mentioned, the NJPS has had a great deal of influence on the American public. Its findings are cited in numerous publications. When NJPS tabulated the statistics from its three-hundred-item questionnaire, the authors assembled the data in a way that emphasizes the contrast between Jewish and mixed households: "In-married and intermarried Jews differ dramatically in the extent to which they raise their children as Jews. Nearly all children (96%) in households with two Jewish spouses are being raised Jewish, compared to a third (33%) of the children in households with one non-Jewish spouse."[21] This statement is very misleading because it does not reveal all of the information the survey gathered. The survey questionnaire specifically asked whether children were being raised Jewish, partially Jewish or non-Jewish.[22] Yet the study did not report the percentages of children being raised partially Jewish and those being raised non-Jewish. This is a significant omission, since in its consideration of adults, NJPS counts as "Jewish" all who are partially Jewish:

> For purposes of this report, a Jew is defined as a person:
> - Whose religion is Jewish, or
> - Whose religion is Jewish and something else, or
> - Who has no religion and has at least one Jewish parent or a Jewish upbringing, or
> - Who has a non-monotheistic religion, and has at least one Jewish parent or a Jewish upbringing.[23]

If the same criteria of Jewishness were applied to the children as to the adults, then any child not raised exclusively in another monotheistic religion would have to be counted as Jewish. Whatever the number of such children, it is far higher than the one-third reported in the survey.

Even though NJPS did not report the numbers of children being raised as partial Jews and as non-Jews, I did obtain such data from face to face interviews I conducted with approximately eight hundred Jewish–gentile engaged and married couples in the Washington, D.C., area between 1986 and 2006 as part of an ongoing study of interfaith relationships. The results indicate that fewer than one-fifth of Jewish-Christian couples intend to raise their children exclusively as gentiles. If a third of intermarried couples raise their children as Jewish, as reported by the NJPS, then about half of the couples intend to raise their children as partial Jews. This proportion is consistent with my own research findings.

There is no precedent for deciding how to count partial Jews, and the NJPS report even acknowledges that "how the children of intermarriages will identify themselves when they grow up is unknown now."[24] Some will consider themselves Jewish, while others will consider themselves Jewish enough to be counted as Jews by the NJPS, based on its definition of a Jew. The fact that the percentage of children raised as non-Jews is much smaller than the other two categories could be construed as reassurance that the offspring of intermarriage are not entirely lost to Judaism.

RESPONSES OF THE JEWISH COMMUNITY

Overall, the Jewish community's response to the perceived crisis of intermarriage is inconsistent at best. According to most Jewish leaders, the first step is to do everything possible to inoculate Jews against intermarriage: Young people's ties to Judaism must be encouraged, and dating non-Jews must be discouraged. Where intermarriage *does* occur, the Jewish community must take action. Some rabbis recommend quarantine—ostracizing intermarried Jews and their children—but most recommend "outreach" to the non-Jewish partner as an antidote to gentile influence in the household. As part of this outreach, synagogues and Jewish community centers offer special classes and support groups for intermarried couples aimed at introducing the non-Jewish partners to Judaism and strengthening the Jewish identity of the family. InterfaithFamily.com (www.interfaithfamily.com) is a national organization and publishing house, funded by the Jewish community, whose mission is to "encourage Jewish choices." The idea, of course, is to make sure that the children of intermarried Jews remain in the fold.

Even though some Jewish leaders advocate a welcoming attitude to interfaith families, all denominations call on their affiliated rabbis *not* to perform wedding ceremonies between Jews and gentiles. Indeed, as I have mentioned, the Conservative movement's Rabbinical Assembly will expel any member who does so. The denominations take the position that the rabbi is automatically the representative of the Jewish community (or at least of the denomination), and therefore the rabbi's mere presence at such a wedding would lend tacit approval to intermarriage. Some rabbis will not even attend mixed weddings as guests.

There is no evidence that rabbis' refusal to officiate at mixed weddings has done anything to abate the rising rate of intermarriage other than to make a statement of community disapproval. There is, however, ample evidence that families that are denied service feel considerable resentment and alienation. The denominations have a right to stand firm in their belief that Jews should not marry outside the community of Israel, but why have they singled out intermarriage for public rejection? No denomination has issued a similar edict regarding Jews who work on the Sabbath, who eat pork or who commit felonies; they can get married by a rabbi as long as both partners say they are Jewish.[25] The difference, of course, is that the denominations see intermarriage as endangering the community of Israel. If intermarriage were in fact such a threat, it might make sense for Judaism to censure those Jews who violate this policy, but as I have shown, there is no evidence that intermarriage actually thins the Jewish population or diminishes Jewish life. Some rabbis will find this statement hard to believe, but I would be pleased to share my research findings with them.

Curiously, while the denominational bodies refuse to perform weddings or co-officiated "welcoming" ceremonies for babies for interfaith couples, they do not necessarily refuse congregational membership to Jews who intermarry. In other words, an intermarried Jew can be a formal member of a Conservative congregation but the gentile spouse cannot, whereas Reform congregations do extend formal membership to the gentile spouses of Jewish members. These policies are consistent with denominational Judaism's practice of enforcing its authority by withholding rabbinic services rather than refusing membership. It may be that the rivalry among the denominations makes them so conscious of their membership numbers that they want to enroll as many Jews as possible, even those whom they have repudiated in some ways. And, as I discussed in chapter 6, the typical household can bring in tens of thousands of dollars in dues. The couples themselves, of course, are perplexed when the same rabbi who refused to marry them encourages them to join the congregation *after* they are married.

The Jewish community's first concern about the impact of intermarriage is the identity of the children. In the 1970s and 1980s, when the rising rate of intermarriage was far more surprising to the Jewish community than it is today, most interfaith couples assumed they had to choose one religion or the other for their children. Jews tended to express stronger feelings about maintaining cultural links with their children than did their gentile spouses (regardless of the gender of the Jewish parent), and the majority of couples opted for raising their children as Jews. By the 1990s, intermarried families were far more common—and more accepted—even within the Jewish community. Even though Jewish and gentile clerics continue to advocate strongly that couples rear their children within a specific religious community, my survey of interfaith couples in Washington, D.C., shows that a clear trend has developed to choose dual Jewish–Christian identities for their children, even though they are not certain either how to define that identity or how to provide it.

When interfaith couples who adopt the dual-identity path for raising their children are interviewed about the motives behind their decision, many reveal that they simply find this approach preferable to choosing one parent's religion over the other's. These couples are seeking to avoid a win-lose situation where one parent's religious identity is selected for the children's nominal identity and the other parent's religious identity is, in effect, deselected. Thus, often the decision to raise the children with a dual identity is based not on the desire to pass on two distinct religious traditions but on the desire to avoid having to make a choice. These couples' reluctance is understandable. Psychologically, when any mixed couple decides to raise its children with one faith, there is both loss and gain: Some aspect of one parent's life is being preserved in ways in which the comparable aspect from the other parent is not.

Although most Jewish authorities continue to view the identity of the children of intermarriage in binary terms, as either Jewish or gentile, dual identity for the offspring is becoming the most common solution among interfaith couples today. Unfortunately for them, denominational Judaism's congregations will not support parents who want to raise their children with both a Jewish and a non-Jewish identity. There are two reasons for this policy. First of all, regarding Christianity specifically, Judaism insists that belief in the divinity of Jesus is incompatible with Judaism; any child who accepts basic Christian teachings is automatically considered to be a Christian and therefore not a Jew. Second, dual identity is incompatible with the basic educational goal of all Jewish religious schools: to instill in their students a complete and exclusive Jewish identity. Even the Reform Movement is uncompromising on this issue and has established a strict policy that any child who is receiving Christian education is not permitted to attend Reform religious school classes.

Ironically, few congregations would refuse membership to a Jew who denies the existence of God, even though belief in God is central to Judaism. But they would reject a Jew, even a child, who believes that Jesus was more than an ordinary human being. It is the right of the Jewish community to decide who is a member and who is not. And in light of the aggressiveness of some Christian missionaries who seek to convert Jews, it makes sense for the Jewish community to insist that belief in the divinity of Jesus is incompatible with Jewish identity. But it is self-defeating for a people worried about being an endangered species to deny education to children of Jewish parentage, even those who are receiving Christian education. Whether the concern is demographic survival of the Jewish people or the authenticity of Jewish identity, it makes better sense to provide impressionable children with a Jewish educational experience than to abandon them to Christianity.

The study I conducted in Washington shows that most intermarried Jews have a desire to pass on at least some Jewish identity to their children. Even when a child is being raised within the practices of the gentile parent's religion, the Jewish parent typically wants the child to retain a Jewish identity. The good news for intermarried Jewish parents is that membership in a Christian denomination is based on religious conviction, not ethnic identity.

Churches typically do not require coverts to renounce their Jewish identity. In fact, in recent years Christian groups have become very interested in Judaism because Jesus was a Jew. As a result, some Christian Sunday school teachers and clerics actually encourage the preservation of their members' Jewish identity. Yet the churches also require their members to accept Jesus as the Messiah, a belief that is, as I mentioned, unacceptable to the Jewish community.

Most Jews believe that children of intermarried couples are more likely to be raised as Christians because Christians are the majority in the United States. There is no actual evidence that the Christianness of America has anything to do with how Jewish–gentile couples raise their children. Couples for the most part make these decisions from their personal perspectives, their allegiance to their own religion and their allegiance to their parents.

Many Jewish leaders cite the decline in formal affiliation with denominational Judaism as an indicator of the weakening loyalty of American Jews. They point out that the children of intermarried Jews, as a class, have lower levels of affiliation than Jews in general.[26] The statistics do not indicate how many children of mixed marriages actually have been disqualified from membership by the denominations themselves.

The Holocaust is one area of modern Judaism where attitudes about intermarriage have a soft edge. Jews who differ about their belief in God, the interpretation of the Torah or the authority of Jewish law are united in their reverence for the Jews who were murdered by the Nazis. Each denomination has endorsed the observance of Yom Hashoah (Holocaust Day), which occurs in the spring on the twenty-seventh day of the Hebrew month of Nisan, and their rabbinic bodies have written liturgies for the occasion. The "Six Million" has become sacrosanct shorthand for a particular group exterminated by the Nazis—a group that includes both Jews and partial Jews. The Jewish community has made it a point of honor to memorialize all the victims of Nazi anti-Semitism, meticulously gathering and recording every name. Even partial Jews, even Jews who had assimilated, even Jews who had become Christians are included among the Six Million. It is ironic that American Judaism accepts the children and grandchildren of intermarriage among those it honors as Jewish victims of the Holocaust, but sets aside the precedent of inclusion when it comes to the offspring of interfaith couples living in America today. A rabbi who will chant the kaddish for a victim of the Holocaust might not conduct a Jewish funeral if that same individual died in America today.

It is especially ironic that many Reform, Reconstructionist and even Conservative rabbis will bless same-gender couples if both partners are Jewish, but not interfaith couples. This is a significant distinction, because homosexuality is condemned in the Torah, whereas intermarriage is not. If by modifying a few words rabbis can conduct the equivalent of a Jewish wedding ceremony for a same-gender couple, why would they deny the same service to an interfaith couple? The reason may be that some rabbis wish to signal their support for sexual minorities in America, but not for mixed marriages. Just as the Reform, Conservative and Reconstructionist movements incrementally accepted the full inclusion of women over the course of the twentieth century, they are accepting the full inclusion of sexual minorities in the twenty-first. Many congregations welcome gay and lesbian members. Rabbis who understand that laws cannot direct sexual orientation and that therapy cannot alter it accept gays and lesbians and provide ceremonies for same-gender couples, as long as both partners are Jewish. But many of these same rabbis do not approve of intermarriage and therefore will not be part of ceremonies that consecrate religiously mixed relationships.

No matter how rabbis justify such inconsistencies theologically, reasonable people will find their justifications confusing. American rabbis cannot afford to hold on to them because doing so diminishes the laity's respect for the rabbinate. We must move forward from our accustomed flexing of clerical muscle in the name of Jewish law lest we marginalize the American rabbinate and decrease its influence.

SOLUTIONS TO THE
CHALLENGE OF INTERMARRIAGE

All the denominations have responded to the perceived threat of intermarriage by setting up programs to encourage intermarried couples to raise their children as Jews. Although this makes sense, it is a narrow approach: There is no reason that partial Jews and mixed households cannot serve as conduits for the transmission of Jewish identity to future generations. Secular Jewish organizations and most independent congregations accept partial Jews and mixed families. If *all* congregations were willing to include partial Jews, a greater number of Americans of Jewish ancestry would then be affiliated with Judaism. A greater number could be encouraged to lead Jewish lives, support Jewish causes and raise their children as Jews.

While Judaism is clear that any Jew who becomes a Christian is outside the Jewish fold, the same is not true in Christianity. Since both Protestants and Catholics define themselves by faith, not ethnicity, Jews who formally accept Christianity are permitted to retain their Jewish identity. Some Christians believe that their faith completes, rather than replaces, Judaism. The Jewish community disagrees with Christianity on this point, but there is no reason to view engagement with Christianity as the end of the story for Jewish identity. It is important to keep in mind the fact that even Jews who join Christian denominations continue to think of themselves as Jewish in some way or other. Therefore, Judaism will always have a potential influence—however small—on their lives. The Jewish community may be able to bring them back into the fold by adopting a less rejecting attitude.

Nor is it a given that children of intermarriage being raised with no religion are lost to Judaism. To the extent that they find Jewish life both accepting and acceptable, Jews who accept Christianity may return to the community, and partial Jews may metamorphose into pure Jews.

Regarding the children being raised as partial Jews, it would be quite logical for rabbinic authorities to state that no minor child of a Jew can be considered a Christian under any circumstance, since religious vows of underage Jews are not binding. This policy is consistent with Jewish law. Invoking it now would normalize dual-identity Jewish children and increase the possibility that they will be members of the household of Israel in the future.

But what happens when these Jewish–Christian children grow up? Currently American Judaism employs a coercive response regarding Jews and Christian faith: This is not what Jews believe; if you believe this, you are no longer a Jew. As more and more children of intermarriage become adults with Jewish–Christian identities, this approach will weaken Judaism's influence in many American households. American Judaism might consider a persuasive response: You are a Jew, and this is not what Jews believe. A persuasive approach is just as firm as a coercive approach, but it promotes more active engagement with the individual, which is exactly what the Jewish community wants.

It is in the interest of the Jewish community to promote Jewish education for all who are interested. Non-Catholics have been attending Catholic schools for years in America, and their presence does not appear to have weakened the Church. It can cause no real harm to American Judaism to welcome all children of Jewish parentage into its schools. Because Jewish law discounts the import of vows made by minors, there is no reason to bar dual-identity children from learning about Judaism.

The issue of rabbinic officiation at life-cycle ceremonies for interfaith families has been highly problematic, but it does not have to be. Many rabbis serving in Reconstructionist or Reform denominations, which do not explicitly bar them from performing mixed weddings, offer an additional reason for refusing to officiate at such ceremonies: the content of the Jewish wedding liturgy itself, which makes reference to God's commandments to Israel and states that the couple is bound to each other under Jewish law. If one of the partners is not a member of the House of Israel, they argue, how can the ceremony having any meaning? Yet there is ample precedent for resolving this issue.

As mentioned, American rabbis have devised solutions to other liturgical problems brought about by changing social conditions. For instance, traditional Hebrew prayers have been reworded to make them gender inclusive. References to animal sacrifice have been eliminated or reinterpreted. As I have shown, in the English-language prayer books of various denominations, the traditional references to Satan and to Paradise have been replaced. Modern rabbis—including Orthodox ones—have even modified the Jewish wedding liturgy.

In the traditional ceremony, only the groom pronounces a vow, and only the bride receives a ring. When social norms changed, it was a simple matter for American rabbis to show respect for society's views about the equality of women and men by composing a vow for the bride while presenting a ring to the groom. All they had to do was replace the specific Hebrew words which invoke Jewish law, *kidat mosheh viyisrael*, with more general language for the woman to recite as she places a ring on the man's hand. Today it is commonplace for a Jewish bride to offer a ring and a vow to her groom. Similarly, rabbis who conduct commitment ceremonies for same-gender couples routinely reword the traditional marriage vow to acknowledge both the gender of the partners and the fact that the ceremony is not in accordance with traditional Jewish law.

With the same modification—eliminating the words about the law of Moses and Israel—the Jewish wedding ceremony could accommodate a marriage between a Jew and a gentile. The reference to Jewish law, although central to the traditional ritual, is not entirely necessary because it does not really convey any legal status today. All weddings in America take place under the authority of the state. Indeed, it is state law, not any religion, which empowers clerics in the United States to marry people. In most other countries, clerics are not routinely authorized to legalize marriages; couples must register their relationship civilly prior to any religious rites. Furthermore, Jewish law does not explicitly bar any rabbi from reciting appropriate prayers and blessings during a

COMMUNITY, INTERMARRIAGE AND OPTIMISM

wedding as long as it is made clear whether the ritual conforms to tradition or not.

Similar solutions can be found for other Jewish life-cycle ceremonies, such the birth of a child or a funeral. American rabbis know how to adapt traditional rituals and liturgies for new situations. Our recent efforts to adapt Jewish tradition to changing times have strengthened, rather than weakened, American Judaism. And the same will hold true as American rabbis find ways to find channels for the preservation of Jewish heritage within an intermarried community.

INTERMARRIAGE IN PERSPECTIVE

It may be true that intermarriage impedes the transmission of Jewish identity from one generation to another. If the Jewish community is determined to avoid intermarriage, it has a reliable if extreme method at its disposal: Jews must avoid dating gentiles, and the only way to do this is to abstain from even the most casual forms of socializing between Jews and gentiles. Indeed, many Orthodox communities practice such social isolation, with the result that intermarriage is less common within that segment of American Jewry. The other major denominations are not prepared to take the same steps. They are not about to recommend that their members not chat with gentile coworkers during coffee breaks. For the foreseeable future, American Judaism will be a self-contained subculture or it will be an intermarried community.

If Jewish congregations are to thrive as wholesome communities, they must move forward from viewing some of their member households as illicit, inferior or impaired. Intermarriage and religiously blended households have become a permanent part of Jewish life. A new American Judaism will serve the community effectively and have broad influence over the lives of Jews in this country by accepting intermarried families as *normal* Jewish households. It will decriminalize and depathologize both mixed couples and partial Jews. This may seem like a radical suggestion, but it will enhance the viability of American Judaism. It will alter the landscape of Jewish civilization in America in ways that cannot be predicted, but the other approach—marginalizing intermarried Jews and rejecting their children—is certain to weaken American Judaism in the long run.

The phenomenon of intermarriage has the potential to increase the number of Jews in America within a generation or two, but right now there are two major barriers to a wider engagement with Judaism: the policies of denominational Judaism and the old American Judaism's fear of annihilation.

If the high rate of intermarriage represents a crisis for the Jewish community, the crisis resides in the possibility that the thread of Jewish identity will be stretched too thin to adequately transmit the heritage of Israel to future generations. If this is so, then the logical response is to do what is necessary to preserve Jewish identity across generations. Penalizing Jews who intermarry by denying denominational resources and professional services does not preserve Jewish identity; denying their children a Jewish education destroys Jewish identity.

Even people who are not alarmist about intermarriage may believe that in-marriage is the best way to ensure Jewish survival. However, as I have discussed, this is not necessarily the case. If the current trend of low fertility among Jewish women continues, then Jewish in-marriage will lead to a decline in Jewish numbers. If the low Jewish birthrate is attributable, even in part, to biological factors—Jewish couples who want to have children fail at a greater rate than the population in general—a different policy might be called for than advocating exclusive in-marriage. In the face of a biological basis to low Jewish infertility, which is indicated by the clinical research discussed in chapter 3, intermarriage is a viable solution to Jewish survival.

Generations of in-marriage among Jews of Eastern European background have resulted in the proliferation of a number of serious medical disorders that could have been lessened by the introduction of genes from outside the Ashkenazi Jewish community.

The implication for the physical welfare of American Jewry is obvious, yet how many American rabbis would be willing to encourage intermarriage as a way to strengthen the Jewish people?

As I have mentioned, intermarriage is neither a modern aberration of Jewish life in America nor a threat to its survival. It has always been a part of the history of the Jewish people as they have dispersed around the world. Jews who marry gentiles can no more be blamed for diluting Jewish life in America through assimilation than Jews who marry Jews can be blamed for diluting the vitality of the Jewish population through inbreeding.

Intermarriage well may be the greatest challenge American Judaism faces today, if only because no one knows its long-range effect on the Jewish community. Nonetheless, for the sake of its own vitality and the welfare of its membership, American Judaism must give up the myth that intermarriage is a threat to its survival.

9

JUDAISM IN AMERICA TODAY

The myths I have been discussing in these pages were born out of the historical events of the twentieth century and the emotional upheaval of a transplanted population. The founders of American Judaism incorporated these concepts into the ideology of the new institutions they were creating to serve the needs of the immigrant generation. But how did the Jewish people in America come to accept these particular myths so readily? And why do so many Jews continue to accept them today despite the intimations of guilt and anxiety the myths bring with them?

The reason is that each of these concepts—as fictional or as factual as they may be—nonetheless speaks to how the Jewish people in America understand their own existence as a civilization. American Jews have embraced these myths not just because generations of rabbis and community leaders have taught them as truth, but also because they resonate with the religion of the Jews in America today. However, the religion I am speaking of is not the formal Judaism of rabbis or the official Judaism of denominations. It is not the Judaism that is described in classrooms or discussed in textbooks. Rather it is the constellation of concepts and practices at work within the American Jewish community today. Most of those elements overlap with formal Judaism. Others—though not discussed with the same reverence—are vivid and powerful aspects of contemporary Jewish civilization. Just as each of the myths makes a statement about the thoughts and emotions of the leaders who produced them, disassembling them uncovers a great deal about the people who preserve them now. By recognizing them as myths, American Judaism can move forward to find within each of them enduring and healing truths that can be embraced in celebration of Jewish civilization.

HISTORY AND FATE

Although it is a fiction that Judaism is four thousand years old, it is a fact that American Jews venerate their ancestors and that they practice a form of mysticism where every ritual points back in time to the origins of the Jewish people. The patriarchs and matriarchs of the stories in Genesis are Judaism's liturgical icons. Though no synagogue contains their statues, their spirits are invoked during every prayer service: "Blessed are You, Lord, our God and God of our ancestors; God of Abraham, God of Isaac and God of Jacob." For most American Jews today, religious observance has far more to do with reverence for the generations that have gone before than with obedience to God's commandments. Jews recite prayers more in the spirit of tending the fire of an altar built at the beginning of history than in the sense of speaking to God. References to the ancestors are central to every ritual within Judaism. Passover matzah is the "bread of suffering our ancestors ate in the land of Egypt." Circumcision is the "Covenant of Abraham." Moses and David are *ushpizin*, invited guests during the festival of Sukkot.

Although the textbooks declare that the Sabbath is Judaism's most sacred time, far more Jews attend services on the High Holy Days than on any other occasion. Synagogues across America are filled beyond capacity during Rosh Hashanah and Yom Kippur, but not necessarily because Jews want to honor a new liturgical year or observe a day of atonement. Most Jews come to services on those days to connect with the Jewish community during a significant time—or to say kaddish in memory of the dead.

The practice of reciting this Aramaic chant in honor of a deceased family member began at a time when Jews no longer spoke Hebrew. The words themselves have nothing to do with death, but the consonance and the cadence of the phrases make kaddish a prayer of mourning: *yit-ga-dal vi-yit-ka-dash vi-yit-ba-rakh vi-yish-ta-bakh vi-yit-pa-ar vi-yit-ro-mam vi-yit-na-sey vi-yit-ha-dar vi-yit-a-leh vi-yit-ha-lal.*[1]

By tradition, kaddish is recited in memory of a parent or a child, a sibling or a spouse. As a result, although it is not officially recognized as such, saying kaddish for the first time is a sacred life-cycle event. It is the American Jew's real coming of age, when the individual joins the congregation of those who have experienced profound loss. Most people enter this holy place when well into middle age, after a mother or father has passed away, though of course some come there sooner. It is the custom to say kaddish for a family member three times daily, beginning with the day of the funeral, for thirty days. But when a mother or a father dies, the child says kaddish until eleven months and one day have passed. Thereafter, kaddish is recited on major holidays and on the anniversary of the death.[2] Many Jews make it a point of personal honor to say kaddish for a parent, though worship of God has little if anything to do with it.

Judaism's most sacred prayers, such as kaddish, are recited only in the presence of a minyan, a quorum of ten adult Jews. And so Jews who might never otherwise set foot in a synagogue will find their way to a Jewish congregation—without regard to its denomination—when it is time to say kaddish.[3] American Jews traveling in foreign countries may seek out local synagogues to say kaddish, knowing that every Jewish congregation on the planet treats mourners with great deference.

Saying kaddish for a parent may well be American Judaism's most honored custom; certainly it is one of the most familiar of its prayers. The same is probably true for Jews in other countries. Indeed, the weekday worship services of most synagogues are populated by people saying kaddish for their parents. The practice implies a bond of honor reaching back through time from generation to generation.

Another religious practice, nearly universal among American Jews, underscores the importance Judaism places on the memory of forebears: the custom of giving "Jewish" names to children in addition to their regular names. Most often these are Hebrew names, though sometimes they are Yiddish[4]. Occasionally they are corruptions of misremembered Yiddish dialectical variations of Hebrew names. Hebrew names are used on marriage certificates and on grave markers; they are used in Hebrew memorial prayers and when formally announcing the *aliyah* in synagogue to call someone to participate in the Torah reading. Names from the Hebrew Bible are the most common religious names for American Jews. It is the custom among Jews of eastern European decent (the vast majority of American Jews) to choose a Hebrew name for a child that recalls a deceased relative, typically a great-grandparent. Presumably, the great-grandparent was named for his or her great-grandparent, and so on in a chain extending back through the generations to the first "David" or the first "Sarah." Some American Jews never have occasion to use their Hebrew names, and a few may not even remember what they are. But most American Jews—whether practicing Judaism or not—have a second, religious name in honor of a family member they never knew and, in theory, a direct ancestor from the beginnings of the Jewish people. Like saying kaddish for parents, giving Hebrew names to children is a sign of the sacredness of Judaism's ancestors.

Thoughts about ancestors lead to thoughts about descendants and to the expectation that future generations will maintain the chain of tradition. While it is not true that American Jews are vanishing, it is true that they are keenly dedicated to the survival of Jewish identity. It is precisely this fervor that makes Jews so vulnerable to alarmist theories about disappearance. Their passion for survival is fueled by their desire to preserve the memory of generations that have passed.

Another reason why Jews in America are so vigilant about their fate and so ready to accept the myth of disappearance is that Judaism has no definitive concept of individual life after death. Some Jews may believe that the soul somehow survives the death of the body, but many believe the opposite: that people's individual consciousness ends when they die; that their awareness of themselves, their personality, their ability to act in the world, their communication with living beings—everything that constitutes daily existence—ceases. Even according to the traditional Jewish belief in *michayei hameitim* (revival of the dead), a person does not immediately go to another world after leaving this one. During the future messianic age, when the world will be made perfect, the dead will come back to life; but until that time, they do not participate in the workings of the universe.[5]

As individuals, modern Jews may entertain different notions about life after death, but as a group, they generally have not been taught to expect that upon death some part of their being will continue to exist. Whatever their individual beliefs, however, the fact is that modern American Jews do not conduct themselves as if this life were merely the preparation for next. In the realm of behavior and morality, Judaism places its emphasis firmly in this life, in this world. All human actions must be directed toward the perfection of human society and collective life on earth.

Other religions do teach that the individual's personality and self-awareness—what some call the soul—survives death. They believe that some aspect of the individual remains conscious forever in a realm beyond this world. Some religions teach that people's life force survives, though not their consciousness or their personality. When a person dies, their life force either becomes part of a new living being or simply merges with the universe. And certain cultures teach that individual life and death are an illusion, that all consciousness is part of the unity of existence.

Such beliefs about immortality are palliative. They relieve the basic human anxiety about death. Judaism provides no such psychological balm to its adherents. Modern Jews are free to speculate about the nature of existence, but modern American Judaism in effect accepts the finality of death. The inevitability of death is a sobering—and potentially immobilizing—thought. Judaism responds to the existential angst by shifting the emphasis from the mortality of the individual to the collective immortality of the Jewish people. What it does offer is the idea that Judaism has existed since the beginning of human civilization and will endure as long as people live on earth. The antiquity of Judaism implies its eternity as well. By being part of the Jewish people, individual Jews participate in the timelessness of Jewish civilization. Everlasting Jewish identity is the life after death that Judaism provides. The perpetuation of Judaism promises that the memory of every Jew will be revered.

People who subscribe to belief systems that emphasize life after death are concerned with how their actions in this world will affect their status in the next world. For example, will they merit eternal life? Will they be reincarnated or not, and how will they be reincarnated? Or where will they go after death, to Heaven or to Hell? The question for Jews is how to conduct their lives in this world so that Jewish identity is perpetuated. It gives rise to what appears to be a circular proposition: continue to practice Judaism in order that Judaism will continue to be practiced. The actual message is this: Keep Jewish identity alive so that you will have life after death.

The theme of keeping Judaism alive is often expressed in terms of numbers. Jews are insecure about their status in America and concerned lest they become too small a minority to protect themselves. That protection is twofold. Jews want to have sufficient power as an organized community to defend their separateness from the encroachments of the majority. At the same time, they are aware that by being separate, they risk being a target of prejudice. So they monitor the Jewish population not just by its absolute numbers but by its growth relative to other groups. However, self-interest is not the only reason Jews seek influence in America. They also want to have a voice in the world, an impact on society. Dreading oblivion and embracing life are two faces of a single coin. The notion of leaving the world a better place may be a platitude, but it is highly motivating for Jews today. Enduring influence is the other form of life after death the Jewish people offer its members.

It is a basic concept of American Judaism that the individual achieves immortality through membership with an eternal people. Whether understood as an explicit philosophical formulation or merely assumed as a part of general cultural outlook, the belief has a tangible effect on how many Jews live their lives. Individuals who are strongly self-identified as Jews observe no absolute boundary between the fate of each Jew and the fate of the Jewish people. Because the memory of the ancestors is sacred above all things, every Jew's individual identity is subsumed within the identity of the Jews as a civilization, and Jews can continue to exist as a civilization only if Jewish identity is preserved throughout future generations. This is why the survival of Judaism assumes the immediacy of a life-or-death struggle and why the Jewish community constantly monitors its vital signs for the slightest indication of trouble. With so much at stake, false alarms about disappearance are inevitable, and the myth of Jewish disappearance is quickly believed.

THE OLD WORLD AND THE NEW

It is no surprise that the myth of the shtetl is also part of American Judaism's veneration for its forbears. While only a relatively small percentage of the millions of Eastern European Jews actually lived in little Jewish towns, the bearded fathers and kerchiefed mothers that populate shtetl literature are icons for the entire immigrant generation. The shtetl is the psychological process by which American

Jewry's real grandparents and great-grandparents are transported back to the venerated Old World and the imagined realm of unadulterated Jewish life. Although the shtetl is as much a literary genre as a fact, it has the power to bestow sanctity upon the memory of millions of Jews who came to America at the beginning of the twentieth century, along with the memory of the millions who died in the Holocaust.

The myth of the shtetl may be a twentieth-century creation, but it also reveals the modern Jew's conception of what an ideal world would be like. When Jews imagine utopia, they think of an earthly society where ordinary people treat each other with love and respect as they go about their daily lives. The shtetl is a projection of important Jewish social values, and fictional or not, the ideals it represents are a very real part of Judaism's outlook on life today.

There has been a range of utopian beliefs throughout the history of religion, and Judaism itself has considered different concepts. Some systems teach that the world—or human society—started out perfect and then declined. In the story of the Garden of Eden, for example, life at first is idyllic and harmonious. When human corruption disrupts that harmony, life becomes painful and chaotic. From this perspective, utopia means restoring the world to its original state of perfection. Some religious philosophies teach that the perfect life exists in another world altogether and that some people will enter that paradise after they die. Other religions also believe that utopia already exists in some other place; by some means or another, a particular class of people can escape this world and be transported to the other one without dying. Certain philosophical systems assume that the external world can never be perfect. Instead, the goal is perfection of the inner life. The purpose of life is to retreat from the physical world and create perfection within the mind. A classical Jewish view—one shared by many Christians—is the belief in the messianic age: Utopia will occur in the future, when God will suspend the laws of nature and transform this world into paradise.

Modern American Judaism is also messianic, but with an important difference: God did not create a world that is perfect, but rather a world that can be made perfect. By cooperating, human beings can use the means already at their disposal to transform this world into a utopia—the Hebrew term is *tikkun olam*, perfecting the world. According to this concept, utopia is earthly; its scale is human. The shtetl is one way of imagining it.

Because the fictionalized shtetl serves as a concrete model of a just and caring society, it is inspiring to Jews. Because it offers a microcosm of the Jews as a nation, it is also didactic. The shtetl is a prescription for a world where religious beliefs and practices, universal social ideals and cultural details of ethnicity all harmonize. Deeply-held Jewish values—venerating the ancestors, transmitting ethnic identity from generation to generation, human reason, social justice, knowledge—these ideals populate the stage of the shtetl along with the stereotypical scenes and stock characters. In the stories that are reenacted there day after day, all the pieces of Judaism as civilization fit together.

For this reason alone, the myth of the shtetl is especially appealing to Jewish educators who want to encourage their students to lead totally Jewish lives as they go about their daily business in America today. Because of its cultural familiarity and its manageable scale, the sentimentalized world of the shtetl provides an effective classroom model of the ideal Jewish community. The myth of the shtetl appeals to educators not only because it is a diorama of a familiar culture frozen in time, but also because it is a miniature that can be taken in by a sweep of the eyes. This may explain the tendency in shtetl literature to portray the Jewish towns as much smaller than they actually were. The romanticized image of shtetl life may be a fiction, but the Jewish dream of a harmonious society is very real.

The highly sentimentalized picture of shtetl life provides an image of their ancestors that American Jews find comfortably recognizable. The Jews of earlier ages, however, would barely be recognizable at all today, so different was the world of ancient Canaan or even the society of Judea during the period of the Talmud. As mentioned, at one time Jews believed in supernatural realms and resorted to magic, but today they depend on reason to understand life on earth. There is no history of any great schism within Judaism about the nature of truth; there was no day when Satan and Heaven and Hell were officially renounced. Over time, Jews simply shifted from sorcery to science as the best method to figure out how the world works.

Yet American rabbis and scholars have suppressed a great deal of information about ancient Jewish society. They are embarrassed by their ancestors' belief in magic and divination, and they simply do not trust the public to sort out for themselves Jewish theories about the afterlife or the forces of evil. American Jews are complicit in this sanitizing of Jewish history. The myth that the Jews of ancient times were as rational and scientific as people today creates the impression of ancestors whose thinking is similar to that of modern American Jews. It is easier to revere ancient sages who spent their days discussing moral values and principles of Jewish law than ancestors who routinely pronounced incantations to ward off witchcraft. The myth that Judaism was founded by rational people helps to preserve the sacredness of Judaism's ancestors.

THE JEWISH COMMUNITY

As I have explained, the denominations are twentieth-century creations. As much as they claim to be the evolved form of Old World Judaism, the fact is that they are institutions copied from modern Christian practice. At the same time, denominational Judaism meets an important historical need of Jews: their desire to live within their own organized society. Denominational Judaism reflects the fact that the Jewish people see themselves as a nation. Nations have territories, capitals, armies. The Jewish people had all these at one time, and the modern State of Israel has them now. The Jews of the Diaspora, on the other hand, possessed none of these physical symbols of nationhood. Of course, they enjoyed many of the riches of a great civilization: literature, law, music, art, language, history and religion. But they had neither palaces nor kings because they had no country of their own. So when the denominations invented themselves as the shadow government of American Jewry, they filled a thousand-year-old longing for national legitimacy. When the denominations were founded, the concept of a restored Jewish homeland in the ancestral territory was little more than a tentative hope. In its stead, each denomination offered American Jews the opportunity to belong to an organized civic body: central and regional offices, laws and regulations, taxes and benefits, flags and insignia, national heads and world ambassadors, prestige and power. Even though in reality denominational Judaism was as green as the immigrants themselves, the idea of a national Jewish establishment was very appealing.

Each of the denominations promised the immigrant generation that tradition would be preserved and reassured them that the innovations of American Judaism were necessary to keep Judaism alive. The Jewish community quickly accepted the myth of denominational authority a hundred years ago, and continues to accept it, because its institutions are strong and enduring. American Judaism trusts the power and their stability of its denominational structure to safeguard its most sacred possession: the memory of its ancestors.

To the extent that we are the representatives of denominational Judaism, the ministers of congregations and the celebrants of Jewish ceremonies, the American rabbinate is a product of the twentieth century. Modern American rabbis also serve as exemplars of the Jewish people's love of ancient learning. Like the rabbis of other countries and other eras, our leadership within the Jewish community derives from our expertise, our power to receive and transmit the knowledge of Jewish civilization. Whether our claims of ancestral authority are justified in the light of history or not, rabbis represent the connection to Judaism's founding sages. We are respected because the Jewish people revere the ancient knowledge we possess. In some religions, clerics have power because they represent channels to God. The myth of rabbinic authority, in contrast, is very powerful because rabbis represent channels to what American Judaism holds most sacred: its ancestors.

The power of the rabbis and the authority of the denominations play a different role when it comes to questions of marriage. It may seem like a tautology that when a Jew marries another Jew, the couple and their children—at least in theory—share the same ancestors. To the extent that it is a civilization dedicated to the veneration of its own bloodline, American Judaism depends on in-marriage. Once a Jew marries outside the community, however, there are two sets of ancestors. The gentile spouse may convert to Judaism, but his or her forbears remain gentile. The perpetual link from Jewish ancestor to Jewish descendent is disrupted by the introduction of a second ancestry. While intermarriage does not threaten the survival of Judaism as a *formal* religion any more than it reduces the Jewish population, it is unsettling to the Jewish community because it threatens the *informal* religion of American Jews: ancestor veneration.

Intermarriage is blamed for the imagined declining Jewish population because Judaism depends on in-marriage exclusively to maintain its numbers while other religious systems actively bring new members into their communities through proselytizing. If American Jews were to engage in missionary work to increase their numbers, intermarriage would not seem to be such a threat. But the fact is that even though Jewish law allows for the conversion of non-Jews, the Jewish community has a strong distaste for proselytizing of any kind. Jewish civilization reproduces itself by transmitting identity from generation to generation. For Jews, no other way seems natural. There are Jewish missionary organizations today, such as Chabad, but they focus on bringing marginal Jews more firmly into the fold.

Despite fears about a declining Jewish population in America, and a concomitant loss of Jewish influence on American public policy, no major Jewish organization has tried to increase the number of Jews in America by aggressively seeking converts. Even though a well-organized national conversion campaign would guarantee both increased membership for the denominations and increased influence for the secular organizations, American Judaism continues to look toward in-marriage to preserve its civilization. Intermarriage simply does not fit in with Judaism's traditional strategy for survival.

The alternative—seeking converts to Judaism—is not appealing because conversion does not mean exactly the same thing within Judaism as in other religious systems. In many ways conversion to Judaism resembles adoption. Preparation programs typically place more emphasis on becoming part of the Jewish people—and being familiar with its customs and ceremonies—than they do on teaching Jewish philosophical concepts. Judaism is not as much a religion as it is a civilization, and people do not convert to a civilization; rather, they become naturalized citizens of the Jewish nation. They accept the Jewish people's ancestors as their own. It may be appropriate for religious systems that are based on ideology to seek converts; it does not seem appropriate to Jews to seek adoptees, and indeed American Judaism resists doing so.

Almost all gentiles who do convert to Judaism already have some familial connection to the Jewish people, typically a fiancé or fiancée. The conversion ceremony always concludes with the bestowal of a Hebrew name on the new member of the Jewish people. When used in Jewish ritual life, Hebrew names have two parts: the person's own name, followed by the Hebrew name of their parent or parents. By tradition, all converts to Judaism become the sons and daughters the *first* Jewish parents, Abraham and Sarah. In this way, they are adopted by the Jewish people and share in preserving the sacredness if its ancestors.

Jews who intermarry are paying a price for Judaism's discomfort with proselytizing. If the denominations devoted as much of their organizational skills and spiritual resources to an aggressive missionary campaign as they now do to combating the threat of intermarriage, their fears about the survival of Judaism in America would vanish as the Jewish population soared. And Jews who marry gentiles would become important allies in that process of Jewish growth.

THE TWENTIETH CENTURY
AND THE TWENTY-FIRST

The first half of the twentieth century was the most transforming period in the entire history of the Jewish people. The migration of Eastern European Jewry to the New World, the creation of denominational Judaism and the integration of the Jewish people into America society—these are phases of a metamorphosis that unfolded within a mere two generations. The transmutation that began with World War II is still unfolding. It too has three phases: the Holocaust, the State of Israel and the Six-Day War.

There have been massacres and exiles throughout Jewish history, but nothing like what the Jewish people experienced in the middle of the twentieth century. When much of the population of Judea was exiled to Babylonia in 586 BCE, they managed to keep their Jewish identity alive and even created new and enduring ways to practice their religion. When the Jews were expelled from Spain in 1492, they found refuge in Holland and the New World. Thousands of Jews were massacred in the Middle Ages, and Jewish towns were devastated during the pogroms, but the extermination of 6 million people during World War II simply because they were Jews was unfathomable. The horrifying photographs of the victims of the Holocaust—those who were murdered and those who survived—formed a new and indelible image of twentieth-century Jews. These were not the faces of the grandparents in the old family photographs from Eastern Europe. These were not the faces of the patriarchs in the Hebrew school textbooks. These were Jewish faces no one had ever seen before. These were the Six Million. The sheer incomprehensibility of the numbers and the depth of the psychological trauma such an atrocity carves into the souls of the survivors changed how the Jewish people would see themselves. Even in the safety of America, the Holocaust changed the meaning of Jewish identity.

As much as the Holocaust altered how Jews viewed themselves during the generation following World War II, the founding of the State of Israel in 1947 also profoundly affected Jewish consciousness by reawakening the awareness of the Jews as a nation with a historical homeland. Although the archeological evidence from ancient times is sparse, it is likely that the kingdom of Judea was conquered by the Babylonian empire in the sixth century BCE. A second monarchy was formed fifty years later and lasted—tenuously—for another five hundred years until it was finally destroyed by the Roman empire. The establishment in 1947 of a third Jewish state as a modern democracy located in the ancestral homeland was an amazing event, barely imaginable during the preceding two-thousand-year Diaspora. In the year 71, the Roman emperor Vespasian commemorated his conquest of Judea by striking a bronze coin "Iudaea Capta." In 1958, the modern State of Israel struck a new coin with "Iudaea Capta" on one side and "Israel Liberata" on the other. The end of the Jewish state and the beginning of the Jewish state, the beginning of the Diaspora and the end of the Diaspora—at the turn of a coin.

Twenty years after the founding of the new Jewish state, the Six-Day War added a completely new dimension to the self-concept of the Jews around the world. Israel's stunning victory over the combined Arab military forces in 1967 created something the Jewish community had never experienced: a Jewish state as a force to be reckoned with. Except for brief periods, the ancient Jewish state of Judea had been a small and militarily weak country surrounded by large and powerful and aggressive empires. Suddenly, in less than a week's time, the world became aware of Jewish muscle. The Jewish homeland had asserted itself into history as a world power. The establishment of the Jewish state reversed the image of the Jew as alien. The Six-Day War reversed the image of the Jew as victim.

American Judaism has not been shaped by historical cataclysms alone. Ongoing social forces have influenced it as well. Concerns about intermarriage and assimilation have preoccupied the American Jewish community since the middle of the twentieth century. Gender issues have challenged the religious community in America—both Jewish and gentile—for a long time. Since their inception, the progressive movements have had to address the role of women in religious life. The arc of this philosophical process was not completed until nearly the end of the twentieth century, when the Conservative movement finally allowed women to become rabbis. Issues of gender continue to challenge American Judaism in the twenty-first century as the denominations grapple with the inclusion of sexual minorities and the acceptance of same-gender relationships.

The individuals who invented American Judaism at the beginning of the twentieth century could not have foreseen the dramatic events that would alter Jewish life within fifty years. They certainly could not have predicted what American Judaism would look like by the end of the century. As tempting as it may be now to speculate about the social forces that will shape American Judaism as it moves forward in the years ahead, it makes no sense to do so. For one thing is sure: When the twenty-first century comes to a close, American Judaism will be very different from what it is today.

EPILOGUE

If I have pulled back slightly the curtain that protects organized Jewish religion in America from the scrutiny of the skeptical mind, then I have done no more than reveal what is already known to exist. We all have our myths. The line that separates fiction from fact is itself an illusion.

In the end, there is only one myth that contains no truth: the myth that there are no myths.

Appendix

JUDAISM'S SACRED TEXTS

The core of Jewish sacred literature is the Torah, the first five books of the Bible: Genesis, Exodus, Leviticus, Numbers and Deuteronomy. Also called the Law or the Pentateuch, the Torah contains the commandments and forms the basis of Jewish law. In Judaism, the Bible means the books of the Old Testament, which Jews refer to as the Hebrew Bible or as the Tanakh. Although the other sections of the Hebrew Bible are considered sacred, the commandments are found only in the Bible.

After the biblical canon comes a large body of rabbinic material. Because the rabbinic literature originally was developed through discussions in academies, it is sometimes referred to as the oral Torah. There are two classes of rabbinic writings: legal and allegorical. The Talmud, consisting of the Mishnah and the Gemmarah, is the encyclopedic compilation of discussions that took place in rabbinic academies from about a century before the year 1 until the 500s. There are two editions of the Talmud, the Babylonian and the Jerusalem. Because it is more extensive than the Jerusalem version, the Babylonian Talmud is considered to be authoritative. Although the Jerusalem edition is of occasional interest to textual scholars for purposes of comparison, most people study the Babylonian Talmud.

The material in the Talmud consists mostly of legal discussions and therefore is considered authoritative in Jewish law, but there is a great deal of allegorical material as well. The Midrash is an encyclopedic compilation of rabbinic interpretations of the Hebrew Bible. Although its content is mostly allegorical, it does refer to matters concerning Jewish law. There are numerous other works from the later rabbinic period, both legal and allegorical. The Talmud and Midrash were written in a combination of Hebrew and Aramaic.

Later generations of scholars extracted the legal decisions from the rabbinic discourses of the Talmud and organized them by topic. Maimonides' Mishneh Torah, compiled in the 1100s, was one of the first of these codes of Jewish law. The most authoritative code of Jewish law is the Shulchan Aruch. Compiled in the 1500s, it is the basis of Orthodox Judaism.

NOTES

CHAPTER 1—INVENTING
JUDAISM IN AMERICA

1. *American Jewish Yearbook*, vol. 1 (New York: American Jewish Committee, 1899), 283–285.
2. *American Jewish Yearbook*, vol. 101, 533–569.
3. Cited in Neil Gillman, *Conservative Judaism* (New York: Behrman House, 1993), 48.

CHAPTER 2—HISTORY,
CONTINUITY AND PERSPECTIVE

1. Milton Steinberg, *Basic Judaism* (San Diego: Harvest/HBJ, 1975), 4.
2. See www.uscj.org/intmar/shouldi.html.
3. See www.aish.com/shabbatthemes/candlelighting.
4. Morris Kertzer, *What Is a Jew?* (New York: Touchstone, 1996), xviii.
5. See www.judaism.about.com/mbiopage.htm.
6. From their Web site, the Office of Chaplains and Religious Life, www.brown.edu/Administration/Chaplains/Communities/Descriptions/judaism.html.
7. See www.bbc.co.uk/worldservice/people/features/world_religions/judaism_core.shtml.
8. Rebecca Alpert and Jacob J. Staub, *Exploring Judaism* (Elkins Park, PA: Reconstructionist Press, 2000), 23–24.
9. Gunter W. Plaut, *The Rise of Reform Judaism* (New York: World Union for Progressive Judaism, 1963), 95.
10. Arthur Green, *Seek My Face, Speak My Name* (Northvale, NJ: Jason Aronson, 1992), 166.

11. See www.myjewishlearning.com/daily_life/Prayer/Ritual_Garb/Tallit.htm.
12. Paul Johnson, *A History of the Jews* (New York: Harper & Row, 1987), 83.
13. Ibid.
14. *Jewish Encyclopedia* vol. 10 (New York: Funk and Wagnalls, 1902), 171.
15. The original work by Joseph Karo applied to the Sephardic Jews; it was adapted for the Ashkenazic community by Moses Isserles.
16. The Greek equivalent appears in the Apocryphal Book of Maccabees and in the New Testament books of Galatians and Acts.
17. *Declaration of Principles* (Pittsburgh: Central Conference of American Rabbis, 1885).
18. *The Guiding Principles of Reform Judaism* (Columbus, OH: Central Conference of American Rabbis,1937).
19. *Emet Ve-emunah: Statement of Principles of Conservative Judaism* (The Jewish Theological Seminary of America, The Rabbinical Assembly of America, United Synagogue of America, Women's League for Conservative Judaism, and Federation of Jewish Men's Clubs, 1988), 39.
20. Cited in Johnson, *History of the Jews*, 108–109.
21. *A Statement of Principles for Reform Judaism* (Pittsburgh: Central Conference of American Rabbis, 1999).
22. See the Reconstructionist movement Web site at www.jrf.org.
23. Johnson, *History of the Jews*, 83.
24. Bernard J. Bamberger, *The Story of Judaism* (New York: Schocken Books, 1970), 6.

CHAPTER 3—FATE, SURVIVAL AND CONFIDENCE

1. *The National Jewish Population Survey 2000–2001* (New York: United Jewish Communities, 2003), 7.
2. See Ephraim Buchwald, Jewish Intermarriage Statistics at www.lilithgallery.com.
3. Thomas B. Morgan, "The Vanishing American Jew," *Look*, May 5, 1964, 42.
4. *The Future of the Jewish Community in America: Essays prepared for a Task Force on the Future of the Jewish Community in America of the American Jewish Committee* (New York: Basic Books, 1973), 150.

5. *American Jewish Yearbook*, vols. 1–72 (New York: American Jewish Committee, 1899–1972).
6. Richard Siegel, Michael Strassfeld and Sharon Strassfeld, eds. *The Jewish Catalog* (Philadelphia: The Jewish Publication Society of America, 1973).
7. Sales figures according to the Jewish Publication Society, which is also the major publisher of English editions of the Jewish Bible.
8. *A Centenary Perspective* (San Francisco: Central Conference of American Rabbis, 1976). See www.ccarnet.org/documentsand-positions/platforms.
9. *American Jewish Yearbook*, vols. 73–101.
10. Although Dershowitz briefly refers to the *Look* magazine article in a footnote, he does say not say anything about the fact that his book has the same title.
11. Alan M. Dershowitz, *The Vanishing American Jew* (Boston: Little, Brown and Company, 1997), 1–2, 24.
12. Paul Johnson, *A History of the Jews* (New York: Harper & Row, 1987), 365.
13. Solomon Schechter, *Seminary Addresses and Other Papers* (New York: Burning Bush Press, 1959), 94.
14. Ibid., 95–96.
15. Former Jewish Theological Seminary dean Louis Finkelstein, cited in Gillman, *Conservative Judaism*, 64.
16. Dershowitz, *The Vanishing American Jew*, 70.
17. See the NFTY Web site at www.nfty.org.
18. All three documents can be found at www.ccarnet.org/documents-andpositions/platforms.
19. See the Union for Reform Judaism Web site at www.urj.org.
20. Joel Lurie Grishaver, *40 Things You Can Do to Save the Jewish People* (Northvale, NJ: Jason Aronson, 1993).
21. See statistics at www.jewishdatabank.org.
22. *National Jewish Population Survey 2000–2001*, viii.
23. Ibid., 2, 31.
24. J. J. Goldberg, "A Jewish Recount," *New York Times*, September 17, 2003.
25. *American Jewish Year Book*, vol. 91.
26. Ibid., vols. 101–106.
27. Elliot Abrams, *Faith or Fear* (New York: The Free Press, 1997), 1–2.
28. Ibid., 7.
29. Charles Krautheimer, *Washington Post*, May 5, 2006.

30. *National Jewish Population Survey 2000–2001*, 10, 27.
31. Ibid., 26.
32. Abrams, *Faith or Fear*, 184–185.
33. See www.sephardicstudies.org/komunita.html.
34. See www.jewishencyclopedia.com.
35. See www.kodesh.snunit.k12.il.
36. Herbert Rosenblum, *Conservative Judaism* (New York: United Synagogue of America, 1983), 136.

CHAPTER 4—AUTHENTICITY, SENTIMENT AND SOPHISTICATION

1. Ted Falcon, *Judaism for Dummies* (New York: Hungry Minds, Inc., 2001), 170.
2. Ibid., 341.
3. Abraham Joshua Heschel, *The Earth Is the Lord's: The Inner World of the Jew in Eastern Europe* (Woodstock, VT: Jewish Lights Publishing, 1949), 10, 97.
4. Ibid., 89, 92, 97, 101.
5. Ibid., 17, 44, 47–48.
6. Ibid., 15–16, 67–68, 89–90, 93.
7. Ibid., 47.
8. Jonathan D. Sarna, *American Judaism* (New Haven, CT: Yale University Press, 2004), 295.
9. Mark Zborowski and Elizabeth Herzog, *Life Is with People: The Jewish Little-Town of Eastern Europe* (New York: International Universities Press, 1952).
10. Online book services such as Amazon and Questia can be searched for occurrences of a book title within other works.
11. Zborowski and Herzog, *Life Is with People*, 25.
12. Ibid., 38.
13. Ibid., 291.
14. Ibid., 293–294.
15. Ibid., 297.
16. Ibid., 310.
17. Ibid., 271.
18. Benjamin Blech, *Complete Idiot's Guide to Understanding Judaism* (New York: Alpha Books, 2004), 249.
19. Ibid., 102.
20. *Jewish Encyclopedia*, vol. 10 (New York: Funk and Wagnalls, 1902), 50–51; S.M. Dubnow, *History of the Jews in Russia and Poland, from*

the Earliest Times until the Present Day, trans. I. Friedlaender, vol. 2 (Philadelphia: Jewish Publication Society of America, 1918), 372.

21. *Jewish Encyclopedia*, vol. 8 (New York: Funk and Wagnalls, 1902), 201.
22. *Jewish Encyclopedia*, vol. 3, 355.
23. Zborowski and Herzog, *Life Is with People*, 25, 144.
24. Ibid., 160–161.
25. Dubnow, *History of the Jews*, 112–113.
26. Ben-Cion Pinchuk, "How Jewish Was the Shtetl," in *Polin Volume Seventeen, The Shtetl: Myth and Reality*, ed. Anthony Polonsky (Oxford: Littman Library of Jewish Civilization, 2005), 118.
27. *Emet Ve-emunah: Statement of Principles of Conservative Judaism* (New York: The Jewish Theological Seminary of America, 1988), 56.
28. Hayim Halevy Donin, *To Be a Jew* (New York: Basic Books, 1972), 4.
29. Susan A. Glenn, *Daughters of the Shtetl* (Ithaca, NY: Cornell University Press, 1991), 261.
30. Isaac Metzker, *A Bintal Brief* (New York: Schocken, 1990), 68.

CHAPTER 5—IDENTITY, REASON AND SELF-ACCEPTANCE

1. Paul Johnson, *A History of the Jews* (New York: Harper & Row, 1987), 337.
2. Joseph Telushkin, *Jewish Literacy* (New York: HarperCollins, 2001), 603.
3. Morris Kertzer, *What Is a Jew?* (New York: Touchstone, 1996), 117.
4. The Central Conference of American Rabbis, *Declaration of Principles* (Pittsburgh, 1885).
5. Morris Adler, *The World of the Talmud*, 2nd ed. (New York: Schocken Books, 1963), 22.
6. Hayim Halevy Donin, *To Be a Jew: A Guide to Jewish Observance in Contemporary Life* (New York: Basic Books, 1972), 333.
7. Alfred J. Kolatch, *The Jewish Book of Why* (Middle Village, NY: Jonathan David Publishers, 2004), 72.
8. Ted Falcon and David Blatner, *Judaism for Dummies* (New York: Hungry Minds, Inc., 2001), 28.
9. Neil Gillman, *The Death of Death: Resurrection and Immortality in Jewish Thought* (Woodstock, VT: Jewish Lights Publishing, 1997).

10. *Siddur Sim Shalom: A Prayerbook for Shabbat, Festivals, and Weekdays*, ed. Jules Harlow (New York: The Rabbinical Assembly, The United Synagogue of America, 1985), 522.
11. Maurice Lamm, *The Jewish Way in Death and Mourning* (New York: Jonathan David Publishers, 1969), 226.
12. Louis Ginzberg, *Legends of the Jews* (New York: Jewish Publication Society, 2003), 13.
13. Ibid., 503–506.
14. Dennis Prager and Joseph Telushkin, *Nine Questions People Ask About Judaism* (New York: Simon & Schuster, Inc, 1981), 81.
15. Hayim Halevy Donin, *To Pray as a Jew: A Guide to the Prayer Book and the Synagogue Service* (New York: Basic Books, 1980), 164.
16. *Siddur Sim Shalom*, 293.
17. Kaufman Kohler, *Jewish Theology: Systematically and Historically Considered* (New York: MacMillan, 1918), 190; Louis Jacobs, *The Jewish Religion: A Companion* (Oxford: Oxford University Press, 1995), 116; Abraham Cohen, *Everyman's Talmud* (New York: Schocken Books, 1995), 54.
18. Scholars are not certain of the exact meaning of these phrases. It is possible that they mean that the woman's reproductive organs will not function properly.
19. Richard Elliot Friedman, *Commentary on the Torah* (San Francisco: Harper, 2001), 437.
20. Gunther W. Plaut, ed., *The Torah: A Modern Commentary* (New York: Union of American Hebrew Congregation, 1981), 1054–1055.
21. Joshua Trachtenberg, *Jewish Magic and Superstition* (Philadelphia: University of Pennsylvania Press, 2004), 219–222.
22. Paul Johnson, *A History of the Jews*, 265.

CHAPTER 6—DENOMINATIONS, AUTHORITY AND INDEPENDENCE

1. See the Web sites www.shj.org and www.aleph.org.
2. See www.am-kolel.org/html_site/partners.htm.
3. See www.havurah.org/directory/.
4. National Jewish Population Survey 2000–1 Questionnaire (New York: Audits and Surveys Worldwide, 2002), 45.
5. NJPS 2000–1 (New York: United Jewish Communities, 2003), 7.
6. It is estimated that there are 5 to 6 million Jews in America. If 46 percent are affiliated, then 5 percent of the affiliated Jews amount to 115,000–138,000.

7. Mordecai Waxman, "The Ideology of the Conservative Movement," *Sectors of American Judaism: Reform, Orthodoxy, Conservatism, and Reconstructionism,* ed. Jacob Neusner (New York: KTAV Publishing House, 1975), 249.

8. Jonathan D. Sarna, *American Judaism* (New Haven, CT: Yale University Press, 2004), 185–186.

9. Ibid., 246–247.

10. The fact that the Reform and Conservative women's groups modified their names in exactly the same fashion indicates the extent to which the movements follow parallel paths.

11. *A Centenary Perspective* (San Francisco: The Central Conference of American Rabbis, 1976).

12. Quoted in Herbert Rosenblum, *Conservative Judaism: A Contemporary History* (New York: United Synagogue of America, 1983), 26.

13. Rebecca Alpert and Jacob J. Staub, *Exploring Judaism* (Elkins Park, PA: Reconstructionist Press, 2000), 162.

14. Hayim Halevy Donin, *To Be a Jew* (New York: Basic Books, 1972), 186–188.

15. Rosenblum, *Conservative Judaism,* 103.

16. Gershon Cohen, "The Present State of Conservative Judaism," *Judaism* 26, no. 3 (Summer 1977), 272.

17. During Passover, special restrictions apply to grain products.

18. Haym Solovetchik, "Rupture and Reconstruction: The Transformation of Contemporary Orthodoxy," *Tradition* 28, no. 4 (Summer 1994).

19. One frequently used site is ucalgary.ca/~elsegal/Cantillation/Chanting.html. Webaissance.com/judaica/trope/torahtrope.htm provides MP3 files for the chants.

20. A recent search for "Judaica" on Amazon.com returned nearly fifty thousand entries. This daunting number makes it hard for a new reader to know where to begin. The educational organization Nextbook.com provides a sensible, up-to-date guide to contemporary Jewish literature.

CHAPTER 7—RABBIS, KNOWLEDGE AND SELF-RELIANCE

1. For a detailed analysis, see Stuart A. Cohen, *The Three Crowns* (Cambridge: Cambridge University Press, 1990).

2. Ibid., 67.

3. The Torah, however, is read facing the people.

4. As mentioned, prior to the opening of the Reconstructionist Rabbinical College in Philadelphia in 1970, Reconstructionism tended to be a subset of Conservative Judaism, and Reconstructionist rabbis typically were graduates of the Conservative movement's Jewish Theological Seminary in New York.

5. The practice of Jewish men wearing head coverings, which now symbolizes membership in the community of Israel, began with the custom of sages who covered their heads as a sign of their special piety.

6. Three particularly handy guides, *The Jewish Baby Handbook*, *The Bride and Groom Handbook* and *The Jewish Mourner's Handbook* are published by Behrman House of Springfield, NJ. They are available by calling 800–221–2755, or going to www.behrmanhouse.com. More complete information will be found in Anita Diamant's *The New Jewish Baby Book* (Woodstock, VT: Jewish Lights Publishing, 2005) and *The New Jewish Wedding* (New York: Fireside, 2001).

7. Out of compliance with state laws, clergy usually refrain from using the terms "marry" or "wed" when they perform ceremonies for same-gender couples.

CHAPTER 8—COMMUNITY, INTERMARRIAGE AND OPTIMISM

1. Jonathan Rosenblum, *Baltimore Jewish Times*, November 1, 2002, quoted in www.jewishmediaresources.org/article/528.

2. Jack Wertheimer, "Surrendering to Intermarriage," *Commentary*, vol. 111, issue 3 (2001): 25.

3. American Jewish Committee, "Jewish Continuity: Policy Statement and Action Plan," December 8, 1997. See www.ajc.org.

4. Stated on the Orthodox educational network Ohr Somayach; www.ohr.edu/ask_db/ask_main.php/191/Q1/.

5. Deuteronomy 7:3 does forbid Israelites from marrying one specific tribe: the Canaanites.

6. Because the Reform and Reconstructionist denominations do not consider rabbinic law to be fully binding on modern Jews, they also recognize the biblical policy of patrilineal descent. In practice, these branches of Judaism state that if either the mother *or* the father is Jewish, then the child is Jewish. The Conservative and Orthodox branches follow rabbinic law: The mother must be Jewish for the child to be considered Jewish at birth.

7. Solomon Grayzel, *A History of the Jews* (New York: Mentor, 1968), 267, 274, 481, 530.

8. Several examples can be found in *A Historical Atlas of the Jewish People*, ed. Eli Barnavi (New York: Schocken Books, 1992), 166, 182–183; *Pictorial History of the Jewish People*, ed. Nathan Ausubel (New York: Crown Publishers, 1953), 222, 223; and *Jewish Encyclopedia*, vol. 4 (New York: Funk and Wagnalls, 1902), 36.
9. *Jewish Encyclopedia*, vol. 6, 162.
10. Jonathan D. Sarna, *American Judaism* (New Haven, CT: Yale University Press, 2004), 222.
11. The National Jewish Population Survey 2000–2001 (New York: United Jewish Communities, 2003), 16–17.
12. Ibid.
13. Wertheimer, "Surrendering to Intermarriage."
14. The National Jewish Population Survey 2000–01, 4.
15. Ibid.
16. See United States Centers for Disease Control, www.cdc.gov/genomics/famhistory/o_cancer.htm.
17. See *The Internet Journal of Gastroenterology*, www.ispub.com/ostia.
18. See the Chicago Center for Jewish Genetic Disorders, www.jewishgeneticscenter.org.
19. National Jewish Population Survey 2000–2001, ix.
20. Ibid.
21. Ibid., 18.
22. National Jewish Population Survey Questionnaire, item 10.
23. National Jewish Population Survey 2000–2001, 2.
24. Ibid., 19.
25. Jews have no universal system for documenting Jewish identity; most rabbis simply accept someone's word.
26. National Jewish Population Survey 2000–2001, 27.

CHAPTER 9—
JUDAISM IN AMERICA TODAY

1. The words of kaddish originated in the ancient rabbinic academies. Typical of legal language, it consists of strings of synonyms: may God's Name be made great, be made sacred, be made blessed, be made majestic, be made beautiful, be made powerful, be made glorious, be made gracious, be made mighty, be made holy.
2. A memorial candle is lit for seven days after the funeral, and for one day on major holidays and on the anniversary of the death.
3. In traditional settings, where mourners remain at home for seven days after a death, the minyan is convened in the house.

4. Now that Hebrew is recognized as the international language of the Jewish people, it is the practice of most congregational schools to insist on Hebrew names rather than Yiddish ones. Most rabbis encourage parents to choose correct Hebrew names for their children.

5. The traditional belief that the bones of the dead will be restored to life during the messianic age is one of the reasons Jewish law forbids cremation.

BIBLIOGRAPHY

Abrams, Elliot. *Faith or Fear.* New York: The Free Press, 1997.

Adler, Morris. *The World of the Talmud,* 2nd ed. New York: Schocken Books, 1963.

Aharoni, Yohanan, and Michael Avi-Yonah. *The Macmillan Bible Atlas.* New York: The Macmillan Company, 1968.

Albright, W. F. *The Biblical Period From Abraham to Ezra.* New York: Harper & Row, 1963.

Allitt, Patrick. *Religion in America.* New York: Columbia University Press, 2003.

Alpert, Rebecca T., and Jacob J. Staub. *Exploring Judaism.* Elkins Park, PA: Reconstructionist Press, 2000.

Ammerman, Nancy. *Pillars of Faith.* Los Angeles: University of California Press, 2005.

Armstrong, Karen. *A History of God.* New York: Alfred A. Knopf, 1994.

Ausubel, Nathan. *Pictorial History of the Jewish People.* New York: Crown Publishers, 1953.

Bach, Alice, ed. *Women in the Hebrew Bible.* New York: Routledge, 1999.

Baeck, Leo. *Judaism and Christianity.* Philadelphia: Jewish Publication Society of America, 1960.

Bamberger, Bernard J. *The Story of Judaism.* New York: Schocken Books, 1970.

Barnavi, Eli ed. *A Historical Atlas of the Jewish People.* New York: Schocken Books, 1992.

Bauer, Yehuda. *Rethinking the Holocaust.* New Haven, CT: Yale University Press, 2001.

Beck, Aaron T. *Cognitive Therapy and the Emotional Disorders.* New York: Penguin Books, 1979.

———. *Love Is Never Enough.* New York: HarperPerennial, 1968.

———. *Depression.* Philadelphia: University of Pennsylvania Press, 1967.

Berger, Michael S. *Rabbinic Authority.* New York: Oxford University Press, 1998.

Berger, Milton, Joel S. Geffen and M. David Hoffman. *Roads to Jewish Survival*. New York: Bloch Publishing Company, 1967.

Berger, Peter L. *The Scared Canopy*. Garden City, NY: Anchor Books, 1969.

Berlinerblau, Jacques. *The Secular Bible*. New York: Cambridge University Press, 2005.

Berman, Rochel U. *Dignity Beyond Death*. Brooklyn: Urim Publishers, 2005.

Bickerman, Elias. *From Ezra to the Last of the Maccabees*. New York: Schocken, 1987.

Blech, Benjamin. *Complete Idiot's Guide to Jewish History*, 2nd ed. New York: Alpha Books, 2004.

———. *Complete Idiot's Guide to Understanding Judaism*. New York: Alpha Books, 2003.

Blecher, Arthur C. *A Teacher's Guide to Stories from Our Living Past*. New York: Behrman House, 1974.

———. *A Teacher's Guide to Jewish Biblical Exegesis*. New York: Behrman House, 1973.

———, and Francis Butwin. *The Jews of America: History and Sources*. New York: Behrman House, 1976.

Bloom, Jack H. *The Rabbi as Symbolic Exemplar*. Binghamton, NY: Haworth Press, 2002.

Bokser, Ben Zion, and Baruch M. Bokser, eds. *Selected Writings*. New York: Paulist Press, 1989.

Borowitz, Eugene B. *Renewing the Covenant: A Theology for the Postmodern Jew*. Philadelphia: Jewish Publication Society of America, 1991.

Bos, Pascale R. *German-Jewish Literature in the Wake of the Holocaust: Grete Weil, Ruth Klueger, and the Politics of Address*. New York: Palgrave Macmillan, 2005.

Breines, Paul. *Tough Jews: Political Fantasies and the Moral Dilemma of American Jewry*. New York: Basic Books, 1990.

Bright, John. *A History of Israel*. Louisville, KY: Westminster John Knox Press, 2000.

Buber, Martin. *On Judaism*. New York: Schocken Books, 1967.

Cahnman, Werner J. ed. *Intermarriage and Jewish Life*. New York: Herzel Press, 1963.

Caplan, Samuel, and Harold U. Ribalow. *The Great Jewish Books*. New York: Washington Square Press, 1963.

Ciarrocchi, Joseph W. *The Doubting Disease*. New York: Paulist Press, 1995.

Cohen, Abraham. *Everyman's Talmud: The Major Teachings of the Rabbinic Sages.* New York: Schocken Books, 1995.

Cohen, Hermann. *Religion of Reason.* Atlanta, GA: American Institute of Religion, 1994.

Cohen, Rich. *Tough Jews.* New York: Vintage Books, 1999.

Cohen, Shaye J. D. *The Beginnings of Jewishness.* Los Angeles: University of California Press, 1999.

Cohen, Stuart A. *The Three Crowns.* Cambridge: Cambridge University Press, 1990.

Cohn-Sherbok, Dan. *Fifty Key Jewish Thinkers.* London: Routledge, 1997.

Couliano, Elaide, Ioan P. and Mircea Eliade. *The Elaide Guide to World Religions.* San Francisco: HarperSanFrancisco, 1991.

Cowan, Paul, and Rachel Cowan. *Mixed Blessings.* New York: Penguin Books, 1987.

Danby, Herbert. *The Mishnah.* New York: Oxford University Press, 1933.

Davis, Moshe. *The Emergence of Conservative Judaism: The Historical School in 19th Century America.* Philadelphia: Jewish Publication Society of America, 1963.

Dawidowicz, Lucy S. *The Golden Tradition: Jewish Life and Thought in Eastern Europe.* Boston: Beacon Press, 1967.

Dershowitz, Alan M. *The Vanishing American Jew.* Boston: Little, Brown and Company, 1997.

De Veaux, Roland. *Ancient Israel: Religious Institutions.* New York: McGraw-Hill, 1965.

Diamant, Anita. *The New Jewish Baby Book: Names, Ceremonies, & Customs: A Guide for Today's Families.* Woodstock, VT: Jewish Lights Publishing, 2005.

———. *The New Jewish Wedding.* New York: Fireside, 2001.

———. *Saying Kaddish.* New York: Schocken Books, 1999.

Dillon, Michele. *Handbook of the Sociology of Religion.* New York: Cambridge University Press, 2003.

Diner, Hasia R., and Beryl Lieff Benderly. *Her Works Praise Her: A History of Jewish Women in America from Colonial Times to the Present.* New York: Basic Books, 2002.

Donin, Hayim Halevy. *To Pray as a Jew: A Guide to the Prayer Book and the Synagogue Service.* New York: Basic Books, 1980.

———. *To Be a Jew: A Guide to Jewish Observance in Contemporary Life.* New York: Basic Books, 1972.

Dorff, Elliot N. *The Unfolding Tradition.* New York: Aviv Press, 2005.

Dubnow, S. M. *History of the Jews in Russia and Poland, from the Earliest Times until the Present Day.* Trans. I. Friedlander. Philadelphia: Jewish Publication Society of America, 1918.

Edelman, Marsha Bryan. *Discovering Jewish Music.* Philadelphia: Jewish Publication Society of America, 2003.

Elazar, Daniel J. *Community and Polity: The Organizational Dynamics of American Jewry,* revised ed. Philadelphia: Jewish Publication Society of America, 1995.

Elbogen, Ismar. *Jewish Liturgy: A Comprehensive History.* New York: Jewish Publication Society of America, 1993.

Eliade, Mircea. *The Sacred and The Profane.* Fort Washington, PA: Harvest Books, 1968.

———. *Myth and Reality.* Prospect Heights: Waveland Press, 1963.

El-Or, Tamar. *Educated and Ignorant: Ultraorthodox Jewish Women and Their World.* Trans. Haim Watzman. Boulder, CO: Lynne Rienner Publishers, 1994.

Emet Ve-emunah: Statement of Principles of Conservative Judaism. New York: Jewish Theological Seminary of America, 1988.

Falcon, Ted, and David Blatner. *Judaism for Dummies.* New York: Hungry Minds, Inc., 2001.

Fine, Lawrence. *Judaism in Practice.* Princeton, NJ: Princeton University Press, 2001.

Finkelstein, Louis. *The Jews: Their History, Culture, and Religion.* Westport, CT: Greenwood Publishing, 1979.

———. *Pharisaism in the Making.* New York: KTAV Publishing House, 1972.

———. *The Jews: Their Role in Civilization.* New York: Schocken Books, 1971.

———. *The Pharisees.* New York: Jewish Publication Society of America, 1966.

Finkelstein, Norman G. *The Holocaust Industry: Reflections on the Exploitation of Jewish Suffering.* London: Verso, 2000.

Frankel, Ellen. *The Five Books of Miriam.* San Francisco: HarperSanFrancisco, 1996.

Frankel, Jonathan, ed. *Jews and Gender: The Challenge to Hierarchy.* New York: Oxford University Press, 2000.

Frankfort, Henri. *The Birth of Civilization in the Near East.* Garden City, NY: Doubleday Anchor Books, 1956.

Freedman, Samuel G. *Jew vs. Jew.* New York: Simon & Schuster, 2000.

Friedman, Edwin H. *Generation to Generation.* New York: Guilford Press, 1985.

Friedman, Rabbi Dayle A. *Jewish Pastoral Care*. Woodstock, VT: Jewish Lights Publishing, 2005.

Friedman, Richard Elliot. *Commentary on the Torah*. San Francisco: HarperSanFrancisco, 2001.

Friedman, Theodore, and Robert Gordis, eds. *Jewish Life in America*. New York: Horizon Press, 1955.

Fromm, Erich. *Psychoanalysis and Religion*. New York: Bantam Books, 1967.

———. *You Shall Be as Gods*. Greenwich, CT: Fawcett Publications, 1966.

Gabaccia, Donna. *From the Other Side: Women, Gender, and Immigrant Life in the U.S., 1820–1990*. Bloomington, IN: Indiana University Press, 1994.

Ganzfried, Shlomo. *Kitzur Schulchan Oruch*. Brooklyn: Moznaim Publishers Corporation, 1991.

Gaster, Theodor H. *The Holy and the Profane: Evolution of Jewish Folkways*. New York: William Sloane Associate Publishers, 1955.

———. *Festivals of the Jewish Year*. New York: William Sloane Associate Publishers, 1953.

Gay, Ruth. *The Jews of Germany*. New Haven, CT: Yale University Press, 1992.

Geffen, Rela M., ed. *Celebration & Renewal: Rites of Passage in Judaism*. Philadelphia: Jewish Publication Society of America, 1993.

Gilbert, Martin. *The Jews in the Twentieth Century*. New York: Schocken Books, 2001.

Gillman, Neil. *Conservative Judaism*. New York: Behrman House, 1993.

———. *The Death of Death*. Woodstock, NY: Jewish Lights Publishing, 2000.

———. *Sacred Fragments*. Philadelphia: Jewish Publication Society of America, 1990.

Ginzberg, Louis. *Legends of the Jews*. New York: Jewish Publication Society of America, 2003.

———. *Students, Scholars, and Saints*. New York: Meridian Books, 1958.

Glatzer, Nahum N. *Essays in Jewish Thought*. Tuscaloosa: University of Alabama Press, 1978.

———. *American Judaism*. Chicago: University of Chicago Press, 1972.

———. *The Judaic Tradition*. Boston: Beacon Press, 1969.

Glazer, Nathan. *American Judaism*. Chicago: University of Chicago Press, 1989.

Glenn, Susan A. *Daughters of the Shtetl*. Ithaca, NY: Cornell University Press, 1991.

Gold, Michael. *And Hannah Wept: Infertility, Adoption, and the Jewish Couple*. Philadelphia: Jewish Publication Society of America, 1988.

Goldberg, Harvey E., ed. *The Life of Judaism*. Berkeley: University of California Press, 2001.

Goldman, Ari. *Living a Year of Kaddish*. New York: Schocken Books, 2003.

Gottlieb, Lynn. *She Who Dwells Within*. New York: HarperCollins, 1995.

Grabbe, Lester L. *Judaic Religion in the Second Temple Period: Belief and Practice from the Exile to Yavneh*. London: Routledge, 2000.

Grayzel, Solomon. *A History of the Jews*. New York: Mentor, 1968.

Green, Arthur. *Seek My Face, Speak My Name*. Northvale, NJ: Jason Aronson, 1992.

Greenberg, Sidney, ed. *A Modern Treasury of Jewish Thoughts*. New York: Thomas Yoseloff, 1960.

Greenberg, Sidney, and Jonathan D. Levine. *The New Mahzor*. Bridgeport, CT: Prayerbook Press, 1977.

Grishaver, Joel Lurie. *40 Things You Can Do to Save the Jewish People*. Northvale, NJ: Jason Aronson, 1993.

Guttmann, Joseph. *Divorce in Psychosocial Perspective: Theory and Research*. Hillsdale, NJ: Lawrence Erlbaum Associates, 1993.

Guttmann, Julius. *Philosophies of Judaism*. New York: Schocken Books, 1964.

Hamilton, E. *Spokesmen for God*. New York: W. W. Norton & Co., 1962.

Harlow, Jules, ed. *Siddur Sim Shalom*. New York: The Rabbinical Assembly, 1985.

Harris, Sam. *The End of Faith*. New York: W. W. Norton & Co., 2004.

Hawxhurst, Joan C. *The Interfaith Family Guidebook*. Kalamazoo, MI: Dovetail Publishing, 1998.

Hayes, Christine E. *Gentile Impurities and Jewish Identities: Intermarriage and Conversion from the Bible to the Talmud*. New York: Oxford University Press, 2002.

Heidel, Alexander. *The Babylonian Genesis*. Chicago: University of Chicago Press, 1951.

Herberg, Will. *Protestant—Catholic—Jew*. Chicago: University of Chicago Press, 1983.

Hertz, Joseph H. *The Authorized Daily Prayer Book*. New York: Bloch Publishing Company, 1961.

———. *The Pentateuch and Haftorahs*. New York: Oxford University Press, 1936.

Heschel, Abraham J. *The Earth Is the Lord's: The Inner World of the Jew in Eastern Europe*. Woodstock, VT: Jewish Lights Publishing, 2001.

———. *Man's Quest for God*. Santa Fe, NM: Aurora Press, 1998.

———. *God in Search of Man*. Northvale: Jason Aronson, 1987.

———. *The Prophets*. New York: HarperCollins, 1962.

———. *Between God and Man*. New York: Harper & Row, 1959.

Heskes, Irene. *Passport to Jewish Music*. Westport, CT: Greenwood Press, 1994.

Hoffman, Eva. *Shtetl: The Life and Death*. New York: Mariner Books, 1998.

Holtz, Barry W., ed. *Back to the Sources*. New York: Touchstone, 1984.

Howe, Irving, and Kenneth Libo. *How We Lived*. New York: New American Library, 1979.

Howe, Irving. *World of Our Fathers*. New York: Harcourt Brace Jovanovich, 1976.

Idelsohn, A. Z. *Jewish Liturgy and Its Development*. Mineola, NY: Dover Publications, 1995.

———. *Jewish Music*. Mineola, NY: Dover Publications, 1992.

Jacobs, Janet Liebman, and Donald Capps, eds. *Religion, Society of America, and Psychoanalysis: Readings in Contemporary Theory*. Boulder, CO: Westview Press, 1997.

Jacobs, Louis. *The Jewish Religion: A Companion*. Oxford: Oxford University Press, 1995.

Jacobson, Kenneth. *Embattled Selves*. Washington: Atlantic Monthly Press, 1994.

Jennings, Theodore W. *Beyond Theism: A Grammar of God Language*. New York: Oxford University Press, 1985.

Johnson, Paul. *A History of the Jews*. New York: Harper & Row, 1987.

Kalmin, Richard. *The Sage in Jewish Society of Late Antiquity*. New York: Routledge, 1999.

Kaplan, Dana Evan. *The Cambridge Companion to American Judaism*. New York: Cambridge University Press, 2005.

———. *American Reform Judaism*. Camden, NJ: Rutgers University Press, 2003.

Kaplan, Mordecai M. *The Meaning of God in Modern Jewish Religion*. Detroit, MI: Wayne State University Press, 1994.

———. *Judaism as a Civilization*. New York: Jewish Publication Society of America, 1989.

Katz, Steven T. *The Shtetl*. New York: New York University Press, 2006.

Kaufman, Walter. *Religions in Four Dimensions*. New York: Reader's Digest Press, 1976.

Kaufman, Yehezkiel. *The Religion of Israel*. New York: Schocken, 1972.

Kepnes, Stephen, Peter Ochs and Robert Gibbs. *Reasoning After Revelation*. Boulder, CO: Westview Press, 1998.

Kertzer, David I. *The Kidnapping of Edgardo Mortara*. New York: Alfred A. Knopf, 1997.

Kertzer, Morris. *What Is a Jew?* New York: Touchstone, 1996.

King, Winston. *Introduction to Religion*. New York: Harper & Row, 1954.

Kirsch, Jonathan. *The Woman Who Laughed at God*. New York: Viking Compass, 2001.

———. *The Harlot by the Side of the Road*. New York: Ballantine Books, 1997.

Kohler, Kaufman. *Jewish Theology: Systematically and Historically Considered*. New York: Macmillan, 1918.

Kolatch, Alfred J. *The Jewish Book of Why*. Middle Village, NY: Jonathan David Publishers, 2004.

Lamm, Maurice. *The Jewish Way in Death and Mourning*. New York: Jonathan David Publishers, 1969.

Lazar, Moshe. *The Sephardic Tradition*. New York: Viking Press, 1973.

Lazarus, M. *The Ethics of Judaism*, vol. 2. Trans. Henrietta Szold. Philadelphia: Jewish Publication Society of America, 1900.

Lederhendler, Eli, ed. *Who Owns Judaism? Public Religion and Private Faith in America and Israel*. New York: Oxford University Press, 2001.

Leedom, Tim C. *The Book Your Church Doesn't Want You to Read*. San Diego: Truth Seeker Books, 2003.

Lerner, Michael. *The Left Hand of God*. San Francisco: HarperSanFrancisco, 2006.

———. *Jewish Renewal*. New York: Grosset/Putnam, 1994.

Liptzin, Sol. *A History of Yiddish Literature*. Middle Village, NY: Jonathan David Publishers, 1972.

MacQuarrie, John. *Scope of Demythologizing*. New York: Harper & Row, 1960.

Maimonides, Moses. *The Guide for the Perplexed*, 2nd rev. ed. Translated by M. Friedlander. New York: Dover Publications, 1956.

Marcus, Jacob Rader. *The Dynamics of Modern Judaism*. Boston: Brandeis University Press, 2003.

———. *The Jew in the American World*. Detroit, MI: Wayne State University Press, 1996.

———. *This I Believe*. Lanham, MO: Jason Aronson, 1996.

———. *The America Jew*. New York: Carlson Publishing, 1995.

———. *The Colonial America Jew*. Detroit, MI: Wayne State University Press, 1994.

———. *United States Jewry 1776–1985*. Detroit: Wayne State University Press, 1993.

———. *To Count a People*. New York: University Press of America, 1990.

Maslow, Abraham H. *Religions, Values, and Peak Experiences.* New York: Viking Press, 1970.

———. *Toward a Psychology of Being.* Princeton, NJ: Van Nostrand, 1962.

Mayer, Egon. *Marriage Between Jews & Christians.* New York: Plenum Press, 1985

Mays, James L., ed. *Harper's Bible Commentary.* San Francisco: Harper & Row, 1988.

Mead, Frank S., and Samuel S. Hill. *Handbook of Denominations.* Nashville, TN: Abingdon Press, 2001.

Metzker, Isaac. *A Bintal Brief.* New York: Schocken, 1990.

Meyer, Michael A. *Response to Modernity.* Detroit, MI: Wayne State University Press, 1995.

Milgram, Goldie. *Reclaiming Judaism as a Spiritual Practice.* Woodstock, VT: Jewish Lights Publishing, 2004.

Millgram, Abraham E. *Jewish Worship.* Philadelphia: Jewish Publication Society of America, 1971.

Mills, David. *Atheist Universe.* New York: Xlibris, 2003.

Miron, Dan. *The Image of the Shtetl and Other Studies of Modern Jewish Liturgy Imagination.* Syracuse, NY: Syracuse University Press, 2001.

Montefiore, C. G., and H. Loewe, eds. *A Rabbinic Anthology.* Philadelphia: Meridian Books, 1963.

Nelson-Pallmeyer, Jack. *Is Religion Killing Us?* New York: Continuum, 2003.

Neugroschel, Joachim. *The Shtetl: A Creative Anthology.* New York: Overlook Press, 2001.

Neusner, Jacob. *Handbook of Rabbinic Theology: Language, System, Structure.* Boston: Brill, 2002.

———. *Rabbinic Judaism: The Theological System.* Boston: Brill, 2002.

———. *Judaism When Christianity Began.* Louisville, KY: Westminster John Knox Press, 2002.

———. *The Reader's Guide to the Talmud.* Boston: Brill, 2001.

———. *A Rabbi Talks with Jesus.* New York: Doubleday, 1993.

———. *Telling Tales.* Louisville, KY: Westminster/John Knox Press, 1993.

———. *A Life of Yohanan Ben Zakkai, Ca.1–80 C.E.,* 2nd ed. Leiden, The Netherlands: E. J. Brill, 1970.

———, ed. *Sectors of American Judaism: Reform, Orthodoxy, Conservatism, and Reconstructionism.* New York: KTAV Publishing House, 1975.

Newman, Louis I., ed. *The Talmudic Anthology.* West Orange, NJ: Behrman House, 1945.

Novak, David. *Jewish-Christian Dialogue: A Jewish Justification.* New York: Oxford University Press, 1992.

Olitzky, Kerry M., ed. *Reform Judaism in America.* Westport, CT: Greenwood Press, 1993.

Oppehnheimer, Mark. *Thirteen and a Day.* New York: Farrar, Straus and Giroux, 2005.

Parrinder, Geoffrey. *World Religions: From Ancient History to Present.* New York: Checkmark Books, 1985.

Pasternak, Velvel. *The Jewish Music Companion.* Owings Mills, MD: Tara Publications, 2003.

Payant, Katherine B., and Toby Rose, eds. *The Immigrant Experience in North American Literature: Carving out a Niche.* Westport, CT: Greenwood Press, 1999.

Peli, Pinchas H. *Torah Today.* Washington: B'nai B'rith Books, 1987.

Petuchowski, Jakob Josef. *Heirs of the Pharisees.* New York: University Press of America, 1986.

Plaut, Gunther W. *The Rise of Reform Judaism.* New York: World Union for Progressive Judaism, 1963.

———, ed. *The Torah: A Modern Commentary.* New York: Union of American Hebrew Congregation, 1981.

Polonsky, Anthony, ed. *Polin Volume Seventeen.* Oxford: Littman Library of Jewish Civilization, 2005.

Prager, Dennis, and Joseph Telushkin. *Nine Questions People Ask About Judaism.* New York: Simon & Schuster, Inc, 1981.

Raphael, Marc Lee. *Judaism in America.* New York: Columbia University Press, 2005.

Rawidowicz, Simon. *Israel: The Ever-Dying People.* Cranbury, NJ: Associated University Presses, 1986.

Rosenberg, David, and Harold Bloom. *The Book of J.* New York: Grove Weidenfeld, 1990.

Rosenberg, Stuart E. *The New Jewish Identity in America.* New York: Hippocrene Books, 1985.

Rosenblum, Herbert. *Conservative Judaism: A Contemporary History.* New York: United Synagogue of America, 1983.

Rowley, H. H. *The Growth of the Old Testament.* New York: Harper & Row, 1963.

Rubenstein, Richard L. *After Auschwitz.* Baltimore, MD: Johns Hopkins University Press, 1966.

Rubenstein, Richard. *Thus Saith the Lord: The Revolutionary Moral Vision of Isaiah and Jeremiah.* New York: Harcourt, 2006.

Rushkoff, Douglas. *Nothing Sacred.* New York: Crown Publishers, 2003.

Sachar, Abram Leon. *A History of the Jews.* New York: Alfred A. Knopf, 1964.

Sachar, Howard M. *A History of the Jews in America*. New York: Alfred A. Knopf, 1992.

Salkin, Jeffery K. *Putting God on the Guest List*. Woodstock, VT: Jewish Lights Publishing, 1996.

Samuel, Maurice. *Prince of the Ghetto*. New York: Schocken Books, 1948.

Sarna, Jonathan D. *American Judaism*. New Haven, CT: Yale University Press, 2004.

———, ed. *The American Jewish Experience*. New York: Holmes & Meier, 1986.

Sarna, Nahum M. *Understanding Genesis*. New York: Schocken Books, 1986.

Saussy, Carroll. *God Images and Self Esteem*. Louisville, KY: Westminster/John Knox Press, 1991.

Schauss, Hayyim. *The Jewish Festivals*. New York: Schocken Books, 1938.

Schechter, Solomon. *Seminary Addresses and Other Papers*. New York: Burning Bush Press, 1959.

Scheindlin, Raymond P. *A Short History of the Jewish People*. New York: Oxford University Press, 1998.

Schlossberg, Eli W. *The World of Orthodox Judaism*. Lanham, MD: Jason Aronson, 1997.

Schneider, Susan Weidman. *Intermarriage*. New York: The Free Press, 1989.

Schochet, Elijah Judah. *The Hasidic Movement*. Northvale, NJ: Jason Aronson, 1994.

Scholem, Gershom. *Kabbalah*. New York: Meridian, 1974.

———. *Major Trends in Jewish Mysticism*. New York: Schocken Books, 1974.

———. *The Messianic Idea in Judaism*. New York: Schocken Books, 1971.

———. *On the Kabbalah Its and Symbolism*. New York: Schocken Books, 1965.

———. *Zohar: The Book of Splendor*. New York: Schocken Books, 1949.

Schwartz, Howard. *Reimagining the Bible: The Storytelling of the Rabbis*. New York: Oxford University Press, 1998.

Schwartz, Leo W. *Great Ages & Ideas of the Jewish People*. New York: Modern Library, 1956.

Shanks, Hershel, ed. *Christianity and Rabbinic Judaism*. Washington: Biblical Archaeology Society of America, 1992.

Sherman, Moshe D. *Orthodox Judaism in America*. Westport, CT: Greenwood Press, 1996.

Shermis, Michael. *Jewish-Christian Relations*. Bloomington: Indiana University Press, 1988.

Sherwin, Byron L. *Sparks Amidst the Ashes: The Spiritual Legacy of Polish Jewry.* New York: Oxford University Press, 1997.

Sidorsky, David, ed. *The Future of the Jewish Community in America.* New York: Basic Books, 1973.

Siegel, Richard, Michael Strassfeld and Sharon Strassfeld, ed. *The Jewish Catalog.* Philadelphia: Jewish Publication Society of America, 1973.

Slobin, Mark. *American Klezmer.* Berkeley: University of California Press, 2001.

Smith, Huston. *The Religions of Man.* New York: Harper & Row, 1965.

Snyder, Howard A. *Models of the Kingdom.* Eugene, OR: Wipf & Stock Publishers, 2001.

Speiser, E. A. *The Anchor Bible: Genesis.* New York: Doubleday, 1964.

Spitz, Elie Kaplan. *Does the Soul Survive?* Woodstock, VT: Jewish Lights Publishing, 2002.

Steinberg, Milton. *Basic Judaism.* San Diego: Harvest/HBJ, 1975.

Steinsaltz, Adin. *The Essential Talmud.* Trans. Chaya Galai. New York: Basic Books, 1976.

Steketee, Gai, and Teresa Pigott, ed. *Obsessive Compulsive Disorder.* Kansas City, MO: Compact Clinicals, 1999.

Susser, Bernard, and Charles S. Liebman. *Choosing Survival: Strategies for a Jewish Future.* New York: Oxford University Press, 1999.

Tanakh: The Holy Scriptures. Philadelphia: Jewish Publication Society of America, 1985.

Tcherikover, Victor. *Hellenistic Civilization and the Jews.* Peabody, MA: Hendrickson Publishers, 1999.

Telushkin, Joseph. *Jewish Literacy.* New York: HarperCollins, 2001.

Thomas, D. Winton, ed. *Documents from Old Testament Times.* New York: Harper & Row, 1958.

Tillich, Paul. *Systematic Theology.* Chicago: University of Chicago Press, 1967.

Trachtenberg, Joshua. *Jewish Magic and Superstition.* Philadelphia: University of Pennsylvania Press, 2004.

Trepp, Leo. *The Complete Book of Jewish Observance.* New York: Behrman House, 1980.

———. *Eternal Faith, Eternal People: A Journey into Judaism.* Englewood Cliffs, NJ: Prentice-Hall, 1962.

Vermes, G. *The Dead Sea Scrolls in English.* Baltimore, MD: Penguin Books, 1962.

Viorst, Milton. *What Shall I Do with This People?* New York: The Free Press, 2002.

Visotzky, Burton L. *The Genesis of Ethics.* New York: Crown, 1996.

————. *Reading the Book*. New York: Anchor Books, 1991.

————, and David E. Fishman, eds. *From Mesopotamia to Modernity: Ten Introductions to Jewish History and Literature*. Boulder, CO: Westview Press, 1999.

Wald, Kenneth D. *Religions and Politics in the United States*. Lanham, MD: Rowman & Littlefield Publishers, 2006.

Walsh, Froma. *Normal Family Processes*. New York: Guilford Press, 1993.

Warner, R. Stephen. *Gatherings in Diaspora*. Philadelphia: Temple University Press, 1998.

Weinberg, Sydney Stahl. *The World of Our Mothers: The Lives of Jewish Immigrant Women*. New York: Schocken Books, 1990

Weinreich, Uriel. *College Yiddish: An Introduction to the Yiddish Language*. New York: YIVO Institute for Jewish Research, 1999.

Weiss-Rosmarin, Trude. *Judaism and Christianity: The Differences*. New York: Jonathan David Publishers, 1997.

Wertheimer, Jack, ed. *The American Synagogue*. New York: Cambridge University Press, 2003.

Wieseltier, Leon. *Kaddish*. New York: Alfred A. Knopf, 1998.

Wilkes, Paul. *And They Shall Be My People*. New York: Grove Press, 2000.

Wilson, Edmund. *The Scrolls from the Dead Sea*. New York: Meridian Books, 1959.

Zborowski, Mark, and Elizabeth Herzog. *Life Is with People: The Jewish Little-Town of Eastern Europe*. New York: International Universities Press, 1952.

Zborowski, Mark, Elizabeth Herzog, and Margaret Mead. *Life Is with People: The Culture of the Shtetl*. New York: Schocken Brooks, 1962.

Zeitlin, Solomon. *The Rise and Fall of the Judean State*. New York: Jewish Publication Society of America, 1978.

INDEX